NOW AND FOREVER

Now
AND
Forever

A Theological
Aesthetics
of Time

JOHN E. THIEL

University of Notre Dame Press
Notre Dame, Indiana

Copyright © 2023 by the University of Notre Dame
Notre Dame, Indiana 46556
undpress.nd.edu
All Rights Reserved

Published in the United States of America

Paperback edition published in 2026

Library of Congress Control Number: 2022951003

ISBN: 978-0-268-20523-2 (Hardback)
ISBN: 978-0-268-20575-1 (Paperback)
ISBN: 978-0-268-20524-9 (WebPDF)
ISBN: 978-0-268-20522-5 (Epub)

GPSR Compliance Inquiries:
Lightning Source France, 1 Av. Johannes Gutenberg, 78310 Maurepas, France
compliance@lightningsource.fr | Phone: +33 1 30 49 23 42

AMDG

CONTENTS

	Acknowledgments	ix
CHAPTER 1	Eschatology, Time, and the Continuity of Grace	1
CHAPTER 2	The Virtues in Time: An Eschatological Anthropology	25
CHAPTER 3	Toward a Theology of Events in Time	49
CHAPTER 4	Tragic Time in an Eschatological Aesthetic	81
CHAPTER 5	The Aesthetics of Tradition and the Styles of Theology	117
CHAPTER 6	Forever and a Day: Resurrected Time in a Heavenly Imaginary	143
	Notes	179
	Index	197

ACKNOWLEDGMENTS

Writing the acknowledgments for a book about to appear is always a delightful way to conclude the project. The work is done, and one pauses to appreciate all the intellectual and emotional support, the many acts of kindness, that enabled the writing to reach its end. For this book on grace, the expression of gratitude for the generosity of friends and family is a way of revisiting the very topic on which I wrote.

I began this book nine years ago when I decided that writing on aesthetics would make me happy—or as happy as one can be ever facing the blank page. Half of these chapters, though, were written between May and December 2020 during the pandemic when I was on sabbatical in the fall semester. I am grateful to Fairfield University for granting me this sabbatical leave. In particular, I am grateful to the Faculty Research Committee and Dean Richard Greenwald for recommending the leave and to Provost Christine Siegel for approving it.

Only chapter 5, on the aesthetics of tradition, has appeared in print before. It was published under the same title it bears here, "The Aesthetics of Tradition and the Styles of Theology" in *Theological Studies* 75 (December 2014): 795–815. It was later reprinted in *Beyond Dogmatism and Innocence: Hermeneutics, Critique, and Catholic Theology*, edited by A. Godzieba and B. Hinze (Collegeville, MN: Liturgical Press, 2017), 56–83. Thanks to SAGE Publications for permissions and to David Schultenover, S.J., for applying his extraordinary editorial skill to the original manuscript.

I am fortunate to be a member of a local, New York–area research group that has its roots in the Constructive Theology Work Group at Vanderbilt Divinity School. We have met together three times annually for sixteen years to share our work-in-progress. Discussion with my friends helped to improve four of the chapters that appear here. I am very grateful to Roger Haight, S.J., Elena Procario-Foley, Michele Saracino, Paul Lakeland, Jeannine Hill-Fletcher, and Brad Hinze for their insights and their company. I presented an earlier version of chapter 2 at the Fall 2018 meeting of the New Haven Theological Discussion Group at Yale Divinity School. As is their wont, the members offered valuable criticism that enabled me to refine my reflection on the theological virtues. Kathy Tanner, Kate Sonderegger, Roger Jackson, and Tom Schmidt gave their time and talent to read particular chapters and offer advice that made them better. Julia Lamm offered helpful direction on the arc of my argument from chapter to chapter, which I happily followed. My good friend Paul Lakeland read the entire manuscript all the way through, some chapters multiple times, a favor that he has done for me many times throughout our shared careers and for which I am extraordinarily grateful. In all sorts of ways, conversations I have had through the years with David Kelsey and Cyril O'Regan have shaped my theological work. Their influence is here, in and between the lines. I am grateful to Eli Bortz, former editor-in-chief at the University of Notre Dame Press, for bringing my pages to publication, to Robert Banning for his fine copyediting skill, and to Matthew Dowd, Wendy McMillan, Kathryn Pitts, and the staff of the UNDP for all their good work.

There are those who did not read these pages along the way and who are just as important to the book's completion as those who did. The topic of this book is time, and Greg Schopen has taught me how time can matter much more than the proximity of space in a lifelong friendship. Even from afar, though, he has provided an inspiring example of scholarly dedication. Susan Rakowitz, Randy Sachs, S.J., Beth Boquet, Alice Fleming, Bill McConville, O.F.M., Joy McDougall, Bob Neville, Ellen Umansky, Wesley Wildman, and Suzanne Wildman have informed my thoughts on grace in this book more than they might imagine or in a way completely beyond their imagination. I trust each will accurately identify his or her imaginative category. I find it hard to imagine a better family than Dorothea, David, Benjamin and Sara, and, indeed, our entire extended family. I am forever grateful to and for you all.

Fairfield, Connecticut
March 3, 2022

CHAPTER ONE

ESCHATOLOGY, TIME, AND THE CONTINUITY OF GRACE

The title of this book announces my intention to write a theological aesthetics of time. As a modern theological theme, time has largely been embraced by process theologians, who in their attention to the present moment tend to avoid talk of the distant temporal past and the distant temporal future, and by more traditionally minded eschatologists, who are eager to reflect on all the ways a future of fulfilled divine promise is yet being realized in the present moment. In these pages, I will follow the path trodden by the eschatologists, who view time not merely as a natural ambience but as a created condition that in every passing moment heralds, in Jürgen Moltmann's phrase, the "coming of God."[1] A traditional eschatology's concern to speak of God's future has pressing implications for the created time in which the future unfolds—here and now. Time, I will argue, is a dimension of creation that mediates God's grace, God's very presence, which brings creaturely existence to resurrected life. In this sacramental quality of time lies its beauty, a beauty whose radiance appears in the gracefulness of events in time that finitely reflects the eternal relations in God's own Trinitarian life. Clearly, such an argument for the sacramental beauty of time will need to address all the ways that events in time are often deeply tragic occasions of loss and human anguish.

Although my eschatology will follow a traditionally minded path in its attention to the ways God's future is always already latent in the present moment, in what I will call "time now," it will pursue an untraditional complement to this view in its claim that the continuity of grace mediated through time requires that resurrected life be imagined as a temporal state, as a "time forever" through which God's graceful presence is ever availed to redeemed creatures. My previous book *Icons of Hope* proposed the theological advantages of imagining heavenly life in a way consistent with the Christian doctrine of bodily resurrection, but did so without a developed account of the role of time in such theological speculation about the heavenly imaginary.[2] Here, I seek to construct a consistent theology of time, at once a theology of grace, that envisages the beauty of time in its created duration from now to forever. If successful, my project will contribute to the mainline theology of grace that has been developing in the Catholic tradition since the mid-twentieth century, as well as to the genre of theological aesthetics that has flourished through the very same years. Eschatology, albeit a somewhat untraditional one eager to consider the theological implications of time forever, will govern my consideration of the beauty of graced time in the pages to come. Let us begin with some introductory observations that attend to the eschatological template of my study.

Eschatology Thick and Thin

An eschatology in the temporal key of hope is the subject matter of this book. Understood as a theological content, as an interpretation of Christian beliefs about death, judgment, and life after death, eschatology has been addressed in the talk and writings of believers since the early days of the tradition. Eschatology as a focused genre of writing, as a theological subdiscipline of its own, is a more recent arrival in the history of theology. This is so because post-Enlightenment theologians began to imagine theology as a variety of differentiated tasks, each characterized by a specific content and method. Not only eschatology, but all theological subdisciplines, such as systematic theology, biblical theology, and historical theology, had their origins in the nineteenth-century project of theological encyclopedia. The theological encyclopedia was not a compendium of entries that briefly explained topics, issues, or technical terms in order to provide an overview of knowledge. The theological encyclopedia was a work on method, concerned to cultivate expertise through the mastery of particular theological concerns, tasks, and skills. The nineteenth-century authors of these works presumed that each theologian could and would garner some measure of accomplishment in all of the theological subdisciplines that the encyclopedia sketched. In the course of the twentieth century, professional specialization increasingly led theologians to concentrate their studies in a particular theological subdiscipline for which they claimed mastery without a professional sense of obligation for the mastery of other fields. By the end of the twentieth century, the Catholic theologian Bernard Lonergan could speak in his own work on method of theological practice transpiring through various "functional specialties,"[3] each of which defined a field of expertise in which a theologian trained and in which a theologian might demonstrate accomplished interpretation. Eschatology, like all of the modern theological subdisciplines, emerged in this way as a discrete field of study, and as the one to which our efforts here will be devoted.

Besides the post-Enlightenment development of disciplinary specialization, there has been a shift in the history of ideas that explains why eschatology specifically has taken shape as a theological subdiscipline in the modern period. In the late nineteenth and early twentieth centuries, the New Testament scholars Johannes Weiss (1863–1914) and Albert Schweitzer (1875–1965) stirred a new awareness of the apocalyptic sensibilities that fueled the preaching of Jesus and the faith of the earliest Christians.[4] In Weiss's and Schweitzer's readings of the Gospels, Jesus was an apocalyptic preacher who expected the imminent end of the present world and who saw his religious message as the harbinger of a new world breaking into time in the coming kingdom of God. Their discovery of what had always lain before the eyes of Christian readers issued from their historical-critical study of the scriptural texts. But their recovery of Christian apocalyptic did much more than fashion a more complete scholarly knowledge of the past. Both scholars recognized that early Christian apocalyptic stood at odds with the views of present-day Christians, many of whom believed that Jesus taught a bourgeois morality that valorized the social status quo. This discrepancy between the apocalyptic worldview of early Christianity and the very unapocalyptic worldview of contemporary liberal Christianity focused theological attention all the more on the distinctive eschatological zeal that animated Jesus and the early church. In the course of the twentieth century, theologians saw the recovery of apocalyptic as a corrective not only to a stilted understanding of Christian origins but also to a reductive regard for Christian faith—one that failed to account for the eschatological ardor of the first Christians. In response, theologians have ventured broader, constructive interpretations of the apocalyptic that appreciate the eschatological dimensions of belief, doctrine, and practice. The works of theologians such as Hans Urs von Balthasar, Karl Rahner, Joseph Ratzinger, Jürgen Moltmann, Miroslav Volf, and Elizabeth Johnson creatively evince this constructive concern. Their contributions to the recent theological genre of eschatology have addressed such topics as the eschatological meaning of the lives of the saints,[5] the symbolic value of eschatological language,[6] the theological importance of the Last Judgment,[7] the Trinitarian God of the eschatological future,[8] forgiveness as eschatological ethics,[9] and the feminist valence of the communion of the saints.[10] There are, of course, other theologians who write in the field of eschatology and who address a host of other eschatological issues.

Even though the past century has seen the emergence of eschatology as a distinctive theological *locus* and as a subdiscipline in its own right, theologians often remain wary of taking up its practice. Christian hope may have otherworldly aims, but modern epistemological commitments defined by the empiricism of the scientific method and the Kantian critique of metaphysics often make theologians quite reluctant to engage in speculation about eschatological events that elude the critical reach of reason and even, perhaps, the power of imagination. Although a few theologians engage eschatology in what Cyril O'Regan has called a "pleromatic" style, one that is not at all reticent about speculatively imagining God's purposes in the "last things,"[11] theologians who take up the task of eschatology more typically do so by teasing out the existential value of traditional symbols. This more customary approach—one that we might metaphorically describe as "thin"—assumes an apophatic stance toward the "last things" in themselves and ventures this-worldly interpretations of their meaning. Purveyors of this thin style of interpretation judge what we might by contrast call a "thick" or pleromatic style of eschatological interpretation to venture far too much in its willingness to speculate about the "last things."

To some degree, the difference between what we might call "thicker" and "thinner" eschatological renditions derives from the difference between supernaturalist and naturalist orientations in theological interpretation. These orientations in turn reflect theological assumptions about (1) the capacity of theological reason and imagination to transcend the realm of empirical experience and (2) the productive theological value of such an enterprise even were it possible. In many ways, these various versions of the same divide concern the nature and scope of temporality—its extent, its limits, its workings, and its possibilities—as the proper ambit for theological interpretation, to say nothing of time as the proper ambit of all creation. In the chapters that follow, I will reflect theologically on the nature and scope of time in order to argue for the value of a speculative approach to eschatology that ventures a thicker description of the "last things." More specifically, I will develop the notion of eschatological time, a time rife with the saving power of God's grace, as a richer field within which theological interpretation might reflect meaningfully on the *eschata*. I will argue that eschatological time pervades every dimension of God's creation, and so this conception of time presumes more continuity than difference between this world and what Christians believe to be the world to come. Additionally, the imaginary I will construct offers a theological aesthetics of time, one that considers time as an eschatological condition for the believer's apprehension of God and that appreciates the beauty of this most fundamental dimension of God's creation.

I have already noted that my argument will present time as a medium of God's grace and that the continuity of God's grace to all things creaturely must then assume a continuity in the created reality of time—a continuity that traverses distinguishable dimensions of eschatological time: "time now" and "time forever." Let us proceed by exploring efforts in twentieth-century theology to configure this-worldly eschatological time—"time now"—and then move on to consider how this gracefully pregnant time might be imagined in the coming world of consummate grace for which believers hope—"time forever."

Time Now

It is interesting to consider how theologies in the past seventy years have imagined worldly time saturated with the divine presence and so, one might say, with eschatological resonance. Two examples—one Catholic and one Protestant—will illustrate this point.

The Catholic *nouvelle théologie* that emerged in Europe after the Second World War reacted against neoscholastic theology's appropriation of the nature-grace distinction by recovering from the ancient Catholic tradition an understanding of the immanence of the eternal in time. The work of the French Jesuit Henri de Lubac (1896–1991) best illustrates this theological direction. De Lubac's ground-breaking *Surnaturel* (1946), as well as his later *Le mystère du surnaturel* (1965), argued that neoscholastic theology's use of the concept of "pure nature" poorly accomplished its theological goal of preserving both the dignity of human nature and the gratuity of God's grace. The notion of "pure nature" postulated a created human nature that, at some imagined point, stood before God graceless, as though the natural order and the supernatural order were two different spheres, each with its own integrity, that would intersect narrowly in the providential economy in order to bring an otherwise graceless but redeemable human nature to the redeeming state of grace. Neoscholastic theology imagined that the sacramental mediation of the institutional church would provide that slender and exclusive channel of grace to join the supernatural order "above" to the natural order "below."

In de Lubac's judgment, there were several problems with this conceptualization. Even though he was willing to admit that the hypothesis of "pure nature" preserved the transcendent gratuity of grace and so God's freedom as the giver of grace,[12] de Lubac concluded that the hypothesis yet fractured the immanent gratuity of grace. Since, he insisted, created human nature never exists outside the ambit of grace, the hypothesis of "pure nature" requires the postulate of a natural order that does not exist and that has never existed. "Indeed," de Lubac asserts, "it is extremely hard—as experience has shown—to pursue this idea of 'pure nature' and make it anything other than a great 'X' for which we have no precise intellectual meaning, and which cannot therefore help our thinking along very much, without our ending up by gradually attributing to it more and more of the qualities and privileges which attach to our present human nature in relation to God."[13] Moreover, what de Lubac pejoratively described as this "nominalist"[14] conceptualization actually made both the natural and supernatural orders different species of a common genus, thus putting both nature and grace on the same level in spite of their affirmed distinctiveness. Though compartmentalized for the sake of their proper distinction, both the natural and supernatural orders yet became homologous in this imaginary because the goal of the distinction was to preserve both the gratuity of grace and the created dignity of humankind in its capacity freely to accept grace. "Thus," de Lubac finds, "the supernatural order loses its unique splendor; and . . . , by a logic whose headlong course we cannot halt, often ends by becoming no more than a kind of shadow of that supposed natural order . . . , a 'supernature' which reproduces, to what is called a 'superior' degree, all the features which characterize nature itself."[15] For de Lubac, nature is always already graced, and the gratuity of grace, to be real, must be gifted to the person as he or she actually stands in graced relation to God if theology is to capture the truth of that relationship.

There was, we should recall, an eschatological dimension to this mid-twentieth century controversy on the relationship between nature and grace. Very much at issue in this debate was the question of whether humankind possessed a natural desire for the Beatific Vision, a theological concern that could be posed as the question "Is humanity created with a predisposition to its eschatological destiny?"[16] Post-Tridentine theology through the neoscholastic tradition answered no, a position grounded on the Aristotelian axiom that a nature's predispositions must be proportionate to their ends. Assuming humanity's creation in a state of pure nature, one could ascribe a desire for natural happiness to human nature, but only grace could elevate the natural desire for beatitude to a desire for the Beatific Vision. For neo-Thomist theology, this sequence of the priority of the gift of creation, followed by the gift of grace, maintained both the gratuity of grace and the moral capacity and responsibility of the human person after the fall. De Lubac answered the question of whether humanity was created with a predisposition to its eschatological destiny with a resounding yes. He insisted that neither the created dignity of humankind nor the gratuity of grace could be secured by appeal to the limit concept of a pure nature. In de Lubac's judgment, such a conceptualization was theologically flawed in its hypothetical construction of a human nature that never existed, since human nature was never not graced. The neo-Thomist fealty to the concept of pure nature resulted in an extrinsicist understanding of grace as a supernatural commodity added to nature. The human desire for the happiness of the Beatific Vision, de Lubac insisted, dwells in the human heart as it is ever graced, the real gratuitousness of grace not requiring that it originally be estranged from nature in some primitive state but only that it be gifted by God to the human nature ever graced.[17]

The category of time never explicitly entered into the critique that de Lubac made of the neoscholastic theology of his day, nor into the controversy that unfolded in the aftermath of his critique. But the category of time actually provides an interesting way of identifying what each party valued in its adjudication of the relationship between nature and grace. The neoscholastic tradition's appropriation of the notion of "pure nature" imagined a temporal sequence in which the original creation of the human person was followed by the divine overture of grace. The gap in this sequence distinguished between a time in the order of creation devoid of grace in which human nature was yet good and morally responsible and a later time in which human nature flourished under the dispensation of grace, the gap in time assuring as well the gratuity of grace and God's gracious freedom. For de Lubac, this imaginary misconceived nature, grace, and, indirectly, time as well. De Lubac denied any temporal sequence in the dispensation of grace. For him, the order of creation is never ungraced, its time so entirely replete with the divine gift that a gap in time between an earlier purely natural and a later graced state would be unthinkable.

The temporal sequence of the pure-nature hypothesis did clearly convey the Council of Trent's teaching on justification, a theological context for the development of the hypothesis in the sixteenth century and thereafter. The sequence clarified the created capacity of the human person to respond to the call of God's grace while avoiding the Pelagian reduction of grace to nature. To the degree that the pure-nature hypothesis served the theological discussion of the desire for God, the temporal sequence affirmed that eschatological fulfillment in the Beatific Vision was not owed to humanity by God, as though God would be constrained to supplement the natural desire for happiness with which God had created humanity. Yet, for de Lubac, these advantages came at the unacceptable cost of positing a temporal gap between the natural and the supernatural that obscured the gratuitousness of grace present to humanity from its incipience. In order for the imaginary of pure nature to be true, he observes, "it would have to be possible to note in the actual course of every real and personal existence . . . a definite moment when God intervenes either to assign an end which till then had been in doubt, or to change the end previously assigned to me." Either scenario, he concludes, would be "absurd," both "supposing a radical extrinsicism which must destroy either the idea of nature or that of finality [grace], or possibly both."[18] In effect, de Lubac concludes, the hypothesis of a time without grace, and so a time without the anticipation of eschatological consummation, disrupts the truth that every temporal moment in the order of creation already stands in the saving ambit of God's infinite love.

We find a parallel concern for the eschatological "now" in the work of the British scripture scholar C. H. Dodd (1884–1973). Dodd developed his understanding of Christian eschatology over the course of his long career, with his first attention to the topic appearing in a 1923 article entitled "The Eschatological Element in the New Testament and Its Permanent Significance." Here Dodd disagreed with the well-known thesis of Albert Schweitzer that Jesus expected the imminent appearance of an otherworldly kingdom of God that would break into history as a transformative interruption, an event about which, Schweitzer claimed, Jesus was mistaken, since it never took place. For Dodd, the problem with this reading of the Gospels was that it understood eschatology exclusively as a futurist event about to overwhelm the present moment. As a corrective to Schweitzer's position, which scholars labeled "consistent eschatology," Dodd proposed what he called in this early article a "transmuted eschatology," one that affirmed the eschatological valence of the present historical moment to some degree rather than an eschatology that interpreted the coming kingdom of God as an utter alternative to the historical now.[19] Jesus, he insisted, did expect the coming of God's kingdom as a consummate event in the very near future but also taught that dimensions of this coming kingdom were already real within the present age, and in such a way that the consummate event would be the fulfillment of saving power that already had begun to unfold in history. Even in this early writing, as throughout his later writings, Dodd parsed the New Testament evidence by distinguishing these two eschatological moments that, he claimed, were intimately related in Jesus's teaching and yet not reducible to each other: a not-yet, consummate eschatological event that lay on the cusp between the present and the future and the already-present eschatological power of God's saving immanence in and through the Christ event.

It was in Dodd's later works, especially his 1935 presidential address to the Oxford Society of Historical Theology, published as an appendix to his book *The Apostolic Preaching and Its Developments* (1936), that these early views were renamed and developed as "realized eschatology." In this essay Dodd again is concerned to correct what he judges to be an unbalanced understanding of biblical eschatology. Undoubtedly, he concedes, the "Day of the Lord" expected by the Hebrew prophets is a "supernatural event" in which the will of God, as "absolute right," will overthrow "the powers of evil, and [bring] judgment upon the sin of men." As a consequence of this divine in-breaking, the Day of the Lord "will bring to those in whom His will is fulfilled a new life which is both glorious and endless."[20] Yet, even here in the Old Testament, all of these otherworldly traits of the *eschaton* do not stand in disjunctive contrast to a historical time before these consummate events transpire. While the Day of the Lord "belongs, in the last resort, to the realm of the 'wholly other,' it is nevertheless not something alien and unrelated to the recorded course of events." "For history," Dodd insists, "depends for its meaning and reality upon that which is other than history. The real, inward, and eternal meaning, striving for expression in the course of history, is completely expressed in the *eschaton*, which is therefore organically related to history."[21]

The New Testament offers this same vision of the organic relation between the imminent eschatological future and the existential eschatological present but with "a profound difference" that intensifies this relation in a unique way. In the New Testament, "the divine event is declared to have happened."[22] For Dodd, of course, what has happened is the life, death, and resurrection of Jesus Christ. Understood as a single divine action, these events form "a particular historical crisis" to which "the characteristics of the Day of the Lord as described in [Old Testament] prophecy and apocalypse are boldly transferred" in the New Testament witness.²³ The New Testament kerygma claims that "the *eschaton* has entered history; the hidden rule of God has been revealed; the Age to Come has come." In Dodd's judgment, "the Gospel of primitive Christianity is a Gospel of realized eschatology."²⁴

Dodd considers this eschatology to be "realized" in several respects. The divine event already accomplished has brought fulfillment to time. Even though this fulfillment awaits a future completion, it is present now in history because the Christ event has already taken place. Jesus's ministry unfolds in miracles that the evangelists narrate as a story of "realized apocalypse."²⁵ The power of God manifest in these events destroys the insidious power of evil in the world and constitutes God's judgment upon the world. Finally, Dodd claims, "eternal life, the 'Life of the Age to Come,' is now realized in experience. Christ is risen from the dead, the first fruits of them that sleep, and we are raised with Him in newness of life. He who believes *has* eternal life."²⁶

These same ideas were developed by Dodd in his book *The Parables of the Kingdom* (1935). The parables of Jesus themselves, he argues, consistently express an eschatology—an account of the coming kingdom of God—that is "realized." Although "Jesus employed the traditional symbolism of apocalypse to indicate the 'other-worldly' or absolute power of the Kingdom of God, He used parables to enforce and illustrate the idea that the Kingdom of God had come upon men [and women] there and then." In Jesus's teaching, "history had become the vehicle of the eternal."²⁷ In calling attention to this important dimension of Jesus's eschatological teaching, Dodd not only identifies something unique about New Testament apocalyptic but also makes normative claims about the belief of the church throughout Christian tradition. "The conviction remains central to the Christian faith," he reminds his readers, "that at a particular point in time and space, the eternal entered decisively into history. . . . To that moment in history our faith always looks back. . . . Above all, in the Sacrament of the Eucharist the Church recapitulates the historic crisis in which Christ came, lived, died, and rose again, and finds in it the 'efficacious sign' of eternal life in the Kingdom of God. In its origin and in its governing ideas it may be described as a sacrament of realized eschatology."²⁸ For Dodd, this means that the meaningful passing of time that we measure as history is neither a secular chronology devoid of eternal significance nor a "veil of illusion" that obscures the eternal from human sight. Rather, historical time "is instrumental, or more properly sacramental, to the eternal order."[29]

Certainly, Dodd's insightfulness as a scripture scholar accounts for his lasting contribution to understanding the character of New Testament apocalyptic, though his own efforts to secure a creative position in opposition to Schweitzer's and the philosophical climate of twentieth-century existentialist philosophy explain to some degree the context in which his insight flourished. Dodd himself admitted that "realized eschatology" was not an "altogether felicitous term" to convey his claim that, in the view of the New Testament writers, eternal life already filled the lives of believers in time. He acknowledged the value of clarifying emendations like Joachim Jeremias's "sich realisierende Eschatologie" and Georges Florovsky's "inaugurated eschatology,"[30] which tried to capture what Dodd had always offered in his fuller scholarly exposition—that although the gift of eternal life was already really in time, the effects of its gracious power had only begun and would be completely actualized in the eschatological future.[31]

Time Forever

In the past seventy years, Christian theology has affirmed the immanence of God's saving love to creation by insisting that time possesses a deep eschatological resonance. Certainly, this theological development is a reaction to the Enlightenment banishment of the supernatural from what it claimed to be the autonomy of the natural world.[32] Our examples of de Lubac and Dodd are simply illustrative of what has become theologically axiomatic—that the natural world, and all of its created qualities including time, cannot rightly be divorced from the supernatural, as though the natural and supernatural were separate compartments of reality. Although distinguishable, the natural and supernatural are deeply interwoven existentially, the power of the supernatural so available to the natural order that isolating some time that stands outside the realm of grace is judged to be theologically deficient.[33]

There are, of course, different Catholic and Protestant ways of locating the graced event that transfigures time. De Lubac, in the spirit of the *nouvelle théologie* that influenced the Second Vatican Council and its heritage, sets the gracing of the natural order in God's act of creation, particularly the creation of humanity, and is unwilling to see humanity's fall into sin as the utter loss of that graced state. Dodd, on the other hand, locates the graced event in Jesus's resurrection from the dead, an act of God that defeats the tragic dimensions of the fall by sacralizing all subsequent time, even to the degree that, in his view, believers already possess resurrected life in existential time. In typically Catholic fashion, de Lubac sees his contribution as a recovery of the ancient tradition of patristic theological reflection, and in typically Protestant fashion, Dodd offers his contribution on graced time as a forgotten truth first expressed by the New Testament writers. However the traditions nuance their views on the eschatological resonance of time, there is now a Christian theological consensus, reflected in the work of de Lubac and Dodd, that worldly time is replete with the power of the life to come. And even though that power has not reached and cannot reach its fulfillment in worldly time, it is the proleptic presence of the eschatological here and now that makes time much more than ordinary.

One might say that this contemporary theological sensibility denies any distinction between "before" and "after" in the temporal order once the event of grace has transpired. In graced time there is no graceless interval. Graced time becomes a continuum in which eschatological fulfillment saturates worldly time even as it yet remains unfulfilled. This denial of the distinction between before and after within graced worldly time extends to any absolute distinction between the natural and the supernatural realms. The sensibility affirms that the graced person and, more generally, graced history possess a supernatural trajectory that makes the popular Christian notion of the "after" life theologically questionable, since heavenly life, the sensibility affirms, already flourishes within earthly life.

It is simply a matter of fact that theology has not pressed its investigations of that graceful continuum in a heavenly direction. Theologians have not imagined an eschatological time in heavenly, resurrected life in the same way that they have insisted that existential time is ever filled with grace. The modern reluctance to speculate about the *eschata* alone would account for this absence. But beyond post-Enlightenment apologetics, there are explicitly theological reasons that account for this hesitancy.

The first reason is that the traditional Christian imaginary has tended to conflate the eternity of God and the metaphysics of heaven, as though heaven and heavenly life were as timeless as the divine nature itself. Thomas Aquinas (1225–74) bespeaks this assumption when he claims that in heavenly life the resurrected body will be conformed to the immutability of the soul transfixed by the glory of the Beatific Vision. The body of the resurrected person, he states, "will be entirely subject to the soul—the divine power will achieve this—not only in regard to its being, but also in regard to action, passion, movements, and bodily qualities."[34] This metaphysics, which envisions heavenly life as a static state, imagines that the saved soul's unchangeable disposition toward the divine will permeates the condition of the resurrected body and, in the heavenly dimension of the communion of the saints, the unchangeable, and so seemingly timeless, character of heavenly life.[35] In some respects, the tradition has imagined that God's timeless being radiates into every dimension of heavenly life to the point that the notion of a heavenly time would be oxymoronic.[36]

A second reason that theologians have not imagined an eschatological time in heavenly life can be attributed to reluctance in at least one important strain of the Christian tradition to concretize the hope of resurrected life in concepts or images. Theologians throughout history have been satisfied to abide by the eschatological reserve commended in Paul's claim that "no eye has seen, nor ear heard, nor the human heart conceived, what God has prepared for those who love him" (1 Cor. 2:9).[37] This reserve has been intensified in modernity by the willingness of theologians to respect the Kantian epistemological concern that knowledge be constructed on the basis of possible objects of sensible experience, a criterion that a theology of heavenly life could not possibly meet. Karl Rahner expresses this heavenly apophasis in an essay on the availability of the blessed dead to believers on earth by noting that "we meet the living dead . . . when we open our hearts to the silent calm of God himself, in which they live; not by calling them back to where we are, but by descending into the silent eternity of our own hearts, and through faith in the risen Lord, creating in time the eternity which they have brought forth forever."[38] Rahner's position perfectly illustrates modern theology's willingness to value the eschatological resonance of existential time and unwillingness to speculate about the temporal resonance of the final eschatological state. Karl Barth expresses the same sort of eschatological reserve in a more dialectical fashion: "Heaven is the boundary which is clearly and distinctly marked off for man [*sic*]. It exists. But in distinction from earth it exists as invisible creaturely reality. It is invisible and therefore incomprehensible and inaccessible, outside the limits of human capacity. . . . It is not merely God who is incomprehensible; the same can also be said of heaven within the creaturely world."[39] This apophatic sensibility would be opposed in principle to any talk of heavenly time as a function of its opposition to talk about all things otherworldly.

The apophasis of this second reluctance has much to commend it. Its unwillingness to qualify the joys of heaven in any way by reducing them to images drawn from worldly experience reflects an avid hope for the life to come and a refusal to place any constraints on the eschatological "more" that constitutes the object of hope. Yet, in spite of the value of this sensibility and its prevalence especially in the modern theological tradition, the representation of heavenly life has a solid footing in the history of Christian art and poetry. The graphic images of heavenly life in medieval art have done much to edify and inspire the hope of generations of believers to the present day, and Dante's (ca. 1265–1321) moving account of heavenly life in the *Paradiso* completes a poem that many consider to be the most accomplished ever written. As untypical as their efforts may be, some of the greatest theologians of the tradition—Augustine (354–430), Aquinas, and Jonathan Edwards (1703–58) among them—have been willing to speculate about the character of heavenly resurrected life, even if none has been willing explicitly to consider the theological value of heavenly time.[40] Even though the apophatic stance offers the advantage of safeguarding the expanse of Christian hope and avoiding any possibility of theological reductionism, there is no reason to think that this mainstream approach to matters eschatological need be the only legitimate one. The Christian tradition has developed a host of interpretive strategies to avoid naïve or even vulgar forms of literalism into which any theology might fall, and these same safeguards could be enlisted in the speculative development of a chthonic eschatology. Finally, the true test of theological adequacy is performance.

If theological speculation about eschatological heavenly time can reap fruitful results, then perhaps such speculation may have a place in the pluralistic range of approaches to eschatological reflection in the modern theological tradition.

The first reluctance considered above is more consequential. The assumption that heaven itself is timeless in its metaphysical constitution has seeped into Christian consciousness so thoroughly that the very thought of a heavenly time seems strange and perhaps even bizarre. As the Christian doctrine of God developed in late Roman antiquity, Greek intellectual thought forms proved to be exceptional philosophical venues for expressing the divine transcendence. Were God timeless, as Plato had described the world of ideas, then God's being escapes the corruption of things in worldly time, experienced by sentient beings as the suffering and death from which the Christian gospel promises redemption. Moreover, the theological category of eternity, understood not only as without beginning or end but also as unchanging timelessness itself, enabled all of God's qualities—God's character, if you will—to be described as fully realized in being and so as consummated metaphysically in a state of absolute perfection. In classical Christian belief to the present day, the claim for divine eternity distinguishes the being of God from all that is less and, lesser still, wanting in God's temporal creation, less because in its metaphysical constitution it is not God, and lesser still because, as Paul taught in Romans 8, all creation, and so all of worldly time, is marred by the sin of humanity.

Even though this difference between God's eternity and created time has been fundamentally important in the Christian worldview, it seems to have become lost in the Christian imaginary of heavenly life. The conflation of heavenly life and God's timelessness wrongly configures the difference as one between this world and the next rather than as a difference between eternity and time, God and creatures. The assumption of heavenly timelessness derives as well from the Christian belief that redemption itself is a changeless state. Since the redemption of the blessed dead in heaven cannot be undone, their wills in redemption are unchangeably conformed to the divine will, a state of heavenly being imagined as timeless. But this imaginary confuses the finitely unchangeable with the eternally unchangeable, which alone is timeless and perfect. The metaphysical constitution of creatures, for example, is unchangeable—they cannot possess natures other than the ones with which they have been endowed—even though the creatures that possess these natures dwell in time and are subject to change in so many other ways. Thus, instances of finite unchangeability flourish in the ambit of temporality. The Christian imaginary would be truer to its classical roots were it to understand the unchangeable volition of the blessed dead in heaven as a kind of finite unchangeableness rather than as the unchanging timelessness that is properly ascribed to God. The irreversibility of the redeemed state in heaven has often been conflated with God's unique unchangeability, but it is theologically important that the Christian imaginary not violate the distinction between God and creatures so that God remains God and creatures remain creatures, even eschatologically. And in order for creatures to remain creatures eschatologically, they must continue to be in time.

The importance of a supernatural time for the integrity of created persons was articulated in a 1992 publication of the Vatican's International Theological Commission (ITC) entitled *Some Current Questions in Eschatology*. Addressing here what it judged to be a number of deficient theological understandings of resurrection and life after death, the ITC explicitly rejected the notion of "resurrection in death," the view that believers are resurrected at the moment of death rather than at the end of worldly time in anticipation of the Last Judgment. The text does not identify a theologian who maintains this position, but certainly it is the theology of Gisbert Greshake that is being called to task. In *Naherwartung, Auferstehung, Unsterblichkeit: Untersuchungen zur christlichen Eschatologie* (1976),[41] Greshake argued that the traditional doctrine of bodily resurrection had become an obstacle for modern believers in its mythological expectation that the bodies of all the dead would be miraculously reconstituted by God and joined with their souls at the Last Judgment. More specifically, he claimed, this belief violated the very holistic anthropology that it affirmed as true. The notion of an interim state between personal death and an end-time bodily resurrection implicitly identified the created person with his or her immaterial soul, and thus encouraged a merely spiritualized understanding of the self. Greshake affirmed that resurrection at death defeats the latent Platonism of the traditional eschatological imaginary by insisting on the unbroken integrity of personal existence in the state of blessedness.

Even before it was questioned by the International Theological Commission, Greshake's theology of resurrected life had already come under the critical scrutiny of Joseph Ratzinger, who would soon become the prefect of the Congregation for the Doctrine of the Faith and then, years later, Pope Benedict XVI. In his *Eschatology: Death and Eternal Life* (1977), Ratzinger argued that Greshake's avowedly holistic anthropology of resurrected life overlooked the need of Christian redemption to embrace all of history just as holistically. The traditional belief in the separation of soul and body at death and the particular judgment of the soul by God deferred bodily resurrection until the universal judgment, when all of history, and not just our individual lives, came to a close. This profound belief, Ratzinger insisted, acknowledges that all of history is invested in each person's life, just as each person's responsibility for history dwells in the vast web of historical relations that stands under God's judgment. "When we die," Ratzinger maintains,

> we step beyond history. In a preliminary fashion, history is concluded—for me. But this does not mean that we lose our relation to history: the network of human relationality belongs to human nature itself. History would be deprived of its seriousness if resurrection occurred at the moment of death. If the resurrection occurs in death then, fundamentally, history is indeed in one sense at an end. Yet the continuing reality of history *and thus the temporal character of life after death* is of quite basic importance for the Christian concept of God as we find that expressed in christology: in God's care for time in the midst of time.[42]

For Ratzinger, Greshake's theology of resurrected life suffered from the myopia of an existentialist individualism that failed to imagine the historical continuity of redemption, a history whose temporality extends even into the heavenly realm.

The criticism of resurrection in death offered by the International Theological Commission enlarges on Ratzinger's provocative suggestion that heavenly life is a temporal state. Like Ratzinger, the ITC faults the notion of resurrection in death for dissolving the "community aspect of the final resurrection" in a resurrection that "would be purely individual." Moreover, some theologians who favor this position imagine this resurrection atemporally by supposing that "after death time can in no way exist, and hold that the deaths of people are successive (viewed from the perspective of this world); whereas the resurrection of those people in the life after death, in which there would be no temporal distinctions, is (they think) simultaneous." But this stance, the ITC insists, "implies recourse to a philosophy of time quite foreign to biblical thought." Time is the created atmosphere for the materiality of God's creation, including the matter that our bodies are now and, in Christian belief, the matter that our bodies will be forever. In the judgment of the ITC, the notion of resurrection in death, which conceives of time as a worldly condition transcended in death, "does not seem to take sufficiently into account the truly corporeal nature of the resurrection; for a true body cannot be said to exist devoid of all notion of temporality." Moreover, even in the interim state between personal death and bodily resurrection, "the souls of the blessed, since they are in communion with the Christ who has been raised in a bodily way, cannot be thought of without any connection with time."[43]

Here we find a serious theological effort to reason through the implications of belief in the resurrection of the body. This effort does not presume that one need approach the doctrine in a naïvely literalist fashion, as though whatever one would say of resurrected selves would be grounded directly in our experience of persons now. The doctrine does not and should not offer a meaning so utterly reductionistic. But however much the reality of eschatological redemption transcends words and thought, the doctrine of bodily resurrection means at least that the human person in the fullness of his or her created being—what the tradition expresses in the ancient categories of body and soul—shares in the eternal life of the resurrected Christ. The doctrine's denial of a merely spiritualized understanding of eternal life and its affirmation of the goodness of the material dimensions of the human person might mean at most that the goodness of the entire material creation shares in eschatological redemption, as Paul envisioned in his talk of a New Creation transfigured by and in the resurrection of Christ (Gal 6:15; 2 Cor 5:17). The International Theological Commission's modest efforts to defend the temporality of heavenly life are an instance of theological faithfulness to the

Christian belief in the integrity of resurrected persons, flourishing as they do in the transfigured temporal theater of God's creation.

Whereas the ancient Christian tradition often embraced Platonic sensibilities on time, regarding time as a measure of corruption and, in Christian values, as the fallen realm of sin and death, the findings of modern physics enable contemporary Christians to appreciate in ways that their ancient forebears simply could not that time is a dimension of energy configured as matter, or, in Christian vocabulary, that time is a dimension of all things created, and so is not in any respect a separable quality of creation.[44] Creation is thoroughly temporal in its created goodness and so much so that, in the language of traditional metaphysics, temporality is enmeshed in the natures of all creatures. What is theologically attractive about the representative views of de Lubac and Dodd that we considered earlier is that they portray the power of eternal life, God's grace, as utterly immanent to the temporality of God's creation, without graceless interval and without objectifying the natural and supernatural as realms incompatible with each other. The notion of heavenly time is theologically attractive for the very same reason. Like the theological sensibilities shared by de Lubac, Dodd, and so many modern theologians, the notion of time in heaven claims that redemption is not incompatible with the conditions of creatureliness, even to the point of rejecting a certain kind of extrinsicism of grace in resurrected life that would require the temporality of resurrected persons to evaporate in the final state of redemption in order for grace to be grace.

The importance of undercutting an extrinsicist understanding of grace even in the traditional Christian imaginary of heavenly life is reason enough for theological attention to the issue of time in heaven. But there are theologically positive, as well as negative, reasons for addressing this issue. How might heavenly time be productively imagined to constructive theological purpose?

If time is the ambience of human creatureliness, the same creatureliness safeguarded in the Christian belief in redemption, then time is an indispensable ingredient in the construction of an eschatological anthropology. Such an anthropology of the redeemed person admittedly would be speculative in its resolve to bring the wider reaches of the Christian imaginary into the scope of theological interpretation. And though speculative, the continuity of graceful time now and forever enables an eschatological anthropology to draw on the evidence of virtue and redemption in existential time in order to speak meaningfully of the joy and fulfillment of resurrected life. In turn, theological initiatives to portray the eschatological "more" of heavenly redemption, however modest they must necessarily be, can shed light on our truthful theological accounts of all things creaturely in the eschatological now.

Theologically explained, the beauty of time lies in its divinely willed difference from God's eternity through which time, in all its created integrity, offers a sequence of becoming that orients creatures toward the consummate becoming of resurrected life. Time is an aesthetical condition for the beauty of all movement in the realm of creation. The beauty of cosmic motion, of music, of dance, of play is simply unimaginable, to say nothing of impossible, apart from time. For created persons in particular, time is the field in which actions transpire that shape character for well or for ill, in consonance with the divine will or in opposition to it. Created persons cannot be who they are, who they have been, and who they will be except within the temporality in which character-building or character-deforming actions unfold.

Time in the eschatological now is at once graced and fallen, burdened by the power of sin and death even as it is filled with the power of resurrected life. Some experiences of time strongly reflect the state of human fallenness. Times of unresolved grieving, times of broken relationship, times of suspicion and fear, times filled with the consequences of hatred, betrayal, and greed, dead time defined by moral paralysis, sinful repetition, despair, and boredom are only some examples of fallen time that appear in existential time, so much of it a consequence of human moral failing, the willed corruption of time in its created state of goodness by God. The emptiness of sin-filled time is redeemed here and now as God graces time in God's ongoing act of creation, and extraordinarily so in the life, death, and resurrection of Jesus Christ. Yet, as human experience testifies, grace-filled time is a time of ardent hope not only because believers yearn for the fullness of the eschatological "more" but also, and tragically, because grace-filled time does not transcend fallen time in the eschatological now.

The grace-filled time of the eschatological forever is a heavenly time that may be judged beautiful in the integrity of its creation by God, in its continuity with grace-filled existential time, and in its capacity to be imagined as a time in which God's redemption ever increases. An eschatological anthropology could be a fertile field for exploration were theologians to follow the ancient lead of Gregory of Nyssa (ca. 335–ca. 395), envisioning heavenly life as a process in which salvational joy, and even the state of redemption itself, increases. This conceptualization is at odds with the traditional Christian imaginary in which resurrected selves, transfixed by the vision of God, seem to enter into the divine eternity itself and pass beyond the conditions of creatureliness. But this common image of heavenly life, in both its Western and Eastern forms, threatens to compromise the most basic assumptions of belief in the resurrection of the body, which require that the character of persons unfolds in temporal action. Gregory's notion of *epektasis* imagines an infinite salvational progress in heavenly life in which the saved self rises in its redemptive state "without ceasing," a heavenly ascent fueled by grace but also by "activity directed toward virtue [that] causes its capacity to grow through exertion."[45] For Gregory, heavenly life is a time—and not an eternity—without end in which resurrected persons exercise virtue.

Gregory does not explain how virtue would transpire in heavenly life, or even why virtue would occur on the favorable side of God's judgment. Indeed, a critic of my proposal would press hard the question of the intelligibility of ongoing heavenly virtue if redemption has already occurred. This question itself expresses the assumptions of the traditional imaginary of heavenly life from which we must depart in order to provide answers. We have already considered a first answer. In order for persons to be persons—even, and perhaps especially, resurrected persons—they must possess character shaped by actions in time. A second possible answer asks us to stretch our eschatological imaginations even further.

Even though a grace-filled time in this imaginary of resurrected life transcends sin, the resurrected selves who enjoy this redemptive time in the glory of the Beatific Vision continue to be defined by the effects of sin just as much as they continue to be defined by the virtue they accomplished in life and might be imagined to accomplish still in heavenly life. Sin, of course, could not transpire in the eschatological forever; otherwise, the redemptive power of grace would be undermined. But the *effects* of the sin that persons both perpetrate and suffer in fallen time must continue to endure in heavenly life if resurrected selves continue to be the persons they were and are in resurrected life, the most basic claim of the doctrine of the resurrection of the body. Although the deathliness of sin has been defeated by grace in heavenly life, the effects of sin in heaven could no more disappear than could the personal histories, the character, the very integrity of resurrected selves. The doctrine of bodily resurrection requires that the effects of sin echo throughout the joys of heavenly time, and as dimensions of saved selves these effects too clamor for redemption.[46]

The beauty of eschatological time lies in its capacity to offer an infinite horizon for resurrected persons to act in order to negotiate morally the sin they have committed and the sin they have suffered, and to do so in the vast proportions of the communion of the saints before and after the Last Judgment. Were we to imagine capaciously the personal, communal, national, international, and transhistorical dimensions of sin whose effects have shaped the character of resurrected selves, then heavenly time opens a graceful duration of endless proportions within which to imagine the workings of heavenly virtue capable of reconciling the eschatological heritage of sin. Were we to dare to hope with Hans Urs von Balthasar that finally the salvation of Christ extends to all so that those whom the traditional imaginary consigns to eternal perdition yet stand too before the Beatific Vision, the moral work of reconciliation in heavenly time increases all the more.[47] And if this reconciliation is a profound dimension of the redemption of Christ itself, then heavenly time is a graceful gift, a transfigured duration as unending as God's love and within which the joy of true reconciliation ever increases with the healing of sinful rifts in the communion of the saints.

We parse time in the categories of past, present, and future, aware that in existential time these moments are implicated in and with each other as they shape the meaningfulness of our lives as they have been, as they are, and as we hope they will be.[48] To be a created person means that the very reality of self ever transpires in the dynamics of this temporal tension in which one's words and deeds configure the person one becomes. When the traditional imaginary of heavenly life does not conflate creatureliness and the divine eternity, it might make room imaginatively for the personal past and present of resurrected selves in heaven. But the traditional imaginary does not posit a heavenly future before which one stands in hope, since hope and the future have evaporated in a redemption timelessly completed. And since a real future has disappeared in the traditional imaginary of heaven, what might remain even of a personal past and present are transformed into a skewed temporality that bears little resemblance to the conditions of creatureliness affirmed in the doctrine of bodily resurrection. The notion of heavenly time only sketched here in this first chapter offers the prospect of a future in the eschatological forever, a future before which one does not hope for a graced time already given but for a future in which grace abounds all the more, as do the moral bonds of relation in the communion of the saints.

Theological speculation about a heavenly time is only of value if its results enhance our appreciation of temporality in the eschatological now as much as they edify our hope for the life to come. God gives us time, and our theological endeavors to reflect on that gift have implications for theological anthropology, ecclesiology, ethics, and even a theology of God. Theological efforts to think through the redemptive resonance of moral endeavor in resurrected life clarify the graceful dimensions of the eschatological now in enlightening ways. Our encounter with graceful redemption now in experiences like love, forgiveness, friendship, understanding, compassion, conversion, commitment, hope, and openness to the stranger might be enriched by considering how the workings of grace continue into the eschatological forever, and how those insights, formed by the deepest Christian hopes, in turn inform our reflections on graceful redemption in the eschatological now.

The continuity of grace in time is an aesthetical judgment that has garnered a consensus in modern theology. I have argued here that the beauty of graced time is more beautiful still if its continuity is imagined to stretch into heavenly life and its ongoing redemption. Such an interpretive course asks Christians to think along with the traditional symbols rather than to translate them into existential states or circumstances to which they are assumed more meaningfully to refer. Yet, even when a traditional imaginary is interpretively reimagined, as it is in my proposal here, the classical symbols of the faith remain rich resources of meaning with an endless capacity to stir our appreciation for the hope of the life to come.

CHAPTER TWO

THE VIRTUES IN TIME

An Eschatological Anthropology

I will continue my theology of time by attending to a particular aspect of the doctrine of creation—the Christian doctrine of the human person created in the image and likeness of God. Our subject matter in this chapter, theological anthropology, will contextualize how we appreciate the theological resonance of time throughout our study. Post-Einsteinian physics has verified that time is a dimension of the physical universe and that matter itself is a configuration of the energy that has animated the universe since its origin nearly fourteen billion years ago. The theological implication of this scientific fact is that time is a quality of created being. Time is the setting in which finite existence flourishes, becoming in all the ways that God's timeless knowledge eternally knew that it would. As a dimension of creation, time is a reality, and thus shares in the transcendental qualities of being that reflect God's own divine qualities. Time is one, true, good, and beautiful. Like all these qualities, the beauty of time, with time itself, extends throughout all of creation.

In this chapter, though, I will not pursue an aesthetical analysis of time through the lens of beauty, as I will in later chapters. Nor will I consider time specifically in its objective reality as a dimension of existence. My approach to anthropology here considers time as a human sensibility, as a way that human subjectivity apprehends the world. The sense of time that accompanies experience, and more particularly the meanings with which persons invest that changing sensibility, will frame my theological anthropology. Rather than venturing an aesthetics of time, an appreciation of its beauty, I will explore an "aesthetic" of time that emerges in the religious experience of Christian believers. The term "aesthetic" in my analysis refers to a field of possible experience. My appeal to this category is inspired by its well-known use by the Enlightenment philosopher Immanuel Kant (1724–1804), though my use of the term will not be beholden to its Kantian employment. I will first examine Kant's influential development of the category and then modify it to serve my purposes here.

Kant begins his major work, the *Critique of Pure Reason* (1787, 2nd ed.), by exploring the conditions under which human subjectivity unfolds and the categories of human understanding that shape and order the vast array of sense experience collected from the empirical apprehension of the world. This starting point is a predictable one for a work that ventured nothing less than a revolution in configuring the constitution of knowledge, the limitations of experience, and the possibilities of reason. Kant's critical Idealism proposes that the problems of traditional metaphysics can be resolved, and the epistemic integrity of modern science assured, by assuming that the objects of experience conform to human understanding rather than that understanding conforms to the objects of experience. It is unsurprising, then, that Kant would begin the first *Critique* with an examination of the subjectivity that molds experience into founded acts of knowledge. The first step that Kant takes in this exposition explores what he calls the "transcendental aesthetic," which he defines as the "science of all principles of *a priori* sensibility."[1] Interestingly, Kant explains in a note that "the Germans are the only people who currently make use of the word 'aesthetic' in order to signify what others call the critique of taste."[2] But Kant rejects this use of the term as a theory of the beautiful, identifying it with what he considered to be the philosopher A. G. Baumgartner's failed attempt to develop necessary, rational rules to govern the judgment of beauty. For Kant, the term "aesthetic" describes the conditions of experience that prescind from the concreteness and specificity of any particular worldly experience or act of understanding, conditions that are a priori, independent of sense experience, but which yet accompany and arrange any actual experience in conscious subjectivity. Space and time are the "two pure forms of sensible intuition" that array possible objects of experience in this aesthetic, in what might be called this subjective theater of moment and place.³ This aesthetic is "transcendental" because the a priori conditions of space and time intuitively frame every possible experience.

For my purposes, there is no need to rehearse in detail Kant's analysis of what for him were the pure intuitions of space and time. I am interested in his notion of an aesthetic, and not the development of his philosophical claims about space and time under the rubric of the transcendental aesthetic. I need only note Kant's claim that space and time lacked any objectivity. They were intuitional forms in which the mind situated experiential representations of things in the world, things that in themselves were inaccessible to experience. Intent on portraying the epistemological relationship between self and world as the conformity of objects to the power of subjectivity, Kant argued that space and time are dimensions of that subjective power, not realities in their own right but "the necessary conditions of all outer and inner experience."⁴ Modern physics, however, knows this not to be true. A scientific configuration of space and time would understand them to be dimensions of objective reality themselves, and not a priori conditions supplied by the mind for the ordering of experience. Kant would have been astonished, as of course would all of his contemporaries, to learn that physical mass curves space and that time slows as it approaches the speed of light, irrespective of the human experience of space and time. In the end, we know that space and time are not as Kant imagined them to be in order to solve certain epistemological problems he addressed in the first *Critique*.

Yet Kant's notion of an "aesthetic" can well serve my theological anthropology in this chapter. Kant employs the term *Ästhetik* to name a field of experience defined by particular kinds of experience, and so a dimension of subjectivity.⁵ I will do the same. My concern in this chapter is time, not space. Here I will not follow Kant's lead in regarding time as an a priori condition of experience. But Kant recognized, as many philosophers have, that there is a subjective dimension to the experience of time that is interpretive. In this regard, I will speak of the meaningful impressions, feelings, and judgments formed subjectively in the experience of time as a "temporal aesthetic." I will speak of this meaningful experience of time—the way that time is apprehended by the experiencer—as "temporality," and distinguish the subjectivity of temporality from the objectivity of time itself.

The temporality of the theological virtues will be my venue for considering the theme of anthropology in this study. Time as a dimension of creation is the ambiance for creation's graceful becoming, which, when fashioned as moral acts by persons created in the image and likeness of God, can be discretely identified as Christian virtues. The very character of human persons is defined by how they perform, or fail to perform, the virtues of faith, hope, and love. Here I will explore the ways in which the theological virtues stir particular determinations of temporality in the believer's subjectivity. Appreciating the temporality of the theological virtues—or, better, the various ways that the believer's religious experience apprehends the virtues in a temporal aesthetic—will enable us as well to appreciate how Christian believers encounter the presence of God in time. Even though we will attend to the temporal sensibility of each of the virtues, and through that analysis to a theological appreciation of the Christian person who believes, hopes, and loves, we will discover that finally the Christian aesthetic can be imagined as a single, unified temporality that embraces all the virtues.

The theological virtues, though engendering temporal sensibilities in the inner life of the believer, are not themselves temporalities. Faith, hope, and love are graceful moral acts that share to some measure in God's redemption. These virtues are ways of living into the divine life. And in this enacted becoming, all of these virtues unfold in time and are experienced by believers in temporally sensible ways. In these respects, and so many others, all the virtues might be characterized by exactly the same traits. In his theological poem *The Portal of the Mystery of Hope*, Charles Péguy imagined the unity of the virtues as a sisterly kinship,[6] capturing through the metaphor the close relationship that all three share. And yet it may be that some relationships between and among the theological virtues are more particular and that such particularity needs to be taken into account when we are exploring the virtues more closely, as we shall here. One particular relationship that we might consider is the close connection between the virtues of faith and hope.

There are some interesting respects in which faith and hope are mutually related, and in a way that distinguishes them from love. Paul was the first to draw such a distinction. It is love, Paul tells us, that is the "greatest" of the three virtues (1 Cor 13:13). In 1 Corinthians, the apostle catalogued all of love's qualities that, to his mind, justified his judgment about love's superiority. But Paul's account of love's lovely qualities—its patience, its kindness, its capacity to transcend envy, arrogance, selfishness, and rudeness, its delight in truth and justice (13:4–7)—finally makes no explicit comparison between love and what he judges to be the lesser virtues of faith and hope. Paul's moving paean to love assumes love's superiority to faith and hope, but does not explain it.

Perhaps we could find cause for love's superiority to faith and hope by reading the New Testament as a single, unified canon and finding direction in 1 John. According to John, "God is love," and love is so indistinguishable from the being of God that "those who abide in love abide in God, and God abides in them" (4:16). God not only loves but is love itself, which makes love the most deeply theological of the theological virtues. Love is the very essence of God's own divine life. It is both what God is and who God is. By comparison, faith and hope are thoroughly creaturely dispositions. They are not possessed by God, nor do they flourish as the divine being itself, at least if one shares the assumptions of a traditional doctrine of God and so eschews the claim of process theology that God too believes and hopes. Faith and hope course in the realm of not-God, as does love, though faith and hope, as more deeply creaturely virtues, meet God at a greater distance than love, at an existential remove that wrestles with God's otherness in faith's affirmation and hope's expectation. Faith and hope are subordinate to love because it is love that "believes all things" and love that "hopes all things" (1 Cor 13:7). Love is the graceful energy of faith and hope. But even as they are empowered by love, faith and hope share a deep affinity for the human limitations that require them, limitations within which faith and hope struggle for relationship to the God who utterly transcends the created realm to which God is yet ever near.

Finally, of course, one cannot reflect on all three theological virtues without considering their perichoretic relationship, a dim reflection perhaps of the divine coinherence of the trinitarian persons.[7] Yet, as we shall see, faith and hope might share a special kinship too in the way they can be imagined to transpire within a temporality defined by eschatological expectation. Though in the tradition they remain clearly distinguishable virtues, perhaps faith and hope often are bound so closely together that the act of faith can be conceived as an act of hope. In my efforts to explore the temporalities of the theological virtues, I will first consider the more deeply creaturely virtues of faith and hope, and then turn to the virtue of love, which, not as virtue but as love itself, is the graceful reality of God.

The Temporality of Faith

Let us begin by considering the temporality of faith. Throughout the Christian tradition, faith has been experienced and described in a variety of ways, and so any attempt to reflect on the temporality of faith must first address the issue of which style of faith is under consideration. Avery Dulles has described this pluralism with his customary clarity and succinctness by identifying seven models of faith.

Under what Dulles calls the propositionalist model, faith is an assent to revealed truths that have been expressed in sentences or propositions. This model flourished in Catholic neo-scholasticism and in conservative Protestant evangelicalism.[8] The transcendental model portrays faith as "a new cognitive horizon, a divinely given perspective, that enables one to see and assent to truths that would otherwise not be accepted."[9] Dulles associates this model with the theologies of Pierre Rousselot, Karl Rahner, and Bernard Lonergan. The fiducial model, which Dulles regards as "characteristically Protestant," regards faith as trust in God's biblical promise. Here, faith is an act of the heart or the will, rather than an act of the intellect.[10] The affective-experiential model finds faith in the immediate apprehension of God and Christ in the inner life, an approach that has gained adherents throughout the tradition in figures as wide-ranging as Maximus the Confessor, the German Pietists, Friedrich Schleiermacher, John Wesley, and Edward Schillebeeckx.[11] The obediential model sees faith as an act of submission to the divine will. It tends to be a Protestant motif that has its origins in Paul and can be found in the theologies of Karl Barth, Rudolf Bultmann, and Dietrich Bonhoeffer, though Dulles also finds this style in the work of the nineteenth-century Catholic theologian Matthias Joseph Scheeben.[12] Faith in the praxis model advocated by political and liberation theologies is faith to the extent that it issues in acts of solidarity with the poor and victims of injustice. Faith itself "is a participation in a social movement that aims to be 'faithful' to God's purposes in history."[13] Finally, the personalist model rebuffs the inclination of the previous models to configure faith in terms of "powers, faculties, and specific modes of action."[14] Here, faith is a relationship, an encounter in which one's own self is drawn transformingly into the personal life of God.

I rehearse Dulles's models to offer not only an overview of the variety of faith but also, through that variety, a way of focusing our reflection on the temporality of faith. In his analysis, Dulles also seeks the unity of faith amid this pluralism. While acknowledging that the various styles of faith may be trying to name very different qualities of the believer's relation to God that finally cross faith's legitimate boundaries, he finally concludes that "theologians discussing faith [in these various ways] have been convinced that they were speaking about the same reality." Moreover, adherents of a particular style of faith typically recognize that the preferred qualities of the other models are yet valued dimensions of their own approach. As Dulles puts it,

> There is a broad consensus to the effect that faith is the basic act or disposition by which human beings respond to revelation and enter into a saving relationship with God. . . . Ideally, faith should take root at the deepest level of the human personality. It should transform believers from within, orienting them in a new way toward God as their creator, savior, and last end. Faith should make a person doctrinally orthodox, trustful, obedient, and socially committed. It should go out to God as one who is to be believed, trusted, obeyed, and loved.[15]

It would be difficult to disagree. The commonality of faith, however, is not exhausted in the combined accents of all seven models. There are other qualities of the richness of faith that are every bit as definitive of the believer's encounter with God, and first among them would be the steadfastness of faith, its capacity to endure throughout the time of its commitment.

The steadfastness of faith appears in the styles of faith in determinate ways. Divine revelation is once-given and closed, and so faith in it reflects those qualities. The divinely created conditions of experience that transcendentally apprehend God are as permanent as the human nature in which they are fixed. The immediate experience of God in the inner life likewise is imagined as a created faculty rooted in the stability of human nature. The biblical promise is ever the same, as timeless as the divine maker of the promise, and so trust in it should abide with the same degree of constancy. Faithful obedience is expected to waver as little as the divine will's immutable command. Faith as liberationist action endures as long as do the sinful structures of systemic injustice and the gospel proclamation that calls for faith's enacted response. Faith as personal relationship to an eternal and omnipresent person would seem to require that the act itself reflect those very divine attributes. And yet, even though the steadfastness of faith appears in different accents that mirror faith's stylistic pluralism, steadfastness is a consistent and definitive quality of faith that has important implications for the temporality of the first theological virtue.

Acts of faith of all sorts—of faith in a spouse, in a friend, and religiously in God—aspire to a constancy that persists over time. If the nature of faith is to remain in faith, then faith's perpetual renewal in the present moment aims to resist the changes that attend the passing of time. The act of faith flourishes in repetition, and in this regard our efforts to describe the temporality of faith can be aided by Søren Kierkegaard's phenomenology of repetition as an analogue for the act of faith.

Repetition, Kierkegaard (1813–55) claims, "is not disturbed by hope nor by the marvelous anxiety of discovery. . . ." "It has instead the blissful security of the moment."[16] Drawing on a vesting metaphor, Kierkegaard proposes that "hope is new attire, stiff and starched and splendid." And "since it has not yet been tried on, one does not know whether it will suit one, or whether it will fit." Repetition, though, "is clothing that never becomes worn, that fits snugly and comfortably, that neither pulls nor hangs too loosely."[17] In repetition, he continues, "one never tires of the old, and when one has it before oneself one is happy, and only a person who does not delude himself that repetition ought to be something new, for then he tires of it, is genuinely happy. It requires youthfulness to hope . . . but it requires courage to will repetition. . . . Hope is the enticing fruit that fails to satisfy . . . but repetition is the daily bread that satisfies through blessing."[18] Thus, faith's stolid repetition is out of sorts with hope's anticipation of a future without familiar precedent. Hope, for Kierkegaard, has its own place in the panoply of responses to the circumstances of life and relation to God. But hope is foreign to faith itself, which steadfastly holds to what it possesses in every instant, taming time, so to speak, by ever repeating an act of commitment that, as repetition, already has been, its goal ever to be again.[19]

Faith, of course, like all things created, is in time. If there is something in the classical conception of faith that seeks to tame time in the constancy of faith's commitment, then that task, as a function of the nature of faith, can never be effectively accomplished. Since faith is in time, it is subject to, and ever reckons with, the vagaries of time. Yet, in its virtuous apprehension of God, faith is imagined to elude time, as though its undeniable temporality were in some fashion atemporal. We can see the resonance of this assumption in Thomas Aquinas's exposition of the virtue of faith in the *Summa Theologiae*.

Aquinas explores the act of faith by considering both its objective and subjective dimensions. The proper object of faith is "the first truth," and so faith "rests upon the divine truth itself as the medium of its assent."[20] It is the reality of the eternal God that faith grasps since God is the truth itself. Unsurprisingly, then, the timeless objectivity of God's own being seems to spill into the subjective appropriation of faith. In the act of believing, Aquinas notes, the believer "is in the same state of mind as one who has science or understanding" to the extent that, as with the knower of a science such as geometry, the content of one's apprehension is fixed in its truthfulness and is not subject to error. Yet, Aquinas observes, the object of faith transcends the powers of the mind in a way that the object of any science does not. And since God eludes the creaturely capacity of the mind, the believer's knowledge "is not completed by a clear vision, and in this respect he [or she] is like one having a doubt, a suspicion, or an opinion."[21] Aquinas does not think that authentic faith is riddled with doubt, vexed by troubling questions, or lost in the confusion of competing views that clamor to be recognized as true. He claims that the believer is only "like" one in doubt, suspicion, or mere opinion because in these mental states the mind does not knowledgeably master the objective truth it seeks, just as the believer's act of faith cannot knowledgeably grasp the inexhaustible mystery of God's divine being.

For Aquinas, the elusiveness of their epistemological object alone configures the very qualified resemblance between faith and doubt.

Considered subjectively, however, faith and doubt in Aquinas's estimation could not be more different. The theological virtue of faith is a most unusual subjective state. Even though the eternal truth it apprehends is consummately beyond its grasp, the act of faith is characterized by a certainty assured by the immutable truth in which faith believes, a certainty brought to fruition in the believer's inner life through God's gift of grace.[22] Since, as we have seen, the believer "is in the same state of mind as one who has science and understanding,"[23] the wavering of doubt is banished in faith's gracefully infused truth. Aquinas offers three reasons for faith's required assent to truths that surpass reason, as well as to truths that lie within reason's domain. The first is "that God's truth [may] be known sooner," and the second "that more people may have knowledge of God." It is the third reason that bears most of all on our efforts to portray the temporality of the classical conception of faith: "The third reason has to do with certitude. The mind of [human persons] falls far short when it comes to the things of God. Look at the philosophers; even in searching into questions about [humanity] they have erred in many points and held contradictory views. To the end, therefore, that a knowledge of God, undoubted and secure, might be present among men [and women], it was necessary that divine things be taught by way of faith, spoken as it were by the word of God who cannot lie."[24] Faith, Aquinas teaches, "is that habit of mind whereby eternal life begins in us and which brings the mind to assent to things that appear not,"[25] as though the divine eternity appropriated in faith is reflected in the certainty that assures faith's subjective truthfulness. "In certitude," he maintains, "faith surpasses [the intellectual virtues of prudence and art] because of its material object; it is about the eternal, which does not admit of contingency."[26] For Aquinas, the steadfastness of faith mirrors the timeless reality of God, who is faith's graceful cause.

As distinctive as Aquinas's scholastic parsing of the act of faith may be, it is materially representative of the traditional Christian belief that the constancy of faith transpires in a kind of atemporal temporality, a passing of time in which time's flux is constrained by an undeniable dimension of the experience of faith—its commitment to continue to be what it is and has been, as though the time in which it flourishes is always the same. So many theologians in the tradition might serve as supportive witnesses to this classical aesthetics of the atemporal steadfastness of faith. But let us cite just one more illustration, closer to our own day, in the work of the twentieth-century German theologian Gerhard Ebeling (1912–2001).

As we would expect, Ebeling speaks of the steadfastness of faith in ways resonant with the claims of his own Lutheran tradition. "Faith," he observes, "determines time," and as it unfolds, faith "is never greedy for time, as we are, who never have time, because it is never dependent upon a certain time. Nor is faith ever sick of time, as we are, who just as often wish it were past, speaking as we do, with a brutality which is no longer noticed as such, of 'killing time.' But for faith every time is right."[27] Every time is right for faith, Ebeling avers, because faith makes every time the same, an ever-recurring moment in which the believer "grasps the promise that God is for us."[28] In its believing act of renewal, faith absorbs time, making each present moment its own, and by so doing witnessing gratefully to the presence of the eternal God in every instant. In Ebeling's judgment, faith so tempers time that there is a sense in which the future is absorbed into faith's immanent affirmation.

Faith, Ebeling attests, is the believer's encounter with justification, nothing less than God's salvation, the unmerited gift of eternal life. This salvation is as timeless as the predestinating decree of God that has brought it about, a consequence that confirms in the believer that "nothing can tear him [or her] from God's hands, but he [or she] has been decided about for all eternity." Faith, he reminds his reader, "is not a pre-condition of salvation, but is the certainty of it; and as such it is itself the event of salvation." Thus, "faith is essentially this certainty concerning the future of one's life, this confident trust that cannot be disappointed or confuted by any future event."[29] There is, of course, an unknown future with regard to all sorts of possible eventualities. But for the concerns of faith the future simply does not matter given what one knows through faith. Every time reiterates this present moment in which grace confirms faith's certainty of predestination, a confessional variant on the phenomenology of faith that is experienced as faith's timelessness even in the midst of time.

However different their historical and confessional contexts may be, these classical accounts of faith share an interesting similarity that even more broadly represents a traditional understanding of this religious act. The beauty of faith flourishes in its paradoxical rebuff of time, in what we have called its atemporal temporality, an imagined duration in which every new moment aspires to be old, in which every new circumstance is embraced by virtuous habit, and in which every nuance of new relationship is absorbed into the character and integrity of principled commitment. An aesthetics of this aesthetic of atemporal temporality appreciates the constancy of ever being in authentic relationship, most consummately in relation to God, the beauty of faithfulness revealing itself in its capacity to abide, to remain in truth, love, obedience, and committed deed, to endure through time in a way that reflects faith's fidelity to its unchanging cause and aim. Faith's steadfastness, its reaffirmation in every passing moment, seeks to defy time, as though its repeated commitment aspires to the impossible goal of appropriating faith's eternal measure in time. Lamenting the limitations of worldly fidelity even as he praises it, Kierkegaard makes this point well by observing that "here only spiritual repetition is possible, even though it cannot be so complete as in eternity where there is true repetition."[30]

Faith, as I have noted, is in time and, like all things creaturely, is utterly subject to time. But in traditional sensibilities the power of faith lies in its resistance to the corrupting temporality of temptation, sin, and perfidy, which would disturb or even rupture its act of fidelity. Epistemically, faith's atemporal steadfastness is portrayed as a certainty that subjectively images the truth of the believer's relation to God, a truth as timeless, and so as unchangeable, as the object of faith. Claims for the certainty of faith announce the experience of a steadfastness that is and has been and the stolid expectation of a future rife with what has already transpired.[31]

How, though, does this classical aesthetic of faith's temporality measure up against the actual workings of faith in the believer's life? Is faith's homologous duration of repeated commitment so continuous that it is uninterrupted by anomalous change, so stalwart that in it faith ever abides untroubled, and so habitual that in it affirmation persists unwavering?

Throughout the tradition, theological testimonies to the life of faith have readily acknowledged the many ways the believer's relationship to

God is beset by trial, temptation, struggle, doubt, and even despair. One need only think of Athanasius's depiction of Antony's frequent battles with the devil in his influential *Life of Antony*,[32] of Teresa of Ávila's claim in *The Interior Castle* that the aspirer to intimate relationship with God inevitably finds herself afflicted by a spiritual depression so deep that it is comparable only to "the torment of those who suffer in hell,"[33] or of St. John of the Cross's account of the despair that attends the mystical journey to God in his treatise *The Dark Night*, the title a metaphor for the pain inevitably experienced by the soul in the course of its contemplative ascent.[34] Or, these well-known accounts of the trials of faith aside, one need only listen to people of faith talk about their struggles to believe in the midst of life's tragedies or even in the course of ordinary time to appreciate just how tenuous the act of faith can be.

A classical aesthetic of faith's temporality does recognize these trials to the religious life, but tends to imagine such struggles ensuing from without, as though faith's essential steadfastness stands beleaguered before all that might prove vexing to its endurance and certainty. And yet, however much assailed by life's tragedies that call it into question, faith in this classical aesthetic is imagined to abide as it has even throughout such tribulations, its resistance a testimony to its valued atemporality.

There have been voices in modern theology, however, that have configured things differently. Paul Tillich (1886–1965), most notably, insisted that doubt is a dimension of faith itself, and not something extraneous to it. Faith, Tillich claims, draws its confidence, its certainty, from its participation in the divine object of faith. This mystical intimacy, though, is ever qualified by a real separation between the believer and God that derives from the finitude and estrangement of the human situation, a separation that requires faith to be a proper acknowledgment of the divine otherness.[35] It is from this metaphysical and moral circumstance of the believer's separation from God that the experience of doubt emerges as a necessary experiential constituent of the act of faith. "Out of the element of participation," Tillich explains, "follows the certainty of faith; out of the element of separation follows the doubt in faith. And each is essential for the nature of faith."[36] Criticizing the traditional aesthetic of faith, Tillich continues: "Faith and doubt have been contrasted in such a way that the quiet certainty of faith has been praised as the complete removal of doubt. There is indeed a serenity of the life in faith beyond the disturbing struggles between faith and doubt. To attain such a state is a natural and justified desire of every human being. But even if it is attained—as in people who are called saints or in others who are described as firm in their faith—the element of doubt, though conquered, is not lacking."[37] In opposition to what he calls "faith as a traditional attitude without tensions," Tillich insists that a truly "living faith includes the doubt about itself, the courage to take this doubt into itself, and the risk of courage."[38]

Tillich intentionally places his theology of faith at odds with the classical imaginary. In doing so, he does not explicitly address the issue of faith's temporality. There may, however, be a temporal aesthetic implicit in Tillich's position. In his claim that the act of faith is constituted not only by steadfast affirmation but also by doubt and the risk of courage, Tillich suggests that that same act is shaped by multiple temporalities. The atemporal temporality of faith's steadfastness is one. But incorporated into that traditional temporality is a more fragmented, anomic temporality, a fractured time of disorientation and disturbance stirred by the encounter with life's tragic dimensions. Loss, alienation, trauma, and betrayal—all the manifestations of brokenness in our lives—lead the believer to doubt what faith affirms. For Tillich, though, this doubting is religiously productive, issuing from and reflecting a realistic, tragic temporality in which our lives ever move and prompting the courageous risk that both dispels faith's complacency and provides occasion for the believer to reaffirm commitment in the face of existential challenge.

Tillich's claim that the act of faith properly incorporates the experience of doubt has been recognized as one of his important theological contributions. Rather than imagining faith's steadfastness as abidingly pacific and supposing that assaults on its atemporal temporality issue from profane quarters extraneous to it, Tillich embraces doubt, and by inference a tragic temporality characterized by disturbing change, into the nature of faith itself. The result is a portrayal of faith that situates the encounter with God in the midst of the confused mix of events and temporalities that transpire in actual life. It is interesting to note, however, that as much as Tillich attempts the existential blend of atemporal and anomic temporalities, he yet conceptualizes the encounter between faith and doubt dialectically, as though faith were an experiential state in which the moments of affirmation and doubt retain their particular identities in their mutual encounter. As Tillich framed it in the passage quoted above, "Out of the element of participation [in God] follows the certainty of faith; out of the element of separation [from God] follows the doubt in faith. And each is essential for the nature of faith."[39] Thus, these two moments in the life of faith, and by inference the temporalities in which they move, remain distinguishable and determinate, in spite of Tillich's creative efforts to describe the act of faith in an existentially fulsome way. Faith's atemporal temporality still abides, even if only as one term in the dialectical life of faith.

A better way to account for the believer's virtuous encounter with God—one that is willing to embrace a tragic and anomic temporality utterly into the act of faith—might be to imagine the act of faith *as* an act of hope. Hope's rendition of time, I propose, may prove to be far more adequate to the claims of faith than the traditional temporal aesthetic of faith.

The Temporality of Hope

As noted in my introductory remarks, faith and hope are the more creaturely of the theological virtues. They issue from the believer's inability to encounter God's mysterious otherness directly. They are subjective responses to the divine moored in the limitations of human finitude. Unlike love, they are not virtues that God possesses, nor are they qualities of God's very own being. This homology provides some justification for reflecting on them together theologically. A stronger justification is the way the temporality of hope illuminates the nature of faith.

Hope is the yearning for a fulfilled future, for a time yet to transpire, a "not-yet" promising a wholeness that completes and redeems the limitations of the present moment. Hope is never in possession of what it hopes for. Hope's yearning dwells in the ambiance of absence, always reaching for what in hope remains ungraspable. And yet, however much the fulfillment for which one hopes is presently elusive, it is imaginable enough to stir hope's desire. Hope's yearning is human initiative. Its experience is not simply given, like the state of consciousness in waking life or grief in the face of overwhelming tragedy. It is something that the one who hopes does. One hopes. Without the aspirant's hoping efforts, there would be no hope, since hope is a relationship formed by the aspirant's willful desire for the object of hope. But that relationship is crafted too by the object of hope, by the fulfilled future that in hope's yearning seems to have a life of its own, even if it can be explained away by the hopeless as the wistful construction of unrealistic longing. The imagined, fulfilled future for which one hopes seems to draw the one who hopes forward, as though the object of hope stretches time, its gravity pulling expectant time toward the completion for which hope yearns.

Parsed theologically, hope yearns for God and for the fulfillment of God's presently given grace. Were we to imagine the believer's encounter with God as the seemingly timeless repetition of steadfast fidelity, then we would readily confess with the New Testament author of Hebrews that faith is "the assurance of things hoped for, the conviction of things not seen" (Heb 11:1). As assurance and conviction, faith affirms the timeless truth of God's divine being and the lasting character of the believer's authentic relationship to God. Such steadfastness, the biblical author claims, is a balm that soothes the believer in the face of divine hiddenness and a motivating respite in hope's long journey toward eschatological fulfillment. Without denying this classical aesthetic of faith, which somewhat linearly assigns faith a stolid priority in all the dimensions of the believer's relationship to God, let us rather imagine hope standing in first place among the more creaturely virtues, even to the point that we imagine faith as hope itself, and faith's temporality as the temporality of hope.

A spiritual phenomenology of hope would never properly speak of hope's certainty, even in the manner of the classical aesthetic of faith, which portrays faith's enduring commitment as a believed certainty.[40] By its very nature, the virtue of hope is full of tentativeness, fragility, and doubt. It skirts the margins of despair, reaching, in deep need and often rather desperately, for the "more" of forgiveness, resolution, and fulfillment. However much hope imaginatively anticipates the reconciled end of its yearning, all that it hopes for stands distant and beyond its grasp as long as hope remains hope. And, for this reason alone, whenever hope abides, it remains incomplete, even in the midst of its most ardent aspirations for a realized future. Both faith and hope, as the more creaturely of the theological virtues, take shape as grace-filled responses to God's mysterious otherness, transcendently in God's aseity or immanently in the incarnation. Both are resigned to encountering God at a distance and flourish in and as that self-acceptance of creaturely limitation. Configured in the classical aesthetic, hope feels this distance more than faith does. Hope does not transpire in the act of repetition, as Kierkegaard observed. It does not find itself confirmed in an ever-renewed present moment that, however dimly, captures the presence of the eternal God. Steadfastness is not a proper quality of hope—not because hope lacks the desire to last but because of the temporality in which hope courses.

Hope most often and intensely moves in anomic time. Unlike faith in the classical aesthetic, in which time conforms to the expected steadfastness of faith, hope waxes and wanes as it faces the consequences of sin in time. As much as hope may struggle to abide, it is not in the nature of hope to remain in hope. Rather, hope twists and turns in the vagaries of tragic time, gaining and losing its virtuous energy as it confronts the power of sin and death in individual lives and in history. It flags in the leaden time of depression, desperately yearns for wholeness in the shocked, frozen time of trauma, retreats overpowered before the confused and angry duration of grief, and ardently aspires for nothing less than a miracle in seemingly hopeless times filled with senseless violence and crushing injustice. God is present to all such anomic times and, as that presence, is the graceful source of hope in all of its manifestations. And yet, even though it is true, as Paul reminds, that "where sin increased, grace abounded all the more" (Rom 5:20), it often seems to hope in the midst of crisis as though the presence of God for which hope yearns has been eclipsed. In the fractured time that calls for hope, the ever-present God who is the source of hope seems to appear, as hope's fulfillment seems founded, or to disappear, as redemption seems illusory. Hope strengthens and weakens unpredictably in this disturbing temporality, for some diminishing and for others increasing in life's most tragic moments, and for all ever in danger of evaporating into an apathy that eclipses all hope.[41]

Hope flourishes too in pacific time, when its expectations for fullness are stirred initially by the truth of realized eschatology—that we already possess eternal life—and then more by the anticipation that what God has already done for creation in Christ will reach consummation in God's future. But pacific time is the blessing of the moment or the blissful ignorance of those whose hope is parochial and self-involved. As one's perspective on time widens beyond the blessedly pacific to face the anomic time that experience knows yet awaits and in which history and the lives of others ever stand, hope's ordinary time shows itself to be a flux within which its virtue ever contends with tragic circumstance to keep the gospel's promise of redemption in sight.

To imagine faith as hope brings the act of faith into the tensive ambiance of hope's consciously eschatological time. All "time now" is eschatological to the degree that it is created, like all creation, in and through the Son of God and so is filled in its very being with his redemptive life (John 1:3–4). All "time now" is eschatological to the degree that it is ever graced and so already in the ambit of eternal life. And all "time now" is eschatological time to the degree that, because it is created and graced, every one of its moments stirs in the believer a sense of an ending, an ending shaped by its very finitude and also by its anticipation of God's consummate victory over the power of sin and death, a victory marked by the end of anomic time in the event of the Last Judgment. Hope begins with the believer's attunement to this resonance of eschatological time and flourishes as it courageously faces the circumstances that unfold in anomic time. Whether hope is diminished before suffering's eclipse of God or strengthened by a glimpse of eschatological consummation, it ever wrestles to be in relation to God in times spoiled by the depths of sin and yet predestined to be completed in the New Creation.

To imagine faith as hope acknowledges that faith ever stands in troubled eschatological time in which gracious virtue cannot be immune to life's tragic dimensions. Unlike faith's atemporal temporality in the classical aesthetic, faith imagined as hope acknowledges the precariousness of the act of faith, its immersion in the sort of time that leads the believer to yearn for a redemption that is not existentially given and that, in spite of hope, often seems to be unrealizable. And even unlike faith as conceived by Tillich, who admirably strove to imagine doubt as a dipolar counterpart to stolid affirmation in the act of faith, faith imagined as hope places the act of faith fully and holistically into a temporality in which the tenuous character of relationship to God is not resisted but embraced.

Faith is not a subjective echo of eternity that transcends fallen time. However much the classical aesthetic makes certainty—even believed certainty—a quality of faith, the atemporal temporality of its imaginary provides no real refuge for an experience resolutely secure in its grasp of God's providential existence. The more deeply creaturely virtues move in the ambit of hope's temporality, engrained in a time of eschatological expectation stirred by profound human need and excited by human yearning's dim apprehension of God's future. This eschatological time offers no certainty at all, whether it be a certainty of God's presence to the crisis of the moment or of God's promised fulfillment. Such is the character of hope's fragility, patience, and perseverance. Unlike faith in the classical aesthetic, hope cannot be imagined to possess qualities analogous to the divine attributes. Whether delineated subjectively as faith or hope, the more creaturely virtues struggle for faithfulness or hopefulness, and always in an eschatological time stretched between the "already" of the graced anticipation of God and the "not-yet" of sin's enduring tragic power. In such a temporal aesthetic, which is intent on remembering that all time is eschatological time, would it not be more productive to imagine the act of faith itself as an act of hope?

This seems to be a rhetorical question that begs for an affirmative answer. But we would not hope for that much from the reader. The evidence of scriptural revelation, the doctrinal tradition, and the long history of Christian spiritual writing has testified to a firm resolve to name two experiences, elevated by their meaningfulness to the level of theological virtues, that are indeed distinguishable. Claiming on the basis of my brief and modest argument that the act of faith could be reduced to the act of hope, to the point that faith could be imagined to disappear, without remainder, would press further than the traditional evidence allows. Rather, my proposal, offered as a thought-experiment, has argued that attention to the temporal aesthetics of the virtues of faith and hope reveals some limitations in the traditional aesthetic of faith that might be remedied by imagining the act of faith in the temporal aesthetic of hope.

Were I nevertheless to press the thought-experiment quite far, I could imagine faith simply as hope itself. The consequence of this strong position would be an imaginary in which the more creaturely act of relationship to God would be anchored not in assent to all dimensions of divine truth but in the fluctuating desire for God's future in the midst of fallen time. In such a configuration of Christian subjectivity, any experience of assent to divine truth or, for that matter, any experience of divine grace at all would be a function of the graceful yearning for God's final victory over the power sin and death. Those inclined to this view might find it attractive for its emphasis on an aesthetic of eschatological time, an aesthetic in which the one who hopes relinquishes any notional claims for certainty and rejects any effort to banish doubt from, or even compartmentalize it productively within, the virtuous apprehension of God. Hope wavers, and authentically so, as it keeps the beat of eschatological time in a troubled key. Finally, imagining faith as hope might be pleasing to those who appreciate the proleptic dimensions of Christian tradition, the capacity of the present moment in the long life of the church to disclose new and surprising ways in which inklings of God's future are in our midst now, and in ways that previously had eluded the community of hope's deepest thoughts, words, and aspirations. The virtue of hope transpires with a keen sense that it lacks the object of its desire. And yet its expectation is stirred by an equally keen sense for the presence of the Spirit of God, whose grace makes time eschatological, drawing it ever into the fulfilled time of resurrected life.

If carrying my thought-experiment to this point be judged too far, then perhaps my proposal that faith be imagined as hope can shed light on a more qualified position that appreciates the bond between the more creaturely virtues not merely in their shared endeavor to grasp God from a distance but also in their properly shared eschatological temporality.

What I have described as hope's temporality is the metier of faith, a faith desiring God's fulfillment as it struggles in fallen time. While faith is a source of strength to the believer, it is not a refuge from all the dimensions of broken finitude that stir the believer's hope. Faith's time is not atemporal in any sense, nor should faith aspire to the kind of permanence in belief that the classical aesthetic imagines. The betrayal of faith is infidelity, but there are corruptions of faith that fall short of its utter loss. The modern error of faith is fundamentalism, which takes the traditional aesthetic of faith so literally that the steadfastness of faith is imagined utterly to transcend the temporality of hope. In that error, hope too is corrupted, its eschatological time reduced to the present moment, and thus to the chiliastic betrayal of hope in an utterly immanentist form of despair. Shades of this insidious and extreme corruption seep into any believer's act of faith, if only as temptation in which one expects faith to mirror the timeless object of eschatological desire. Although faith relies for its content on the givenness of the authoritative past, it is no less oriented in time toward God's future than hope and, so situated, is caught up in the eschatological pull of the New Creation, which promises more to every present moment. In this mutually supportive relationship between faith and hope, faith struggles not to lose hope but to remain faithful to its properly eschatological resolve. This hoping-faith, a faith shaped by the desire for the God, who graciously shares God's own eternal life, aspires for a time beyond the times that so needfully call for its virtue.[42]

The Temporality of Love

I have been intent in these pages to speak about the temporal aesthetics of faith and hope, and I have reached a tentative conclusion in my theological thought-experiment to imagine faith as hope. That thought-experiment was offered as a corrective to the limitations of the classical aesthetic of faith and required a phenomenology of hope's temporality that, I proposed, was a far better setting in which to imagine the first theological virtue. I will conclude my reflection on a temporal aesthetic of the virtues with a demurral of sorts. My analysis of faith and hope could be conducted as it was because these virtues do indeed offer distinctive aesthetics, however adequate or inadequate they are judged to be. The virtue of love, to the contrary, offers no particular aesthetic of time. Paul's famous paean to love in 1 Corinthians names no quality of love that suggests a particular temporal aesthetic, with the possible exception of love's "patience," a quality that, for the apostle, seems rather to refer to love's capacity to suffer—to "bear all things" and to "endure all things" (1 Cor 13:4, 7)—and not at all to a time that is specifically germane to love.

The briefest of meditations on the virtue of love will reveal that it has no time that is uniquely its own. Like all the virtues, love is in time. But unlike the virtues of faith and hope, it seems to course in all possible times in ways that avoid its making a particular configuration of time its own. In time love is subject to all the occasions of sin that plunge love into time's fallen state of tragic flux. It is wounded by betrayal, and sometimes even lost through selfish neglect and apathy. Love courageously takes its stand against the powers of injustice and hatred, passionately struggling for relationship and community in times of violence and division. By the same token, in time love is subject to all the occasions of grace that cause love to fill the moments of life with its joyful commitment to nurturing the bonds of union with the beloved, in communities of love, and to welcoming the stranger into these very same ties. All of love's lovely qualities seem to transcend both serene time and tragic time, or, in what might be another way of saying the same, love's qualities nestle into all times, making all times love's own.

My argument in this chapter has been that all time is eschatological time—time that is laden with God's future, time that anticipates the fullness of Christ's redemption. The believer's sensibility for eschatological time is what shapes and molds the human person into the kind of creature whom God intended the human person to be in "time now": a self hopefully attuned to God's eschatological consummation in the midst of anomic time. Time rightly appreciated as God's creation unfolds in every minute, in every hour, with a keen expectation for that fullness which is grasped only partially now. Were we to imagine a productive aesthetic for the virtue of love, it would be that same eschatological time in which the virtue of hope traditionally moves and in which I have urged the placement of the virtue of faith.[43] Love as virtue is as creaturely as the virtues of faith and hope, and in its creaturely limitations human love too encounters God at a distance, struggling in fallen time to remain in love and ever hoping for the "more" of love's eschatological completion. But even if the virtue of love possesses creaturely dimensions as human endeavor, it is different from faith and hope because the very love that animates its virtue is the being of God itself. If the virtues of faith, hope, and love are graced human actions, the divine love that especially fills the virtue of love is the uncreated grace that stirs the believer's virtuous responses to God and neighbor in faith, hope, and love. Perhaps this is why Paul continues his paean to love in 1 Corinthians by imagining love itself as the power that presses faith to believe and hope to hope. Love, he claims, "believes all things," and love "hopes all things" (1 Cor 13:7).

This interesting difference between faith and hope as the more creaturely virtues, on the one hand, and love, on the other hand, suggests that love as creaturely virtue that mirrors God's own being as love itself might be appropriately imagined through an aesthetic of atemporal temporality, though in a style that differs from the classical aesthetic of faith. Were we to follow Katherine Sonderegger in regarding the divine attributes *as* the very being of God, claiming, as she does, that the divine oneness is God's "foundational perfection,"[44] then the love that God is may not be distinguished from the eternity that God is. Love understood as the grace that constitutes God's own divine life is atemporal not because that love brings us fixed certainty or even because we encounter that love as steadfast. Love as the grace of God's own divine life is atemporal because the perfection of the divine eternity brings God's presence into all created time and into all the temporalities that issue from the human appropriation of time. The believer meets the consummate beauty of divine love in love's temporality as virtue, virtue that is graced by the divine love itself but that, as virtue, struggles as human endeavor in fallen time to endure in acts of love, and faith, and hope. If love is the perichoretic unity of the theological virtues, it is so not as virtue but as grace, a grace that stirs the longing of faith, hope, and love in a time made eschatological by a redemption already accomplished that believers encounter in hope's desire for a time gracefully made more. It is in the midst of eschatological time that the eyes of hope, however clouded by time's fallenness, can perceive the flow of created beauty toward its source and its end in uncreated love.

This temporal aesthetic configures our theological anthropology of Christian subjectivity, an anthropology informed by the unity of the theological virtues in hope's tensive time. Through the vagaries of anomic time, which, like all time, is eschatological time, the believer anticipates time's fulfillment, graced by the love of God's own eternal life, which draws time, and indeed all creation, to redemptive consummation. Viewed through hope's temporal aesthetic, this eschatological anthropology appreciates the believer's experiential encounter with God as a sensibility ever attentive to God's future that unfolds in the virtues of hoping-faith and love, animated, as are all things, by the love who God is.

CHAPTER THREE

TOWARD A THEOLOGY OF EVENTS IN TIME

Faith conceived as hope highlights the way hope's eschatological temporality saturates the theological virtues. My theological thought-experiment in the previous chapter need not lead to the conclusion that the virtue of faith is reducible to the virtue of hope. The testimony of believers throughout the tradition provides ample witness to the integrity of the act of faith in Christian experience. Nevertheless, my thought-experiment may lead us to question the traditional representation of the temporality of faith and to appreciate its steadfastness instead as the ardency of hope in the midst of time both fallen and graced. More broadly, my thought-experiment encourages us to consider too how love as virtue ever moves in eschatological time, struggling in the ambit of sin even as it aspires to the consummate love that is God's own divine self.

These reflections suggest the outlines of an eschatological anthropology, a theological interpretation of the created self in light of the Christian hope of God's redemptive fulfillment. There are many ways in which the theme of Christian anthropology has been developed in recent theology—as the giftedness of human nature created male and female and sacramentally represented in the spousal meaning of the body,[1] as human nature created in the image of Christ, who is the true, revealing image of the Father,[2] or as human nature subject to the sinful deformation of racism, from which the restoration of the *imago Dei* in which all are equally created offers liberation.[3] An eschatological anthropology might appreciate these, and other, theological accents more or less, but will judge those it considers truthful through the hope of resurrected life revealed in Jesus's own resurrection from the dead, an event in which our humanity, like his, has been, is, and consummately will be embraced into the eternal life of God. My exploration of the theological virtues situated virtuous acts of relationship to God and neighbor in an eschatological time stretched between the believer's sinful fallenness and God's graceful consummation of all that is creaturely, a time that shapes the character, and thus the person, that these acts define. To the degree that the virtues, both as actions and ideals, configure what the self is and what the self through its acts might be, their interpretive inflection through the temporality of hope offers the outlines of an eschatological anthropology.

In this chapter, my approach to time shifts from anthropology to metaphysics, from an aesthetic of temporality to an aesthetics of time, from human subjectivity to creation's objectivity, from an account of how time seems to the believer to time's unfolding beauty in events. Although I have appropriated Kant's notion of a temporal aesthetic to develop a theological anthropology of Christian experience, we should resist the temptation to explain time solely through human subjectivity, as though time were simply a function of human perception. Kant's influence on post-Enlightenment thought encourages this experiential understanding of time, as does Kant's more specific influence on modern theology. Transcendental theologies that enter into apologetical dialogue with modernity through broadly Kantian assumptions are inclined to privilege experience as both the source and object of interpretation, finding within the conditions of possible experience, including time, an orientation to the divine, transcendental "whence" of meaning.

Experience, of course, dwells in time as all created existence does, and so any theological aesthetics of time must count the experience of time within its field of explanation. But time is not simply a quality of perception nor merely a human measure of the change that transpires in the world. Time, modern physics has established, is a dimension of existence in the physical universe—what Christians believe to be creation—and so possesses an objectivity as a behavior of the natural world, of creation, that transcends the human apprehension of time. As much as our experience of time may lead us to make judgments about how time seems, and as much as Christian believers do this, say, by ascribing traditional temporalities to the Christian experiences of faith and hope, time remains a dimension of existence itself that must be appreciated in its integrity, and considered theologically in that regard. This is an especially important perspective for a theological aesthetics that attempts to detail the beauty of time in all of its meaningfulness, not only as a human sensibility but also as a dimension of created reality itself.

I will now begin my task in this chapter—to speak theologically of the beauty of time in the way it transpires in the movement of God's creation. In doing so, in making theological judgments about the beauty of time, one cannot escape the realm of sensibility, which is the ambiance of human judgment. To put the matter in Kantian terms, there is no direct access to the thing-in-itself. But whereas my goal in the previous chapter was to explore sensibilities regarding the human apprehension of time in the temporalities of the theological virtues, my aim here is to consider the theological resonance of the eventfulness of time itself, and to consider the graceful beauty of that eventfulness. It would be good for my own modestly constructive efforts toward this end to take their point of departure from Augustine's famous meditation on time in book 11 of the *Confessions*. A theology of time like mine is obliged to take account of Augustine's engaging efforts to wrestle with the mystery of time, which can aid me in clarifying my own theological choices through these issues.

Augustinian Tempo

Aurelius Augustinus (354–430) wrote much of his work the *Confessions* in what in his day was the novel genre of spiritual autobiography. The *Confessions* comprises thirteen "books" or chapters. In the first nine books, Augustine writes a religious memoir, narrating the incidents of his life from his childhood to the death of his mother Monica, soon after his conversion to Christianity at the age of thirty-two. He situates these events in what he believes to have been a providential plan that turned the young, ambitious rhetorician from a public life of status and acclaim to a devotional life in service to the will of God. Augustine wrote the *Confessions* in the years 397–401, long after his conversion in 386, his baptism in 387, and his ordination to the priesthood in 391 and, more recently, after his call to serve as bishop of the Church of Hippo Regius in North Africa in 397.[4] Scholars have noticed that Augustine's portrayal of his life in retrospect reflects more recent changes in his theological mindset. In the mid-390s, Augustine read the New Testament letters of Paul with a new perspective that deeply appreciated Paul's strong theology of grace and God's divine election of the believer. He explained this reading of Paul in a long letter that he wrote in 396 to his friend Simplicianus, who was soon to be Ambrose's successor as bishop of Milan.[5] Scholars see this work as the beginning of a theological trajectory that would traverse the time to Augustine's death in 430 and manifest itself in his insistence on the irresistible power of grace in his battles with the Donatists and the Pelagians, who instead championed the power of moral resolve in the religious life.

The *Confessions* falls within this trajectory. The works Augustine wrote soon after his conversion ardently defended the power of human free choice in relation to God's divine will, and so suggest that Augustine experienced conversion much more as an act of his own free choice. The *Confessions*, however, portrays its author's life to the point of conversion as an obstinate, sinful resistance to God, and conversion as the overwhelming victory of divine power over Augustine's sexual desire and worldly ambitions, as a dramatic change in his life that happened in spite of himself. The *Confessions* is a narrative of God's amazing grace, and so, in the words of the famous hymn so thoroughly Pauline in its sensibilities, its narrative requires the portrayal of the recipient of grace as a moral "wretch" so that the story's plot ever highlights God's transforming power. The fact that Augustine's claims for his preconversion debauchery seem not to align with his own account of his character reify this suspicious reading of the *Confessions* as a literal rendition of Augustine's early life.

It is tempting to read the *Confessions* as two separate works artificially joined into one. In such a view, the first work comprises the nine autobiographical chapters, and the second work comprises the four concluding chapters, meditations on the divine presence in memory, in relation to time, and in biblical revelation. The difference in genres between these two parts of the *Confessions*—spiritual autobiography and theological speculation—alone would seem to justify this conjunctive reading. Nevertheless, the *Confessions* is a single work in which the concluding speculative chapters follow the autobiographical narrative of grace by Augustine's intentional, authorial design. It would be consistent, then, to read the concluding theological speculations in the *Confessions* in light of the autobiographical narrative of grace. For our purposes, this offers an important but often overlooked context for understanding Augustine's meditation on time in book 11.

The concluding, speculative chapters of the *Confessions* catalogue the various avenues Augustine pursues in his search for the God who brought him to conversion. In successive literary meditations, he considers the world, the inner life, the ephemerality of time, and the spiritual meaning of the Scriptures as possible paths to the divine mystery. Even if less directly than the autobiographical chapters of the *Confessions*, these speculative chapters illustrate Augustine's Pauline understanding of how God's own power transformed his life. Strong theologies of grace stir and accentuate the emotion of gratitude, a gratitude Augustine expresses explicitly throughout the autobiographical chapters in the doxological prayers that punctuate his story of conversion. In strong theologies of grace, this gratitude typically incites a yearning, a deep longing for the God who would be so gracious and who is yet so mysteriously elusive. It is not surprising, then, that Augustine brings the autobiographical part of the *Confessions* to a close by telling the story of the mystical experience that he and his mother shared in Ostia shortly before her death, for in this experience Augustine encountered, however briefly, the God of grace who, thankfully, took possession of his life.

The experience had its beginnings in a conversation in which the pious mother and devoted son voiced their curiosity about what the "eternal life of the saints would be like" in heaven. Augustine, and presumably Monica too, assumed that the divine eternity joyfully animates heavenly life, and so it is God's timeless being that quickly became the goal of their mystical ascent. Impelled by the divine love, which "burned stronger in us and raised us higher towards the eternal God," Augustine recounts his and his mother's survey of finite things below and their shared appreciation of the wonders of creation. Moving from the visible to the invisible, they experientially transcended even their "own souls and passed beyond them to that place of everlasting plenty," its unending excess supplied by

God's divine life itself.⁶ Then, but for an instant, mother and son grasped this divine eternity in mystical rapture:

> But that Wisdom [of the divine life] is not made: it is as it has always been, and as it will be for ever—or, rather, I should not say that it *has been* or *will be*, for it simply *is*, because eternity is not in the past or in the future. And while we spoke of the eternal Wisdom, longing for it and straining for it with all the strength of our hearts, for one fleeting instant we reached out and touched it. Then with a sigh, leaving our spiritual harvest bound to it, we returned to the sound of our own speech, in which each word has a beginning and an ending—far, far different from your Word, our Lord, who abides in himself for ever, yet never grows old and gives new life to all things.⁷

In many respects, this spiritual crescendo of the autobiographical chapters defines the subject matter of the concluding speculative chapters, each of which attempts to grasp and recapture intellectually the profundity of that mystical moment, a special revelation marked by the difference between God and creatures, and especially by the radical difference between eternity and time. This difference, most specifically, is the object of Augustine's spiritual wonder in book 11.

Augustine's famous reflection on time begins with an appreciation that "no moment of time passes except by [the divine] will,"⁸ and with repeated expressions of his longing for the God whose eternity he grasped ever so briefly in the mystical moment at Ostia. That appreciation for God's power over all things creaturely and his fascination with the radical difference of divine eternity led Augustine to take the hiddenness of the divine act of creation in eternity as the point of departure for his meditation. The opening words of scripture, "In the Beginning you made heaven and earth,"⁹ offer entry into the mysteries of time and eternity, for, Augustine asks, how could there be a beginning to creation if God is timeless and so not subject to the change that time charts and that any beginning would seem to require? "All these [created] things proclaim your glory as their Creator," Augustine acknowledges. "But how do you create them? How did you make heaven and earth?" God could not have created as a human craftsman does, by fashioning material at hand into a product, since nothing was at hand to God before the act of creation. Whence,

Augustine asks rhetorically, "could you have obtained matter which you had not yet created, in order to use it as material for making something else?"[10] Creation is not its own origin, and so one may not invoke creation to explain how the act of creation transpires in God.

The problem for reason and imagination is that the very notion of "beginning," a temporal marker, is foreign to Augustine's classically Christian understanding of God. Given the assumption of divine eternity, how could the will to create that gave rise to time have originated in God? Augustine recognizes this logical problem, while yet as a believer distancing himself from it, configuring it as an objection to the coherence of the Christian belief in divine eternity on the part of a hostile opponent. "'For the will of God,' the objection goes, 'is not a created thing. It is there before any creation takes place, because nothing could be created unless the will of its Creator preceded its creation. The will of God, then, is part of his substance. Yet if something began to be in God's substance, something which had not existed beforehand, we could not rightly say that his substance was eternal. But if God's will that there should be a creation was there from all eternity, why is it that what he has created is not also eternal?'"[11]

Augustine's response to the unbeliever is modest and simple and derives from the mystical experience that he and his mother shared years earlier. Eternity and time are not the same, and so the opponent's attempt to create an aporia through their conflation fails to appreciate the radical difference of God's eternal being. Augustine concedes that these are "matters of which I am ignorant," though he is confident enough to reply to the questioner that "before [God] made heaven and earth, God made nothing."[12] Creatureliness and temporality have no share in the divine being itself. And should the questioner persist in asking how God could begin the act of creation and thereby change from being a God who did not create to being the creator God, Augustine observes that the questioner has not succeeded in banishing time from a true conception of eternity, falsely imagining a "before" and "after" before time existed. "But if there was no time before heaven and earth were created, how can anyone ask what you were doing 'then' [before the act of creation]? If there was no time, there was no 'then.'"[13]

There is, Augustine proposes, a christological key to this mystery. In the prologue to the Gospel of John, he finds interpretive direction in the traditional belief that God created the universe through the Christ, the eternal Son of God. In a Christian reading, the words of Genesis through which God spoke creation into existence were uttered timelessly in and through the divine Word, who is himself timeless. The divine act of creation that gave birth to time, Augustine suggests, is not itself in time since it is rapt in the mediation of the eternal Word. Though the divine act of creation is itself timeless, finite things, including time itself, do not share in eternity, which is exclusively a divine quality. Even if the divine act of creating eventuates timelessly, creation itself unfolds in time. Addressing God as the source of his inquiry, Augustine observes, "You create [finite things] by your Word alone and in no other way. Yet the things which you create by your Word do not all come into being at one and the same time, nor are they eternal."[14] The mystery of "beginning" is ensconced in the mystery of God's eternal otherness.

For the skeptical questioner, of course, this christological "solution" to the origin of creation solves nothing. Saying, as Augustine does, that God created all things through the eternal Word simply reiterates his belief that every divine act in and of itself transpires timelessly and so is not subject to the creaturely categories of "then" and "now." The same wonderment Augustine experienced in his mystical grasp of eternity appears here to be answer enough to reason's troubled curiosity. And now in book 11, what thus far has amounted to a meditation on the mystery of eternity throws into relief the wonders of time and prompts an ensuing meditation on its puzzling behavior.

"What, then, is time?" In a much-quoted passage, Augustine wrings his hands before the prospect of answering his own question: "I know well enough what it is, provided that nobody asks me; but if I am asked what it is and try to explain, I am baffled."[15] Nevertheless, Augustine ventures tentative answers that together present a phenomenology of time. His initial impulse is to see the ephemeral nature of time as a function of the nothingness from which God brought all creation into being. The past and the future, Augustine proposes, cannot "be," "when the past no longer is and the future is not yet." The same even seems to be true of the transient present. Though one might think that the present's actuality gives it a mooring in being, the present is time only in its capacity instantly to dissipate into the past. Given this temporal behavior, Augustine asks, "how can we say that even the present *is*, when the reason why it *is* is that it is *not to be*?" The logical conclusion is that "we cannot rightly say that time *is*, except by reason of its impending state of *not being*."[16] Here, though, it is important to note that Augustine speaks of the transience of time. Were time identified with nonbeing itself, it would have no standing in creation and, as sheer privation, be judged evil, an incoherent view in Augustine's Christian metaphysics. It would be truer to Augustine's position to say that time is especially beset by the nothingness from which all created things have been drawn, and that is reflected in time's ephemerality.

Augustine reifies his judgment on time's transience by examining the rhetoric of temporality in common parlance. We speak of time as "long" in expressing an awareness of its extended duration. But what in time itself could actually be long? If neither the future nor the past exists, then they could not possess that possible quality of time. And if the present is nothing more than the transience of the in-breaking future or the present-becoming-past, then "the present cannot possibly have duration" because it ever stands at the threshold of nothingness.[17] Yet we do speak of temporal duration. It does seem as though time is "long" or "short," even though philosophical analysis shows this to be impossible. We do measure time, Augustine concedes, but not as the past or as the future, which do not exist, but only from the standpoint of the subjective awareness of time in the receding present. Thus, he concludes, "we can be aware of time and measure it only while it is passing," or, better put, only as we experience its passing.[18] We measure time only in the transient present, and not time as it is but as we apprehend it to be, a judgment neatly consistent with Augustine's belief that time is characterized by what it is not.

This move toward the subjectivity of time governs the remainder of Augustine's analysis in book 11. It may seem as though time is an objective reality. Indeed, the customary division of time into past, present, and future suggests that these words name states of being, each a dimension of actuality. But this, for Augustine, is not the case. In his judgment, what one imagines as time is more truly conceived as temporality, a sensibility regarding time apprehended by a human perceiver. Time can only be measured in its passing because the experience of temporality, finally the experience of transience, transpires in the ever-ephemeral present. Thus, Augustine asserts, "it might be correct to say that there are three times, a present of past things, a present of present things, and a present of future things. Some such different times do exist in the mind, but nowhere else that I can see. The present of past things is the memory; the present of present things is direct perception; and the present of future things is expectation."[19] If time exists, then it exists as the experience of these subjective states that apprehend events, that remember events, and that expect the occurrence of events.

These subjective experiences of temporality, all of which unfold in some passing present moment, also must ground the measuring of time as durations, even if Augustine is hard pressed to account for an objective norm that itself frames the comparative judgments of longer or shorter durations of time. "It seems to me, then," Augustine concludes, "that time is merely an extension, though of what it is an extension I do not know. I begin to wonder whether it is an extension of the mind itself."[20] It is in the mind that time is measured, and for that reason, in consonance with his inclination to associate time with nonbeing, Augustine cautions himself not to "allow [his] mind to insist that time is something objective."[21] Time as the past increases in proportion to the diminishment of the future only as the apprehension of time, since the past and the future do not exist in themselves. These judgments of temporal duration, Augustine claims, and so temporality itself, issue from "the mind, which regulates this process, [and] performs three functions, those of expectation, attention, and memory."[22] Time appears to consciousness as the experience of time's passing.

Augustine's meditation on time explores the mystery of creation. But its purpose finally is to appreciate a deeper mystery highlighted by the vagaries of time—the eternity of God, which stands in metaphysical contrast to all things created and so in time. No wonder, then, that Augustine concludes his meditation on time by marveling at the divine transcendence, the source of the grace that turned him out of himself and toward the eternity that he grasped with his mother in an extraordinary way at Ostia: "In the Beginning you knew heaven and earth, and there was no change in your knowledge. In just the same way, in the Beginning you created heaven and earth, and there was no change in your action. Some understand this and some do not: let all alike praise you. You are supreme above all, yet your dwelling is in the humble of heart. For you comfort the burdened, and none fall who lift their eyes to your high place."[23] Here

Augustine testifies that the same power of God's eternal otherness that rescued him from worldly desire and ambition sets in relief its creaturely beneficiaries, not only the human persons whom grace brings to fulfillment but also the temporality of creation, which evokes the mystery of time's origin. For Augustine, an awareness of time's ephemerality derives from a true understanding of divine eternity, an eternity that paradoxically is as gracefully present to time as it is completely different from it.

Time, Eventfulness, and Beauty

There are several features of Augustine's treatment of time in the *Confessions* that make him an interesting conversation partner for my treatment of time here, even if largely by way of negative counterpoint. Augustine's Platonic metaphysics encourages him to accentuate both the divine transcendence that is time's creative source and time's ephemerality, which stands before God's eternal being as finite contingency. In contrast to the fullness of being that he believes the divine eternity to be, Augustine portrays time as contextualized by nonbeing, as though time were a chimera generated by the experience of an ever-recurring present moment that, in its passing into nonexistence, configures the illusions of past duration and future expectation. Frustration drips from Augustine's rather futile stab at depicting time as an extension of the mind, since this speculative gesture concedes that something seemingly so reified actually possesses a much more tenuous standing in creation. Thus, the metaphysical thinness of time offers no analogy to its divine, creative source—a disappointing realization for a theological mind yearning for a worldly medium through which to grasp again the mystical moment of joy at Ostia. For Augustine, time testifies to the glory of God only through its stark difference from the divine eternity, with which it stands in creaturely contrast.

But even if Augustine's metaphysics of time is at odds with an understanding of time shaped by modern physics, in which time is appreciated as a dimension of the natural world itself, his insistence that a theology of grace accompany his metaphysics of time can be instructive for my efforts to sketch a theological aesthetics of time. My appeal to grace as a resource for my theology of time, however, will swerve from the course set by

Augustine. Augustine developed his later theology of grace in order to address the question of the natural capacity of the human will to contribute to the believer's redemption. Augustine adjudicated this issue by claiming that the human will, powerlessly captive to the history of sin, could only be turned to grace by grace itself. This volitional key to Augustine's later theology of grace appears in the *Confessions*' meditation on time in the sharp contrast Augustine draws between eternity and time, the latter resonant with creaturely fragility and the former with the sheer power of the divine life, from which grace flows. Rather than follow Augustine in this volitional approach to a theology of grace, one that sees grace as transcendent power over the human will, let us instead consider the possibilities of envisaging grace as providential presence, and do so by constructing a theological imaginary that finds analogy, however carefully qualified, between the divine life as uncreated grace and the beauty of God's immanence to all things created—especially, to the eventfulness of creation in time. My proposed analogy will offer a way of imagining the beauty of events in time as a reflection of the beauty of God's graceful presence to creation, and even as a reflection of the eventful beauty of the divine life itself. Before I can explore this analogy between the divine life as grace and the eventfulness of creation in time, there are a number of issues at stake in my framing of the analogy that I must consider.

First among these issues is the association between time and eventfulness posed in my promised analogy. Why turn our attention in a theological aesthetics of time to eventfulness, the transpiring of occurrences in the world? What is the relationship between eventfulness and time, the thematic focus of my entire study? We should note that our most talented physicists have had difficulty saying exactly what time is and, in their reach for words, stand in a long line of philosophers and theologians who, like Augustine, have found the phenomenon of time to be rhetorically elusive. Since time escapes precise definition, framing the relationship between eventfulness and time in principle will prove to be just as difficult. Yet, even though time and events are not reducible to each other, each is a function of the other. Each, so to speak, is a behavior of the natural world that deeply permeates and shapes the behavior of the other. The explanation of time offered by the theoretical physicist Sean Carroll can help us to appreciate this relationship.

While conceding the difficulty of saying exactly what time is, Carroll notes that time seems to be bound up with the events that transpire in the world. First, he proposes, time can be conceived as "a coordinate . . . [that] labels moments in the universe."[24] As "the world *happens*, again and again," time not only marks each event as occurring in this or that moment but also "provides a sequence that puts the different instances in order."[25] Understood as a coordinate, time is inseparable from the three coordinates of space—length, width, and height—to which time adds its own fourth coordinate to comprise the four dimensions of the space-time continuum within which all events unfold. "What we call the 'universe,'" he observes, "is just the set of all events—every point in space, at every moment of time."[26] Carroll adds a second conceptualization that accounts for time's relation to occurrence—time as a measure of "the duration elapsed between events." At first glance, he admits, this notion seems quite like the concept of time as a coordinate since it seems that the measure of duration also would be a certain kind of coordinate. But here the coordinate is of a very different sort from the location of events in four-dimensional space-time. Time as the measure of duration between events broaches the measuring standard of a good clock—a humanly produced machine or a natural process—that is capable of what Carroll calls "synchronized repetition,"[27] a reliable yardstick for cataloguing duration between event x and event y, and in turn their elapsed durations relative to other events. This notion of time as the measure of elapsed duration highlights the difference between space and time. As Carroll puts it, "time has a direction and space doesn't." Time transpires "from the past toward the future, while . . . all directions of space are created equal." Or, in a formulation that clarifies even more, he observes, "We can invert directions in space without doing damage to how physics works, but all sorts of real processes can happen in one direction of time but not the other."[28]

A third conceptualization of time that conveys the inseparable relationship between time and events portrays time as "a medium through which we move."[29] Carroll is quick to note that this is a popular notion of time, and finally a metaphor for how time often seems to human experiencers. As events take place, the experiencer can imagine moving along with them together with all things in time, as though time were a river flowing from the past to the future. Certainly the natural world, the world of things, dwells in the dimension of time. But this sensibility about time strains to imagine time as though it were itself a *thing*, a substance in its own right, though truly this metaphoric concept is only "something we reconstruct from the correlations in these events."[30] This, Carroll's third, conceptualization of time is what I have described as temporality, a subjective sense of time that varies with a person's actual and changing experience in the world. Even though Carroll's first two notions of time are scientific concepts that physicists would quickly embrace, while the third notion of time as a sensibility courses in the realm of poetry, all three conceptualizations are configured through the inextricable relationship between time and eventfulness. The behavior of time is implicated in the behavior of events, and the behavior of events is implicated in the behavior of time. Each is a context within which the other occurs. Time is the ambiance of events, just as events are the ambiance of time. Perhaps this inseparable relationship between eventfulness and time is captured most pointedly by the American physicist John Archibald Wheeler, who, when pressed for a definition of time, thought for a few moments and then replied, "Time is Nature's way of keeping everything from happening at once."[31]

Time is the métier of creation, and its tempo is manifested in events. The boughs of a tree swaying in the wind, the breaking wave that laps the limits of the shore as white foam, the child's laugh, the bird's oscillating song, the mutual outreach of arms that finish in embrace, the disappearance of the sun into a western horizon saturated in orange and pink, the last breath of a life lived well or poorly—all unfold as events stretched out in time, each distinguished in time from other events themselves stretched out in time. All events are in time, but within this creaturely ambit of time each event is itself fixed in time, unfolds within it, and, quite rarely in the history of the universe, is apprehended by a human being as this or that occurrence that is observed, noted, or valorized in this way or that. Time can be imagined in its greatest natural extent as the history of the entire universe from the Big Bang to whatever form its entropic ending takes. Time in this universalizing arc, as all eventfulness from the origin of energy to its complete dissolution, evokes a sense of wonder at its magnitude, and so of the abundant giftedness of creation, even if time's long duration is the history of creation's metaphysical fragility.[32]

The second issue that attends my promised analogy between God's transcendent divine life as uncreated grace and the beauty of God's immanence to creation in time concerns the beauty of eventfulness. It is a bit unusual to reflect aesthetically on the beauty of events as such. Typically, aesthetical theory addresses the beauty of a work of art or the beauty of a natural object or scene. My theological attention to time, however, requires me to consider the beauty of eventfulness itself and to offer a theoretical explanation of time's beauty. The beauty of events in time, I propose, lies in time's individuating power, its capacity to frame a time in which events achieve their particularity in this moment or that, and then, within that same time, are distinguished from each other by the particularities of their own times and by the time that intervenes between them.[33]

Classical aesthetical theories typically explain the human judgment of beauty as an edifying apprehension of the qualities of proportion, coherence, or harmony in the beautiful object. The ancient Greek philosopher Aristotle (384–322 BCE) notes in his work the *Poetics* that "what is beautiful (not only an animal, but anything constructed of parts) ought to have . . . ordered parts."[34] In the *Metaphysics*, he states that "the chief forms of the beautiful are order, symmetry, and definiteness."[35] The medieval theologian Thomas Aquinas (1225–74) expresses this same classical notion by stating that "beauty is a matter of right proportion, for the senses delight in rightly proportioned things as similar to themselves, the sense-faculty being a sort of proportion itself like all other knowing faculties."[36] As difficult as it may be to say what makes the beautiful thing beautiful, these premodern aestheticians portray the quality of beauty as a difference rendered pleasing by its revelation of balance or symmetry among the parts of the beautiful object. As the philosopher Glenn Parsons has observed, this "classical conception of beauty as 'just proportion' remained the dominant way of thinking about beauty in the West from antiquity up until the eighteenth century."[37] Rather than pursue a modern approach to aesthetics, which focuses on the subjective conditions that lead to the judgment of beauty, I will employ the assumptions of this classical aesthetics in order to account for the beauty of events in time in their objectivity. Beauty in this traditional conception is the experience of difference rescued from the centrifugal power of chaos, of difference set in productive relief through its inherently synthetic qualities that raise difference to a sense of an organized whole judged beautiful. Whether the beautiful object be a landscape, a face, or a painting, its perceived beauty appears in the proportioning of difference into a unity that appeals to the perceiver, though a unity in which difference abides and configures the symmetrical beauty.[38]

So explained, time's individuating power in the framing of particular events shapes the conditions for the possibility of the judgment of beauty in the perceived order, proportion, and coherence of an event in time. In classical perspective, the beauty of the particular event dwells in its own propriety as an occurrence, which takes place identifiably and distinctly within the different moments that lend themselves to its unity as event. The beauty of a sunset, for example, might be found in the way that the disappearance of the sun over the horizon in the course of several minutes coheres as a single event, bathed in colors, that announces the end of the day. The beauty of a particular event might also be configured *ad extra*, in the way an occurrence achieves its own symmetry in contrastive difference from other events in time. The beauty of a marriage ceremony, for example, might be found in the way that its meaningfulness stands out in relief from the great multitude of events that shape one's life more ordinarily or routinely, all centered in the love of the couple professed in the spoken words of the marriage promise. Finally, the beauty of a series of events, or even of the imagined series of all events, can be found in the way the multiplicity of occurrences displays a meaningful coherence that draws the many moments of time into the harmonious particularity of event. The beauty of a son's or daughter's childhood, for example, might be found in the way that uncountable events transpiring over years coalesce in memory to achieve a pleasing unity that evokes a parent's smile.

Parsing events in time through classical aesthetical categories can elucidate how events might be judged beautiful. Ancient and medieval theorists like Aristotle and Aquinas did not specifically make events in time the thematic object of their reflection, though both, as illustrators here of the classical sensibility, did include events among their examples of the beautiful. Aristotle offered his explanation of beauty in the *Poetics* to account for the plot of the tragedy, in his judgment the highest form of art.[39] In the *Summa Theologiae*, Aquinas speaks of the beautiful as apprehended by the "most cognitive" senses, seeing and hearing—"thus we speak of beautiful sights and beautiful sounds but not of beautiful tastes and smells; we do not speak of beauty in reference to the other three senses."[40] Although any experience is rightly classified as an event, Aquinas's inclusion of sound in his short list of the sensibly beautiful recognizes the dynamic eventfulness of extension in time required of a beautiful sound, such as a poignant melodic line. More than was the case with Aristotle and Aquinas, though, my analysis is specifically intent on offering an aesthetics of events in time. To do so, I need to consider one other quality of the beauty of events that, together with the individuating power of time, stirs the judgment of beauty.

Events, by their very nature, transpire in motion. This is what it means to say that events are in time and that time is the ambiance of events. As we apprehend the world, this motion is readily perceivable in this event or that, and less perceivable in other objects of possible experience. Everything that exists in an expanding universe, however, is in motion, regardless of how static a particular thing may seem to common sense at a particular moment in time. Moreover, quantum mechanics has established that motion runs deep into the natural order of things. Matter is a configuration of energy and at its subatomic level is constituted by particles in motion, regardless of how static a material object might appear at the macrolevel. The universality of motion in the universe is a function of time's permeation of natural reality. For any event in time to be found beautiful, the motion that characterizes its ordered coherence must be judged graceful. By "graceful" here, at this point in my analysis, I mean nothing theological. Graceful is a quality of movement that—in human judgment, of course—defines an event individuated in time; more specifically, it is a quality of differentiated movements centripetally shaped into a symmetrical unity that makes for the beautiful event, and so, we might say, the beauty of the time in which the event is kept. Grace is a quality of the motion of events ordered in time, a tempo, so to speak, of that motion in time judged for its beauty. Nearly all events in time are not found to be beautiful, since some clearly are not and others that perception might judge to be beautiful do not stand out in relief as ordered difference and so are never noticed. Whether the graceful event in time be one aesthetically self-conscious like a ballet, or the familiar gestures of a friend in animated conversation, so typically him or her, or the daily stroll of an elderly couple, arm-in-arm, each keeping pace, thoughtful of the other's gait and wary not to walk too fast—the movement of the event that harmonizes different moments in time into the time of *this* event will be judged graceful and in that grace beautiful.

Now that I have explored how traditional aesthetical categories might inform an aesthetics of events in time, and before I turn to my proposed theological analogy for imagining God's graceful presence to time, let us consider the Catholic style of the imaginary I will offer.

A Catholic Imaginary of Divine Immanence

God's relationship to the world has been configured in many ways throughout the Christian tradition. All of these theological imaginaries struggle to speak well of the tension between affirming God's providential presence to creation and yet respecting God's uncompromised transcendence. The belief in God as the creator of the universe stands at the heart of the doctrine of providence. The universe itself derives from the creative will of God, the goodness of its being a reflection of the being of God, who is goodness itself. The doctrine of providence extends the belief in the goodness of creation to its God-given worthiness of redemption. In the incarnation, the divine nature assumes creaturely existence in order to bring creation to eternal life, a belief expressed so eloquently in the Gospel of John: "For God so loved the world that he gave his only Son, so that everyone who believes in him may not perish but may have eternal life" (3:16). Yet the Christian tradition insists that God's intimate relationship with the created order in no way diminishes God's divine otherness, God's uncreated difference from all that is not-God. The tradition's deep allergy to the primal sin of idolatry bespeaks this concern that the aseity of God be ever affirmed no matter what degree of sacramentality a particular theological imaginary ascribes to the world's capacity to mediate divine presence.

Denominational differences in negotiating this tension have gravitated around the issue of the depth of human fallenness in sin and, attendant to that theological locus, beliefs about the human capacity to know God through the created world. Maintaining the total depravity of humankind after the fall into sin, the great Protestant Reformers Martin Luther (1483–1546) and John Calvin (1509–64) decried the ability of reason to know God productively through the created order. Luther conceded that reason could know that God exists, but reason could never know who this God is lovingly and salvationally for the believer. The striking motif of the "theology of glory" that Luther presented in his early work the *Heidelberg Disputation* sarcastically portrays any attempt to know God speculatively through creation as a delusional exercise in theological vanity.[41] In book 1 of his theological masterpiece, *Institutes of the Christian Religion*, Calvin acknowledges that there is a knowledge of God inherent in human nature, though its efficacy, he avers, has been vitiated by sin.[42] In rhetorical tones so different from Luther's passionate polemical style, Calvin writes elegantly of reason's encounter with the glory of God in the theater of creation, though, like Luther, Calvin holds that this knowledge only points to the splendor of God as creator and is empty of the liberating message of the gospel.[43] Those who seek God through reason alone, he claims, "are merely toying with idle speculations," since the evidence of creation testifies at most to God's transcendent majesty.[44] The Catholic tradition has addressed these concerns in a different doctrinal key. In light of a theological anthropology that affirmed some integrity of human reason and will even after the fall into sin, medieval, Tridentine, and modern Catholic theologians have regarded creation as a richer theological resource in its capacity to reflect the presence of God in the natural order of things and have considered reason informed by faith as a power able to discern the infinite in the finite. Medieval Christian metaphysics understood the realm of created being to participate, to share, in the divine source of being from which it purposively issued. This metaphysics, grounded in a Christian interpretation of Neoplatonism, encouraged Catholic theologians to imagine the God-world relationship through the doctrine of analogy, a theological rhetoric that mirrored these metaphysical assumptions.[45]

The medieval doctrine of participation is a theological imaginary that affirms a deep coherence in being between Creator and creature, though a coherence that ever assumes the utter dependence of creaturely being on the infinite power of God's being itself. In the categories of medieval theologians who developed this doctrine in nuanced ways, finite essences flourish in their own power of being not merely through a divine act of creation that brings each essence into existence but through an ongoing sharing, a participation, of each finite essence in the power of God's own eternal being that maintains creatures in their own limited acts of being. While the metaphysical coherence affirmed in the doctrine of participation properly finds the creaturely "participant" to be sheerly derivative of and dependent on its divine source, the creature's participation is imagined itself to offer a medium for the reasonable contemplation of God's presence to creation, as well as an intellectually abstractive path for reason to follow in speculating theologically about the being of God. Even though the medievals, and indeed much of the Catholic intellectual tradition, framed the doctrine of participation in a worldview imagined as a hierarchy of being, there is no reason in principle that participation need be imagined this way, except perhaps to define the metaphysical difference between Creator and creature, a most basic Christian belief. The doctrine of participation is a variation on the doctrinal theme of providence, a metaphysical rendition of the divine immanence to all of creation.

Participation is the classically Catholic way of accounting for the divine immanence to creation that affirms as well creation's capacity as a resource for theological reflection. Even though the Lutheran and Reformed traditions have been suspicious of this approach, some styles of Protestant theology have been willing to affirm the same kind of closeness between God and creation heralded in the doctrine of participation, albeit not in that doctrine's categories. A fine example is the recent work of the American theologian Katherine Sonderegger.

In the first volume of her systematic theology, Sonderegger offers an extended reflection on the divine attributes and on what she judges to be the rightful priority of God's oneness among the other divine traits, a focus that configures her portrayal of the God-world relationship in her theological project. As one might expect in a theology concerned with speaking faithfully of the divine unity, Sonderegger ever reminds her readers of the theological need to respect the divine difference from all things creaturely. And yet this affirmation of the divine aseity appears in her theology side by side with a deep regard for God's presence to creation. God's relation to the world, she claims, should be conceived as what she calls the "Transcendental Relation," the "Divine Aseity within the world of creatures."[46] Even though much of the theological tradition would understand God's otherness to define the problematic of knowing God,

Sonderegger moves in a different direction. The problem for believers in knowing God, she states, "does not stem from our being unable to conceive or know or receive Him properly under the conditions of human experience.... Even less does it stem from His seeming 'distance' from or ideality toward the world. The problem, rather, is that the One True God is very *near* to us, *present* in His surpassing Uniqueness."⁴⁷ For Sonderegger, the mystery of God lies not in God's otherness but in God's providential presence to creatures. The challenge for a theology proper that wishes to speak well of the immanence of God's aseity must begin by constructing a theological imaginary that enables the expression of the depths of the divine presence to creatures. In a most creative gesture, Sonderegger proposes a reinterpretation of the theological notion of compatibilism in order to conceptualize God's immanence more truly.

Traditionally, compatibilism has an explanatory home in theological anthropology. It ventures an account of how the power of human free choice can be reconciled with the eternal will and knowledge of God. Sonderegger finds advantage in reconfiguring the anthropological context of this issue so that a capacious compatibilism now explains how God's transcendence can be reconciled with God's radical immanence to all of creation. The theological compatibilism that Sonderegger proposes finds no need to adjudicate long-standing debates about whether "the finite . . . [has a] purported 'capacity' for the Infinite." Compatibilism takes a stand neither on the likeness of God and creatures nor on the dissimilarity of God and creatures. Compatibilism's task is not the resolution of that tradition-long debate. Rather, she maintains, "compatibilism in theology is *sui generis*. It affirms that God's very Reality—His Aseity—resides among us, without contradiction or identity or annihilation. . . . Of course, this is a wonder, the miracle and mystery of all wonders! But the salient affirmation is that God alone can bring this about: that the One who surpasses all thought, beyond all category and form, can dwell with us, yet remain His glorious and true Reality."⁴⁸ Sonderegger portrays compatibilism as a theological affirmation because the grand truth of this imaginary is divinely revealed in the biblical word. In a classically Protestant style, Sonderegger understands theology as the description of scriptural revelation. What she offers under the rubric of "theological compatibilism" is merely a certain accent in the truth to which revelation attests in the mysterious drama of God's love toward creation. "Now all this must mean," she reminds her reader, "that God's compatibility with creatures is His utter Mystery and Unicity, His Hiddenness when He draws near."[49] In effect, the affirmation of this truth is no more than a simple act of faith.

Thus, the theological imaginary that Sonderegger commends is a kind of interpretive pragmatics. She is completely—and refreshingly—unconcerned with justifying her account of the God-world relationship. As she provocatively puts it, "Theological compatibilism describes and reports what it has seen; nothing more." And what the eyes of faith have seen is "the Mystery of God with us." "Such a *relatio*, we must say again and again, is the Lord God's very own Life: God just is His own relation to the world."[50] This is a theological imaginary that shares with the doctrine of participation a strong commitment to conceptualizing the God-world relationship as God's own self-communication to creatures. Whereas the doctrine of participation envisions the divine immanence as metaphysical energy that holds creatures in the willed order of God's creative plan, theological compatibilism imagines a sacramentality "from above" in which God showers God's own attributes, God's very own self, on all that is not-God: "To borrow a term of the philosophers for a moment, we might say that divine predication is a species of 'downward causation': God invades the creation to spread his own properties among creatures and their words. Now, of course, this is only borrowing a term; we do not in fact know how God can communicate His own Perfections, nor how he can make a creaturely term compatible with his own hidden Mystery. But in truth he has done so."[51] While acknowledging that the imagery she invokes is theological poetry, and so that her portrayal of the God-world relationship is an imaginary trying its best to capture in words the God whose existence unfolds in relation to the world, Sonderegger yet boldly affirms a univocal congruence between the imaginary of theological compatibilism and the doctrine of creation. "Such compatibilism," she maintains, "is not merely *like* the doctrine of creation, its formal structure or relations; such compatibilism just *is* the doctrine of creation."[52]

My approach to an aesthetical imaginary of events in time will follow the broadly Catholic sensibilities that we find in the doctrine of participation and in Sonderegger's theological compatibilism. As different as they are, these imaginaries find Christian meaning in a configuration of the God-world relationship that speaks of God's transcendence in and through

God's immanence to creation. As noted, a commitment to the doctrine of participation encourages the theologian to respect the difference between God and creation in language by appealing to analogy as a means of theological expression. Analogy walks a middle path between two false forks in the road of theological rhetoric—one that holds that God and creatures can be spoken of univocally, the other that holds that God and creatures can only be spoken of equivocally. Between these extremes of utter similarity and utter difference, analogy bespeaks the similarity-in-difference between God and creatures that the doctrine of participation, which underlies its assumptions, imagines metaphysically.[53] Sonderegger refers to the poetic images for God she offers in her work as this or that "analogy," though she explicitly distances her compatibilist worldview from the doctrine of participation and is wary of any notion of analogy that claims authenticity on metaphysical grounds.[54] Instead, she commends the use of analogy in a "'deflationary' way, in a commonsense manner that guards against *explaining* just how and why the analogy works in such and such a way." Better, she advises, that one "guard against analogy saying too much."[55] One does not need a theory of analogy in order for an analogy to do its expressive work. When presented with a good analogy for the God-world relationship, "we simply *recognize* its fittingness, its likeness and suggestiveness; we see it is so."[56] Finally for Sonderegger, analogy as a discrete image of God's immanence—or, for that matter, analogy as the grand image of compatibilism—unfolds as a theopoetic pragmatics that modestly ventures words faithful to the character of the biblical God. Her claim that the aptness of an analogy lies in the judgment of its believing audience applies as much to the classical Catholic doctrine of analogy as it does to her own deflationary approach to theological metaphor. The same pragmatic standard will judge the rhetorical performance of my theological aesthetics of time.

An Aesthetics of Graceful Time

How, then, to pose a meaningful analogy for God's presence to the beauty of events in time? Augustinian counterpoint can orient us once again. Recall that Augustine envisaged time as a marker of creaturely difference from the timelessness of God. For all of its interesting speculation on the nature of time, the extended meditation in book 11 of the *Confessions* finally is a reflection on the God who consummately transcends the most creaturely condition of time. Augustine, of course, whose Christian conversion was shaped by his reading of "the books of the Platonists,"[57] did so much theologically to marry the worldviews of Neoplatonism and Christianity, thus charting a course toward the medieval doctrine of participation and its metaphysical account of God's immanence to creation. And, like all Christians, Augustine believed in the miraculous immanence of the incarnation, the Christ event that, as one would expect, stands at the center of his theology. But in the *Confessions*, Augustine does not find God in time. Though created by God, time for Augustine seems to transpire in creation as a moving, ephemeral reminder of the transcendent trait that in its otherness most distinguishes God as God—the divine eternity. Time in an Augustinian tempo is a contrastive measure of divine transcendence. My interpretive efforts have ventured something different. I have regarded time as a dimension of creation that extends from earth to heaven, a realm rife with God's redemptive presence, and I have regarded the experience of this time, its temporality, as charged with eschatological hope. My aim is to appreciate theologically the graceful beauty of time understood as the measure of divine immanence.

Clearly, from a human perspective, all events in time are not beautiful. Nearly every event in time has transpired without the human notice required for the judgment of beauty. So many events that human persons undergo or witness in their own lives, in the lives of others, and in the natural world are violent, painful, emotionally devastating, and tragic and are judged to be anything but beautiful. I will turn to this sad truth in the following chapter. But many events that human persons undergo or witness are judged to be beautiful, just as one might render the same judgment about the eventfulness of time itself. I have proposed that the beauty of the event in time issues from an edifying appreciation of time's individuating power, from time's particularizing of this or that event into an ordered whole that, in its perceived harmony of moments, coalesces difference, which ever yet remains, into a symmetry that elevates its array to beauty. Grace is an adjudged quality of time's individuating motion, the very motion that shapes the harmony of the event valued for its beauty. A doctrine of creation, which is always at once properly a doctrine of providence, must explain the workings of events in time as the work of God, and must do so in a way that accounts for their graceful beauty.

Since God's act of creation brings time into existence and sets the conditions for the behavior of time, it should be unsurprising that the beginning of the universe manifests time's beauty. For testimony to this beauty, we could read again the opening verses of Genesis to find there the ancient author's poetic account of the six days of creation, each of those times the span of a creative event through which God brings a distinctive symmetry to the chaotic—and, we might say, the naturally "timeless"—waters of the void. But instead, let us consider a natural-scientific account of the early formation of the cosmos by the physicist Stephen Hawking. In his book *A Brief History of Time*, Hawking notes that "the concept of time has no meaning before the beginning of the universe," in the event of the "Big Bang."[58] In the aftermath of that singular event, in time's early history over millions of years, the galaxies began to coalesce, each a confluence of billions of stars and each a grand event of its own, slightly resisting the expansion of the universe. "The universe as a whole," Hawking notes,

> would have continued expanding and cooling [in this early period], but in regions that were slightly denser than average, the expansion would have been slowed down by the extra gravitational attraction. This would eventually stop expansion in some regions and cause them to start to recollapse. As they were collapsing, the gravitational pull of matter outside these regions might start them rotating slightly. As the collapsing region got smaller, it would spin faster—just as skaters spinning on ice spin faster as they draw in their arms. Eventually when the region got small enough, it would be spinning fast enough to balance the attraction of gravity, and in this way disklike rotating galaxies were born. Other regions, which did not happen to pick up a rotation, would become oval-shaped objects called elliptical galaxies. In these, the region would stop collapsing because individual parts of the galaxy would be orbiting stably round its center, but the galaxy would have no overall rotation.[59]

Hawking offers no aesthetical judgment in this description of galaxy formation. He ventures only an accessible explanation of how these events took place.[60] But were one to appreciate the beauty of differently configured galaxies in the colored resolution of Webb telescope images and ponder the movement that defines their eventfulness—the very movement that Hawking describes in their formation—it is interesting to consider how Hawking's account can be read through the aesthetical categories for the interpretation of events in time that I have developed here. In a theological frame of explanation, God's act of creation, not only as sheer beginning but also as ongoing providence, brings order and balance, the very symmetry of beauty, to the shapeless differentiation of energy in which the universe had its origin and in which it continues to unfold in time. It is God's grace that fashions this ordered beauty. In such a providential causality, time is the medium of the divine grace that stirs the graceful motion of the beautiful event into its proportionate particularity. Galaxies are fine examples of the beauty of graceful motion in time shaping an eventful unity. No wonder that Dante chose the beauty of stellar motion as the closing metaphor of the *Paradiso* to describe God's providential efficacy as "l'amor che move il sole e l'altre stelle"—"the Love which moves the sun and the other stars."[61]

We have seen that the beauty of a temporally individuated event can also shine forth through contrast with other events that might be judged to lack beauty or to be routine or ordinary. In such an instance the graceful motion judged to be beautiful in the way it brings unitive balance to differentiation exercises aesthetical power over a wider field of multiplicity that includes a host of other events to which the beautiful event stands in contrast, and not simply the motion that defines the meaningful particularity of the beautiful event. My earlier example, the reader may recall, was a marriage ceremony. Of course it is important to note that the differentiation of moments in time or events in time that gracefully coalesce in the symmetry of the event judged beautiful is not negated or erased in the aesthetical proportion of the contrastively beautiful event, any more than it is in any event judged beautiful. Rather, beauty lies in the symmetrical ordering of difference that never ceases to be difference, even as difference assumes a patterned unity in the eye of the beholder of beauty. With regard to the beauty of an event, such elevated difference is the plurality of moments gracefully individuated into the time of this or that event. So it is with the beauty of community, an event distinguished from the events of alienation, estrangement, and loneliness and in which the bonds of friendship, love, or understanding unite the remarkable diversity of the life moments of its members, the diversity itself ever productive of the communal whole.[62] Nor should one think that the beauty of a contrastive event is set in relief only to events judged to be quite unlike the beautiful event, as in the example of community. Contrast may take the form of traditional analogy in which similarity-in-difference defines the relationship between beautiful events. To return to our initial example of the contrastively beautiful event, a marriage ceremony often provides occasion for those who appreciate its beauty to be reminded of their own marriage day in what has proved to be a lifelong, loving relationship.

To imagine the divine immanence to contrastively beautiful events, we need only consider the theological proposal introduced in our consideration of cosmic motion—namely, that we envision the graceful motion through which time individuates events adjudged beautiful as the work of divine grace. And since I have chosen to side with the theological tradition that views grace as uncreated, I may imagine the graceful motion that creates the beauty of events in time as energized by the divine life itself. So understood, the beautiful event in time not only reflects the transcendent beauty of God but also radiates the beauty of God's presence to creation. To imagine the graceful quality of beautiful events as the presence of God's own self-giving means that the time that shapes and measures all events is a gift, and its giftedness is especially on display when the eyes of faith are able to apprehend the beauty of God's eventfulness in time.

As uncreated, as the divine life itself, this grace is self-identically the presence of God as shared with creatures. Yet the effects of this grace manifest themselves differently in the economic acts of creation, redemption, and eschatological consummation. Thus, of all of the events that a believer might judge to be contrastively beautiful, and so to mediate this graced eventfulness, the incarnation would have an unsurpassable pride of place. The incarnation is unlike any other event in time. According to the orthodox teaching of the Council of Chalcedon (451), it is an event in which divine and human difference are united into a single whole, the person of the Savior, in whom the natures are preserved while undergoing "no confusion, no change, no division, no separation."[63] Its beauty lies in the union of God and humanity, itself *the* sacramental event, manifested in the midst of events in time. The graceful motion in time in which the beauty of the event took shape transpired as "the Word became flesh and lived among us" (John 1:14). And yet, although the incarnation is unlike any other event, the incarnate eventfulness of the Savior's life brings ordered beauty to all events in time. The Son of God, who embraced humanity, is the one through whom all things were created (John 1:3). He is the one in whom "all things hold together" (Col. 1:17). In the Cappadocian Christology that secured the Chalcedonian orthodoxy, the divine nature assumed humanity to itself in the event of the incarnation, and in that sacramental embrace all humanity was rescued from the powers of sin and death.[64] The contrastive beauty of the incarnation is itself the source of its immanent beauty as all humanity is drawn into the incarnate unity of the Savior.

The pages of the Gospels offer testimony to the beauty of the Savior's life, the gracefulness of his character shaped by his words and deeds in time. But the most beautiful of these events, the event that most manifests Jesus's character, is his resurrection from the dead, the saving event by which a humanity lost to the anomic powers of sin and death is reconciled to the harmony of God's own eternal life.[65] In the Gospel of John, Jesus anticipates the beauty of his resurrection's graceful reconciliation of sinful difference by declaring to his listeners, "And I, when I am lifted up from the earth, will draw everyone to myself" (John 12:32). The historical-critical study of the Gospels often leads scholars of faith to consider whether the resurrection of Jesus was a historical event, an event in time. The scholarly claim that the resurrection, if yet a real event, did not occur in time typically seeks to bracket the issue of the resurrection's truthfulness from the critical investigation of the texts that record the experience of the early Christians. In spite of the importance of historical-critical investigation, a theological approach to this question should insist that the resurrection, as an incarnational event, indeed occurs in time, as does every dimension of Jesus's human nature. The temporal eventfulness of Jesus's resurrection is a necessary condition for the creedal affirmation of its bodiliness, as it is for the believer's judgment of its redemptive beauty. Time is the created condition of eventfulness, and graceful motion individuated in time configures the circumstances that engender aesthetic judgment. On that first Easter morning, God brought death to the beauty of resurrected life, and, as all are drawn by grace's motion into the resurrected Christ, all are drawn too into the eschatological beauty of what Paul calls the New Creation (2 Cor 5:17).[66]

My final exploration of the eventful beauty of graceful time reprises my example of a series of events individuated in time as a single event, and the series of events I will consider is the most extended possible—the imagined series of all events in time. Here we meet our imaginary of a theological aesthetics of time as such. The twentieth-century Catholic *ressourcement* theology of grace that I explored in chapter 1 in the work of Henri de Lubac, and that I could have explored as well in the work of Karl Rahner, Hans Urs von Balthasar, and Latinx, feminist, and Black liberation theologians, insisted that creaturely reality in time is always already graced. De Lubac's rejection of the neo-Thomist category of "pure nature," an initially graceless state in creation that later is graced by God, implies that there no time that is ungraced, a theological position that has become axiomatic in postconciliar theology. My constructive efforts here have attempted to bolster this theology of grace not simply by erasing an imagined gap between graceless and graced time but by imagining the eventfulness of time itself, motion individuated in and by time, as the medium of that very gracefulness. My proposal aspires to a more deeply sacramental understanding of God's graceful immanence to creation, one that perhaps, by comparison at least, banishes the last bit of extrinsicist residue from de Lubac's astonishing contribution to the modern Catholic tradition. Grace, of course, is not time, and time is not grace. Uncreated grace is the self-giving of the divine life itself, and time is a fundamental dimension of creation and so not-God. Grace, to be grace, must be gratuitous. But to imagine the eventfulness of time as the medium of grace counters the traditional understanding of time as created lack, articulated so well and influentially by Augustine in the *Confessions*. This imaginary also enables us to appreciate the theological beauty of events in time, and so how an aesthetics of grace might capture the dynamic quality of God's immanence to creation.

How, though, to conceptualize this theological intimacy between God and time given my project's commitment to a traditional understanding of God's eternity, and so to the very different modality of God's timeless, uncreated beauty? What analogy will encourage the eyes of faith to see the divine presence in the graceful motion of events individuated in time, or, as is my present concern, of all events together individuated in time? The analogical difficulty lies in the infinite degree of divine difference, though not absence, from created time, as well as in the tradition's tendency to diminish the sacramental capacity of time. Let us instead consider time through the motion of eventfulness that it defines.

Trinitarian doctrine does profess belief in certain kinds of "motion" that transpire in the divine life itself as the relations between and among the persons of Father, Son, and Spirit. In the teaching of the fourth-century creeds, the Father begets the Son and the Son is begotten of the Father. In order to make clear that this motion, this event of begetting and being begotten, flourishes in the timeless nature of God and so is an uncreated motion, the fathers at the Council of Constantinople (381) qualified the profession of faith of the Council of Nicaea (325) by approving a creed that described the Son as begotten of the Father "before all the ages," a phrase often translated by the word "eternally."[67] The "motion" of the Father's generation of the Son dwells within their *homoousion* relationship, in their shared eternal being, and so is an eternal motion not beholden to the individuating limitations of created time, though a "motion," we might say, nonetheless. The person of the Holy Spirit participates in this motion that characterizes the inner life of God, and moves relationally as well in the Holy Spirit's own particular way. Following Jesus's teaching in the Gospel of John (15:26) that the Holy Spirit proceeds from the Father, the creed of Constantinople affirmed the truth of that eventfulness in the divine life. Centuries later, the Western Christian tradition expanded its account of the Spirit's procession to speak of the Holy Spirit's procession "from the Father and the Son" in order to reaffirm that the Father and the Son share the one eternal being of God, as does the Spirit. Beginning with the work of Maximus the Confessor (ca. 580–662), the later theological tradition would portray these relational movements between and among the divine persons as a *perichoresis*, a "going around" that attempts to capture in a single word the dynamic co-inherence of the divine persons in the inner life of God.[68]

Trinitarian theology has also used the metaphor of motion to describe God's relationship to the world. Missions in and from the Trinity, each a distinctive "sending" of the gift of grace *ad extra*, are saving actions that reconcile the world to God. Creation is appropriated to the Father. The Son, sent by the Father on the mission of incarnation, reconciles the fallen universe to God. The Holy Spirit, sent by the Son in the event of Pentecost (John 15:26), continues the Son's saving work through all time by bringing the universe to eschatological consummation. The earliest Trinitarian theology recognized quite clearly that these "motions" of divine outreach to the world finally coalesced into a single divine action. Although the Father's appropriation of creation and the missions of the Son and the Spirit each have their own enacted integrity as the work of a divine person, these giftings of grace yet reflect the perichoretic unity of motion in the eternal life of God. The fourth-century Cappadocian father Gregory of Nyssa (ca. 335–ca. 395) expressed the beauty of the unity-in-difference of the missions by stating, "With regard to the divine nature . . . we do not learn that the Father does something on his own, in which the Son does not co-operate. Or again, that the Son acts on his own without the Spirit. Rather does every operation which extends from God to creation and is designated according to our differing conceptions of it have its origin in the Father, proceed through the Son, and reach its completion by the Holy Spirit."[69] Although the classical Christian tradition rightly insists on the timelessness of God's eternity, it yet speaks of eventfulness in the being of God in order to capture the moving experience of God's graceful providence.

This "motion" in the divine Trinity serves as the analogical point of similarity to the graceful motion of events in time. In this imaginary of grace, the motion that time individuates as events, and finally the motion of all events in time, can be conceptualized as a creaturely image of the uncreated "motion" of the divine processions and missions. Here, Plato's well-known account of time as "the moving image of eternity" in the *Timaeus* can be filled with Christian content to see the imagistic character of time not as metaphysical lack but as gracious plenitude and to see the eternity that time images not dialectically but analogically, as the divine life in which a saving eventfulness flourishes.[70] In such a perspective, time is a creaturely measure of eternal movement that shapes the bonds of divine love—the mutual love of the Trinitarian persons and the love of God for the world. Such an imaginary may offer the modern Catholic theology of grace a richer way of conveying its *ressourcement* insight that grace is everywhere, since the eventfulness of time, itself a dimension of creation, is understood to be the medium of grace. Time bristles with the divine motion in a creaturely way, its difference yet a testimony to its graceful source. The tempo of eventfulness is the resonance of eternity in the created now.

We have seen that graceful motion that coalesces moments of difference into a perceived harmony accounts for the judgment that an event is beautiful. In my proposed analogy, we can understand that beauty as a sharing in the beauty of the Trinitarian life of God, in which the real difference of the divine persons eternally dwells in the oneness of the divine essence. This divine symmetry itself transpires in the uncreated graceful motion that animates the bonds of love between Father, Son, and Spirit.[71] The beauty of events finitely individuated in time reflects that same divine beauty in the immanence of uncreated grace, the self-giving of the divine life itself and the source of the created motion shaped by time into the beautiful event. All the examples of beautiful events in time that we have considered—the formation of a galaxy, a marriage ceremony, communal sharing, an elderly couple's measured stroll, an embrace, an entire childhood—and some of the many others that would serve as well—the rhythmic chants of a crowd calling for social justice, the exchange of words of reconciliation, communal acts of solidarity with the poor—all of these events may be imagined as beautiful in the ways their temporal occurrence manifests the graceful power of divine motion without beginning or end. We may say the same of the beauty of all events in time, abstracting from my aesthetic account of the beauty of particular events. The Christian tradition has imagined all time as a vast expanse of events from creation to the Last Judgment. In the traditional Christian imaginary, this is time measured by the tragic rhythm of redemptive need, as time, with all of creation, "groans" (Rom 8:22) in expectation of the New Creation. So conceived, the beauty of all events, even though they be events in the history of sin and death, lies in the way the providential life of God, the grace of God's own self, moves events in time toward their eschatological destiny, bringing all time to the fulfilled beauty of its created goodness in a future time when God will be all in all (1 Cor 15:28).

My first chapter proposed, and my last chapter will explore, the theological possibilities of considering time, and events in time, more widely, as extending from this world into resurrected, heavenly life. The premise of such an imaginary is that time, though created, is unending, infinite with respect to its future, though not eternal. When time is so conceived, then in this time without end, the beauty of all events in time would not draw to a close with the Last Judgment but would continue ever more. As my study moves toward its close, I will need to consider how this notion of all time as unending, eschatological time yields its own kind of beauty.

CHAPTER FOUR

TRAGIC TIME IN AN ESCHATOLOGICAL AESTHETIC

My reflection on the graceful beauty of time offered a speculative theological aesthetics intent on imagining the depths of God's providential presence to the world. Time, I argued, may be viewed as a medium of God's immanence to eventfulness, to the uncountable occurrences that fill the history of time. The beauty of time itself, what I called the series of all imagined events in time, lies in its sacramental dynamism, in its capacity to provide a tempo for the graceful motion in which all events transpire. The beauty of particular events is a function of the universal beauty of events in time as such. The beauty of particular events, though, arises in human judgment as time individuates an event so that a perceiver appreciates the way its graceful motion brings symmetry to difference. Beauty thus explained is difference transfigured while yet remaining difference—in this case, the different moments in the flow of motion that together constitute the event. Whereas a modern aesthetics strives to account for the vagaries of subjectivity in judging what is beautiful, a premodern aesthetics seeks to explain the qualities of the object that human sensibility judges to be beautiful. Each perspective has its own truth to tell, and both are ingredient to a thoughtful consideration of beauty. The aesthetics of events in time in my previous chapter followed the premodern approach to aesthetics, which suited my attention to time as a dimension of reality—in theological language, time as a dimension of creation and so time as graceful endowment.

But if time is the medium of God's own divine life to creation, and the eventfulness of time itself as creation is beautiful, then how can this claim of faith be reconciled with the way eventfulness and time so often present themselves to faith-filled judgment: as suffering, as loss—in a Pauline phrase, as sin and death, in secular language, as the tragic? I have already noted that so many events in time seem to lack beauty. But more, so many events in time, whether the work of nature or the work of human will, break human bodies or human spirits. They destroy lives or the environments that promote life and liveliness. They are scourges to moral sensibility and affronts to human dignity. Their capriciousness and senselessness are ethically maddening. So many events in time cause death and the deathliness of human suffering. The encounter with the tragic consequences of such events is what human persons call evil. What does the transpiring of such events, not merely occasionally but constantly, again and again in human experience, say about the truthfulness of the theological imaginary proposed in the previous chapter? Is my aesthetics of graceful time faithful to the reality that it purports to represent, or does it present a skewed version of that reality to the point that the imaginary is but a caricature of what the Christian tradition believes about the power of sin and death in fallen creation?

The theological imaginary of graceful time proposed in the last chapter might give the impression that its attention to beauty requires an avoidance, perhaps even a willed ignorance, of the power of sin and death in human lives and indeed in all of creation. Measured against the darkness of human fallenness, my aesthetics might seem to posit a false glory to creation that belies the world in which we actually live, so rampant with evil. And it would be good to point out that such a critique is not entirely a function of the theological genre of aesthetics. The thesis of the most accomplished theological aesthetics, Hans Urs von Balthasar's *The Glory of the Lord*, is that the modern age has lost a traditional sense for the beauty of God sacramentally manifested in the incarnation, in the lives of the saints, in the church, and in creation. In this grand work, Balthasar's discrete studies of theological beauty throughout the Christian tradition attempt to stir in the reader a sense of graceful attunement to the Holy

Spirit, an apprehension that has been corrupted by human vanity and ego.[1] Balthasar's theological aesthetics is as much a theological engagement with the effects of sin as it is an appreciation of sacramental beauty. The same must be true of the present study. I must address the tragic dimension of events in time as much as I appreciate their beauty.

My goal in the previous chapter was to construct an imaginary in which time is conceived as the medium of grace to creatures and as the manifestation of grace's eventful beauty. Intent on that goal, I devoted my efforts to exploring the most basic Christian claims about God's deep immanence to creation in what I called the Catholic style of my theological imaginary. My theological aesthetics of time proposed a new way of imagining the intimacy of God's relation to the world. My efforts to speak well of God's presence did not leave room for more than a mention of what I called the sad truth that so many of the events that transpire in time are judged to be anything but beautiful. Even though talk of beauty of any sort brings us into the realm of human judgment and subjectivity, my focus was on physics, on time as a dimension of reality in the universe, and on what we might call Christian metaphysics, the doctrine of creation, which is faith's profession of the fullest truth of physical reality. Our attention has been on the objective, the real—at least the real affirmed in Christian belief. That objectivist orientation did not lend itself to a fulsome discussion of evil, for in any orthodox Christian worldview, evil does not exist. Evil has no metaphysical standing in reality. If the universe created by God in and eventfully through time exists—and it certainly does!—then in its being it is not evil at all. Evil in Christian belief is a privation, a lack or absence of the goodness that radiates from the being of every created thing, a goodness that reflects the goodness of the divine Creator, who is goodness itself. And yet, though evil does not exist, it fills the world as human persons encounter its death-dealing power.

Now in this chapter, with my imaginary of graceful time as a background, I need to address the prevalence of sin and death, of evil, in the midst of the beauty of eventfulness. The eschatological aesthetic of time that I considered in chapter 2 will help me to chart a course through this difficult issue. Before beginning my investigation of evil, it is important to consider how it will *not* be conducted. A brief exercise in comparative religion will help to elucidate the path I will not follow.

Against Theodicy

All religions address the problem of evil from the perspective of their own salvational desires, naming and negotiating death and deathliness in ways that reflect their own hopes for human fulfillment in the face of these tragic powers that ravage human lives. The ancient religions of South Asia, Hinduism and Buddhism, claim that the realm of ordinary experience is deceptive appearance, as is the universe that experience purports to apprehend. Time is the cycle of samsara, in which sentient beings—gods, humans, animals, and demons—are trapped by their attachment to the seeming reality of the world and, more, the seeming reality of their own existences. These beings labor under the false view that they, as the selves they seem to be, suffer and die again and again and again. In the now dominant Hindu tradition of Advaita Vedanta, the only true reality is Brahman, timeless divine spirit devoid of personal consciousness and so impervious to the delusion of suffering and death that ever accompanies a sense of self. The Hindu believer in this mainline tradition struggles to realize through many rebirths that he or she actually is the divine being of Brahman, in this religious imaginary the only true existent. This realization in turn entails the awareness that one's seemingly suffering self is a deceptive chimera, as is the death and deathliness experienced by the merely apparent selves that course in rebirth. Buddhism pushes this deep cultural suspicion of selves as nesting grounds for suffering and death even further by denying as well the True Self of a divine, deathless Brahman underlying the deceptive veneer of a suffering, individual self. The early Buddhists denied the existence of Brahman and thus maintained that neither an individual self nor a divine True Self exists. What common sense affirms as reality is actually impermanent mental and physical appearances devoid of inherent existence. In these ancient Indian religious traditions, suffering and death are judged to be mere, yet seemingly powerful, illusions from which believers seek escape in the religious realization that personal selves suffering and dying in time do not really exist.

The ancient Mediterranean religion of Gnosticism offers a very different account of reality and the place of evil in it, though its explanatory strategy shares an interesting resemblance to the ancient religions of South

Asia. Gnosticism appeared in a variety of forms as it emerged in the first century of the Common Era alongside the fledgling religion of Christianity, whose stories and symbols the Gnostics drastically reinterpreted in making them their own. In Gnostic belief, the "god" who fashioned the physical universe, the creator God of the Jewish and Christian traditions, is actually an evil monster whose own material being stands in dualistic contrast to a true and good God of timeless divine spirit who created and providentially rules over a spiritual world above. The evil "god," whom the Gnostics called the Demiurge, was the material issue of a primal sin that tragically transpired in the heavenly world. Cast out of heaven by the true God into a netherworld of darkness, the Demiurge, whom Christians and Jews perversely worship, fashioned the universe from the material substance of his own physical, and so evil, body. Thus, the universe in its very physicality is evil, the power of suffering and death identified in this imaginary with material existence itself, and most of all with the fragility of human bodies.

Ancient Gnostics believed that they, and only they, possessed fragments of divine spirit tragically dragged into the lower world when the Demiurge was expelled from the Gnostic heaven. These bits and pieces of divine spirit, lost in the nether world of material evil, were unwittingly shaped into the bodies of Gnostics by the evil god, a belief that defined their religious identities as divine spirits estranged from their heavenly home. For the Gnostics, liberation comes with the realization of one's self-divinity and the extraordinary religious knowledge (*gnosis*) that their divine, spiritual selves stand above the death and deathliness attendant to the material universe and especially to the frailty of human bodies. In their belief, physical death is the release of the Gnostic spirit from the evil world of time and matter and its reintegration into the timeless, heavenly world of the true God above. Even though the ancient religions of South Asia and Gnosticism have remarkably different worldviews—respectively, evil as worldly illusion and evil as material reality—both negotiate evil religiously by the strategy of escape. Both the religions of ancient India and Gnosticism find solace in a religious wisdom that allows the believer to abandon the irredeemable realm of time because, so utterly fraught with evil, the universe—whether seemingly or actually real—is the very problem that the quest for human fulfillment must transcend.

The Abrahamic religions, following the matrix of Jewish belief, define and negotiate the issue of evil quite differently. The ancient monotheistic faiths of Judaism, Christianity, and Islam all claim that the one true God, the Creator of the universe, is, in God's very being, goodness itself and that God's goodness is reflected in the being of the created universe. In these religions, being qua being is good. Evil in these religions, as I have already noted of Christianity, is understood to be a privation of the good, since their shared belief in the goodness of the Creator God undercuts the possibility of metaphysical dualism. Here, evil being is a contradiction in terms. The power of evil, of the death and deathliness that courses through creation, is blamed neither on the illusory character of experience nor on material existence itself but rather on aberrant acts of the human will that are privative of the will's appropriate faithfulness to the will of God. Human moral failure is the source of evil and the human suffering that the encounter with evil engenders.

In Hinduism, Brahman ultimately has no self, no consciousness, and so no purposive actions. Brahman simply is all true reality that the illusion of ordinary experience distorts and that believers seek to realize perfectly in the course of many rebirths. As a consequence, the Hindu belief in Brahman causes no tension in the tradition's efforts to negotiate the problem of evil. In many respects, Hinduism's doctrine of karma deflates the very possibility of such tension since human actions, not Brahman, bring about good or evil consequences from rebirth to rebirth. Ancient Buddhism is a nontheistic religion. No God appears in its religious worldview. As a result, there is no God to be implicated in the tradition's efforts to negotiate the problem of evil, which follow Hinduism's cosmology of karma and rebirth. The true, spiritual God of Gnosticism stands utterly above the sheer evil of the material universe, the domain of the Demiurge who is evil's evil cause. Here too evil rages outside the scope of divine power. But the God of the ancient monotheisms of the Middle East is thoroughly implicated in the problem of evil. Here, God is a divine person who possesses personal traits such as consciousness, self-transcendence, language, relationship, creativity, purposive action, character, knowledge, and love. The beliefs that this one God creates a universe that reflects God's own goodness and that this one God exercises an abiding providential care of creation, directed especially toward human persons, intensify the problem of evil dramatically.

Even if humanity's sinful rebellion against God, the privation of the aberrant will, is the source of evil, and now, in specifically Christian explanation, suffering and death are God's just retribution for the indignity of sin, believers often find themselves scandalized by the ways that the human encounter with evil is so unevenly shared. According to the doctrine of original sin, all human persons sin collectively in the primal sin of Adam and Eve and so are born into the world already tainted by sin's power. More, as Paul notes, "death spread to all because all have sinned" in the course of their lives (Rom 5:12). Sin is inescapable, as is God's just punishment for sin, which, all mainline Christian traditions hold, is death itself. Yet, though the universality of sin tragically bequeaths to humanity the universal punishment of death and the deathliness that saturates the human condition, all persons do not suffer the consequences of the history of sin and death at all in the same way. Life-shattering poverty besets some, and not others. Some are the victims of oppressive discrimination, and others are not. Some children are the victims of physical and emotional abuse, and others enjoy the comforting happiness of their early years. Some lives are destroyed by the workings of unjust political and economic systems, and other lives enjoy the power and wealth of the very same systems. Some pass through life in vigorous health, and others suffer physical and psychological disability. The catalogue of difference in what the Christian doctrinal tradition believes to be the corporate history of sin and death is endless, and each of these differences raises questions about the goodness of God. Although the doctrine of original sin indicts all humanity for the evil encountered in creation, the extreme variation in suffering in the history of human fallenness raises troubling questions about God's goodness, providence, and justice. For believers, the attribute of God's omnipotence typically does not bend under the weight of this scandal. And this affirmation of God's unlimited power over creation presses the question of God's goodness further still.

The Christian belief in one God, Creator of the universe, whose infinite goodness is providentially reflected in the world, powerfully intensifies the problem of evil. This tension is a function of the moral relation between the divine person and human persons, the likes of which one does not find in the other religions I considered as counterpoints to the Abrahamic religions. A Christian imaginary of the beauty of graceful events in time intensifies the problem of evil all the more, since it claims that time's eventfulness itself is a medium of grace, of God's own divine life, and yet the death and deathliness encountered in life as evil, often horrendous evil manifested in unjust and violent acts, unfold in events that present themselves to believers as anything but gracefully beautiful.

There are several ways in which believers have addressed the monotheistic configuration of the problem of evil. Here, I would like to identify two, related responses that we will find unacceptable. The first is emotional consolation that issues from a deep faith in the love, mercy, and goodness of God and that I will call the providential explanation. The second is a modern style of argumentation motivated by a faithful trust in the goodness of God that the philosophical tradition has called theodicy. Let us consider each in turn.

The providential explanation is offered as consolation by believers to believers who have been victimized by tragic loss. The traditional Christian doctrinal account for why such suffering has befallen the grieving victims—say, the parents of a young daughter who has succumbed to cancer—would be utterly insensitive to the point that it would raise real concerns about the truthfulness of the doctrine. According to the legal explanation of the doctrine of original sin, all humankind is implicated in the first sin of Adam and Eve, and this corporate guilt requires the redress of God's divine justice; hence the suffering and death that God has justly judged will beset every human life without exception. All human beings, the doctrine claims, deserve death since all share the guilt of humankind, an explanation that defends God's integrity but at the cost of denying the scandal of innocent suffering endured by the young girl who died and her grieving parents. According to the doctrine of original sin, all suffering is guilty suffering.

It would be heartless to offer this orthodox doctrinal explanation to the grieving parents in the face of their terrible loss. This explains why at the young girl's funeral, the pastor's sensitive homily would never consider mentioning the tradition's doctrinal account for why this terrible death has occurred. As a consequence, well-meaning believers offer the consolation of the providential explanation instead. God, the consoler claims, has good purpose in this death, which, like all things, stands under God's unlimited power. Even though the victim's tragic loss makes it seem as though God has abandoned the believer, the providential consoler assures the victim, or the victim assures him or herself, that the tragic event is wrapped in God's good purpose, even though that providential meaning is mysterious and beyond the believer's understanding. "This is all part of God's plan," the assurance goes, "and even though this hurts terribly, know that this suffering, this death, has a design fashioned in God's infinite wisdom and love." Such consolation, so common to Christian piety, intends to mitigate the scandal of innocent suffering by making the terrible event an act of grace. It intends to relieve the moral tension between divine and creaturely persons by having providential purpose eclipse the scandal of innocent suffering. The providential explanation, though, often has the opposite effect. Its ascription of divine causality to the horrendous death may intensify the problem of evil terribly for victims unable to believe that God's supposedly gracious power could be directed to such tragic ends or that, if it were, God would be a malicious purveyor of death, an enemy to the grieving victim.

The second response to the monotheistic configuration of the problem of evil is the philosophical project of theodicy. A theodicy is a reasonable argument that attempts to justify God in the face of the evil that courses through creation. Theodicies are a product of the modern intellectual tradition and reflect the Enlightenment's confidence in the power of reason. But the reasonable arguments advanced in theodicies are motivated by the faith of the Christian philosophers who produce them. The theodicist is a believer who tries to explain logically how the power and goodness of God can be reconciled with the evil that fills creation. Thus, the classical formulation of the problem that theodicists address: If God is infinitely good and if God is infinitely powerful, then whence evil? Were one of these two attributes denied of God, one could imagine the possibility of evil in God's creation. If God were infinitely good but not infinitely powerful, then God would lack the power to bring God's infinite goodness providentially to bear on creation, and this would explain the presence of evil. If God were infinitely powerful but not infinitely good, then God's intention to extend God's benevolence to creation would be diminished in some way, and this would explain the presence of evil. But if God possesses the attributes of power and goodness infinitely, as the Christian tradition claims, then evil, to say nothing of the prevalence of evil, should not vex creation at all. Here I will address the classical genre of this philosophical project that has come to be known as the "best of all possible worlds" theodicy.

The eighteenth-century German philosopher Gottfried Leibniz (1646–1716) coined the term "theodicy" in the title of his 1710 book *Theodicy: Essays on the Goodness of God, the Freedom of Man and the Origin of Evil*. The argument that he develops astutely addresses the critique of the antitheodicist, one who calls into question God's goodness or power in the face of the evil prevalent in the world. The antitheodicist is able to imagine other possible worlds that an all-good and all-powerful God might have created in which this or that evil did not transpire—a world without disease, a world without the debility of old age, a world without physical or emotional disability, a world without genocide, and so on endlessly— even to the point that one could imagine a world completely devoid of evil. Each of these possible worlds offers a point of comparison to the actual world that God created, and each possibility that was not actualized in creation indicts the goodness or power of God. Leibniz's counterargument is elegantly simple. The antitheodicist's attention to the divine attributes of goodness and power has led the critic to overlook the role of God's knowledge in shaping God's good intention and the exercise of divine power in God's creative plan. Before the creation of the universe, Leibniz argues, God's infinite knowledge contemplated the infinite possible worlds that God might create, comparing them to each other as God decided which to bring to actuality. "The result of all these comparisons and deliberations," he claims, "is the choice of the best from among all these possible systems, which [God's] wisdom makes in order to satisfy goodness completely; and such is precisely the plan of the universe as it is."[2] The divine attributes of infinite goodness, power, and knowledge possess an inseparable unity in the divine character, and their mutual cooperation in the act of creation logically requires the conclusion that the universe God created must necessarily be the best of all possible worlds, even though there is evil in the universe. In God's infinite knowledge God knew what the best of all the possible universes would be; in God's infinite goodness God desired that universe to exist; and in God's infinite power God made the best possible universe real. One might say that the short form of Leibniz's theodicy is that if God is God, then this is the best of all possible worlds. Evil, though problematic, is not a scandal that calls God's goodness into question.

A more recent version of the "best-of-all-possible-worlds" theodicy was offered by the American philosopher John Hick (1922–2012) in his

1978 book *Evil and the God of Love*. Hick grounds his theodicy on a distinction drawn by an early Greek father of the church, Irenaeus of Lyon (ca. 130–ca. 202). Genesis 1:26–27 speaks of God's creation of human persons in God's own "image" and "likeness." While most commentators have seen the words as synonyms, Irenaeus ascribed a different meaning to each. The "image" of God that human persons possess describes their metaphysical nature, and thus the distinct kind of being human persons are. "Likeness," though, describes what human persons might become in the course of their lives by the exercise of moral free choice toward the development of character. Hick observes that God's creation of the entire universe and a humanity bearing the image of God was easy work for an omnipotent being. But the likeness of God toward which morally accomplished human persons might develop could never be finished work on God's part, since moral development requires the exercise of free will in challenging moral circumstances. Thus, because the creation of human persons was a preeminent value in the sort of universe God providentially created, and because human persons to be who they are must be afforded opportunities for their own spiritual growth, God purposively created a universe in which the struggle with evil would allow human persons to grow into spiritual relationship with each other and with God. In Hick's view, the antitheodicist chastises God for not creating a universe free of pain and strife, as though God had the same obligation to humanity as would a pet owner to provide the pet a humane environment in which to flourish. But this way of imagining the problem of evil overlooks the simple fact that human persons are not pets, but persons able to develop into a mature, moral relation with their Creator. Thus, Hick asserts, the right question to pose in considering God's relation to evil is not "Is the architecture of the world the most pleasant and convenient possible?" Rather, the correct question is "Is this the kind of world that God might make as an environment in which moral beings may be fashioned, through their own free responses and insights, into 'children of God'?"[3] Hick assumes that the answer to this rhetorical question is a resounding "yes" that affirms his logical conclusion that God created the best of all possible worlds.

Any time that a theology broaches the issue of the evil endemic to the human condition, as the present chapter does, the specter of theodicy immediately is raised. Whether theodicy takes the form of the reasoned argumentation of philosophers like Leibniz and Hick or, perhaps stretching the category a bit, the pious consolation of the providential explanation, it ardently defends the goodness of God in the face of the evil that courses through the world, especially the evil of innocent suffering that presents the most egregious threat to God's providence.[4] My consideration of these matters, though, roundly rejects theodicy as a viable approach for faith to follow, and thus for my theological aesthetics of time to follow as well. There are several reasons for the avoidance of theodicy.

Strictly speaking, the providential explanation offered as consolation by believers to believers is not a theodicy, since it does not construct a logical argument as a proper theodicy does. There is no doubting, though, that the providential explanation has theodicy-like qualities, both in its eagerness to defend God before evil and to do so in words that attempt to bring closure to the anguish of innocent suffering. As we have seen, the providential explanation seeks such closure by insisting that what seems to be tragedy is actually grace and that the judgment that the victim suffers innocently, however understandable, is emotionally misaligned to the real meaning of the causal event in question. Although the providential consoler does not explicitly go so far in his or her words of comfort, the purport of the consolation is that the suffering victim actually has reason to rejoice. This denial of the victim's actual feelings in a time of crisis, to say nothing of the consoler's assurance that God is the agent of the tragic event, often fails to bring consolation, and instead intensifies the victim's suffering to a feverish pitch.[5]

The best-of-all-possible-worlds theodicies are just as problematic in their unwillingness to engage the actual evil that human persons meet in their lives and in history. Leibniz's version of this logical explanation is an a priori argument, one that prescinds from any empirical evidence of evil in the world. For Leibniz, the actual quality and quantity of evil in the world need not enter into consideration at all in the defense of God. The effective unity of the divine attributes of infinite power, infinite goodness, and infinite knowledge yields the purely theoretical conclusion that God, by God's very nature, had to create the best of all possible worlds. Thus, even the evil in the world that God actually created manifests God's providence, a position Leibniz expresses by affirming Augustine's well-known claim that the evils of the world are "only of such a kind as may tend towards a greater good."[6] The implication of this position is that evil is productive. Its capacity to destroy the bodies and spirits of human persons in individual or systemic acts of overwhelming violence falls into the shadows, and instead evil's deathliness is optimistically transfigured into potential from which God ever draws goodness. Evil, for Leibniz, is not scandalous at all.

Hick's version of this theodicy offers some nuanced differences from Leibniz's but, as a best-of-all-possible-worlds argument, moves in much the same direction. Unlike Leibniz, Hick does not make an a priori argument but rather one that takes account of the evil that one finds in the world. He challenges his reader to imagine that a universe without human persons would be better than the universe that actually exists. Convinced that his reader would never judge such a possible world better, Hick then turns to anthropology to justify his view that an all-good and all-powerful God would create a world just like ours, evil and all. Since human persons, he believes, must be moral, freely willing agents whose decisions allow growth or diminishment in character, and since moral decision transpires in circumstances that face the challenge of evil, God had to create a world with evil in it in order for human persons to be who and what they are by nature. Believer that he is, Hick sees the universe as a providential stage erected in the original act of creation for the performance of moral lives. Like Leibniz, Hick views evil as a resource for the production of a greater good. That Hick could describe human life as a "hazardous adventure in individual freedom"[7] suggests that his is a theodicy for survivors, for persons who encounter evil, negotiate it morally, and, as a consequence, find themselves to be "more" in experience, wisdom, and character. Hick seems to lack the moral imagination to consider how devastating evil would play out in the logic of his argument—the sort of evil that capriciously and overwhelmingly reduces life to death or to a living death from which the victim never recovers. One worries that the implication of Hick's argument is that such horrendous evil would be judged grist for the moral mill of bystanding witnesses, or worse, that the surviving, though devastated, victim would be faulted for not sufficiently rising to the challenge of evil in God's creative plan.

The moral insensitivity of the theodicy project—its unwillingness to confront the actual evil in people's lives and in history—alone would justify our avoidance of this interpretive approach to the tragic announced in this chapter's title. Indeed, some have judged this insensitivity to be so compromised as to render the theodicy project itself an act of evil.[8] Here, though, I would like to address another dimension of the theodicy project's approach that is keenly problematic with regard to our study's theme—the issue of time.

The aspirations of theodicy have everything to do with time, even though time is not a theme explicitly highlighted by theodicists like Leibniz and Hick. Although a theodicy is a logical exercise, an argument whose purpose is the defense of God, the theodicist desires much more than the satisfaction of a cogent conclusion reached by formal logic. To the degree that theodicies view evil in creation as productive of the good, they regard time as a field of potential within which either God (in the case of Leibniz) or humanity (in the case of Hick) can exercise power to draw good from evil. There is a real sense in which theodicists yearn for the reduction of tragic time to an illusion, an ephemeral disguise that hides the workings of providence, whose efficacy cannot be thwarted. Leibniz gestures in this direction by referring to Adam's sin, from which the entire history of suffering proceeded, as *felix culpa*, a "happy fault" in its capacity to bring about the saving incarnation of the Redeemer.[9] Hick refers to the history of time after its origin by divine fiat as the "second stage" of God's creation. Time in this period, actually its entire duration, is both "evolutionary" and "teleological," its development and purposiveness the context for "soul-making," in which evil prods human persons to be the children of God they were created to be.[10] In these respects, Leibniz and Hick imagine tragic time transfigured, its suffering eventfulness transformed into the providential time that the theodicists argue it most truly is.

There is another way in which theodicies address time that undermines its tragic eventfulness and so makes theodicy a deeply deficient interpretive approach for a theology of time. The argumentative venue of theodicy attempts to erase time in the syllogism's logical closure. Intent on achieving epistemic certainty about divine goodness before the troubling prospect of evil, the theodicist fashions a chain of premises that reason logically draws to a conclusion whose purported cogency brings the assurance of knowledge. In the movement from premises to conclusion, in the order of the syllogism, time, and especially time in the deep uncertainty of its tragic dimensions, disappears. In the instant of the logical deduction, the duration of time's actual eventfulness evaporates. The formal logic in which the argument achieves the truth it desires renders time superfluous. And this brings the advantage of not having to negotiate time as one finds it, replete with tragic events that cause terrible innocent suffering.

We see this logical erasure of time most clearly in Leibniz's theodicy. In principle, Leibniz's a priori argument need not consider time, or any other dimension of creation for that matter, in order to arrive at its conclusion that this is the best of all possible worlds. His premise that infinite goodness, power, and knowledge are one in the simplicity of God's being requires the conclusion of his theodicy. In effect, his logic unfolds as a contemplation of God before the creation of time. Thus, time is inconsequential to reaching his argument's conclusion. On its face, Hick's theodicy seems to make the actuality of evil in time vital to its argument. Virtue's dialectical relationship to evil in the time of human lives prompts Hick's conclusion that God created the world, evil and all, in order to permit the greater good of human character. But in its logic, Hick's theodicy never need take the actual eventful circumstances of tragic time into account. Although not presented syllogistically, his argument in effect begins with a major premise that defines his anthropological, rather than theological, orientation—God created human persons with free choice so that they would be capable of the extraordinary good of creaturely moral development. His minor premise, which is actually enfolded in the major, is that moral development through free choice requires the negotiation of evil. Hence, Hick arrives at the conclusion that God created the best of all possible worlds. Evil does appear as an ingredient in the argument. But actual evil in the deeply tragic time of broken lives does not. Real time is syllogistically erased in the instantaneous logical move from major to minor premise, and so to the felicitous conclusion that evil in time is a dimension of God's providential plan.

My interpretive approach to tragic time thus takes a stand against theodicy for several reasons. Theodicies, including the providential explanation, are morally insensitive. In their eagerness to defend God and offer comforting assurance they swerve from the evil before them in order to imagine a palatable evil, one that might be defeated by their words. And their words convey the judgment that the victim is only seemingly a victim, or, in any case, not as much a victim as the victim is thought to be.

As totalizing explanations, theodicies say too much, not only about the victim but also about God. And as one might expect, this superfluity of words issues not from the modest claims of faith but from the theodicist's single-minded desire to know how God's purpose fills evil so as to render it meaningful. Most importantly for our concerns here, theodicies are impatient. They refuse to abide time in its eventful duration since time impedes the logical closure that the theodicist's act of knowing requires. Even more, time's duration presents uncountable events that enter persons' lives as overwhelmingly tragic, the very events that theodicies avoid in order to reduce evil to the morally negotiable. Put simply, theodicies are allergic to tragic time, even though human judgment finds so much of time to be filled with encounters with evil. Theodicies deny time as it is in order to find solace in God's timeless providential will.[11] My interpretive approach will strive to be patient with time, and especially with tragic time, offering theological explanation that recognizes the tragic character of events while yet pressing the argument of my previous chapter that the eventfulness of time is the medium of God's graceful presence to creation.

Eschatological Time

My brief foray into comparative religion demonstrated that Christians face an intensified version of the problem of evil that some religious traditions do not and that this problem issues from the Christian belief in the divine person who Christians claim God is. A sharp tension is stirred in the life of faith as its claims for God's providential goodness meet the insidiousness of tragic suffering in individual lives and in history. An engaged faith confronts this tension as an ongoing emotional struggle. My investigation of theodicy's deficient approach to this problem enabled us to see that this emotional difficulty at the heart of faith is not a problem to be solved. The providential explanation and theodicies try to do just that, and I found their explanatory solutions to be disturbing attempts to deny the tragic dimensions of evil in people's lives. But more, it is the very desire for a solution that distorts the theodicy project from its beginning, for that desire conveys the theodicist's flawed assumptions that just the right words can transform evil into providence and that logic is the best medicine for a believer's troubled heart. As I turn theologically to the issue of tragic events amid the beauty of graced time, it is important to announce at the outset that I will not seek a solution to the problem of evil, especially a solution that attempts to justify God before the evil that courses through creation. My assumptions are that human words can offer no such justification and that evil, though an emotional problem for the life of faith, is not the sort of problem that can be solved. Instead, my reflection will proceed by thinking along with the tradition's doctrine of creation in order to appreciate the depths of God's saving immanence to the world. I can begin by turning again to a claim for which I argued in chapter 2—that all time is eschatological time.

I have imagined the eventfulness of time as sacramental, as the way God's graceful presence manifests itself to the universe. All events in time, in their very act of transpiring as events, radiate the grace that is God's own divine life. And this, I have proposed, is the beauty of creation, there to be appreciated in the gracefulness of motion, a sign of and dynamic testimony to God's providential intimacy to the things that are made. Although the graceful beauty of particular events garners our attention and stirs the believer's sense of the faith to recognize God's presence in an astonishing way, I imagined more comprehensively that time as such, and so all events in time, convey the divine omnipresence. The qualities that medieval Christians ascribed to all created being—that it is beautiful, as well as one, good, and true—apply as much to the time in which being eventfully flourishes. I have argued as well that all "time now" is eschatological time. This claim, I proposed, expresses several basic Christian beliefs. All time now is eschatological because, as created, it has been saturated with the power of eternal life. Like all things, time has been created by God in and through the divine Word and so is predestined from its very origin to share in the New Creation that Christians believe his own resurrected life has inaugurated. All time now is eschatological time because it is always already redeemed, even as its redemption awaits consummation in the midst of the history of sin and death. In other words, all time now is eschatological because all time is graced, or, as I have argued, time itself is the created medium of God's grace, and so, since time is a dimension of created reality, grace, to paraphrase Augustine, is closer to creation than creation is to itself.

As we have seen, there is another respect in which there is an eschatological quality to time. All time now is eschatological because time bears within itself the sense of an ending. Time is creaturely. Like all of creation, time is brought into being by God's creative will out of nothing, a nothingness that enshrouds time, setting the limits of its eventfulness. Time's finitude is defined by its origin, its ending fixed in its very beginning. But earthly time's ending is fixed as well in its duration. Time passes. And as it does, the present moment ever ends as it instantly recedes into the past. Even if understandings of the past and visions of the future may abide in ways the ephemeral present never can, they too are always ending as their configurations shift this way or that in light of the ever-changing present. Time possesses a fragility that a Christian metaphysics affirms in recognizing the difference between God and all that is not-God. Like all creation, time in its very being stands in need. Time now not only passes but also is passing away. The physical law of entropy confirms that the energy in the universe is winding down, and as the energy of that motion finally dissipates, so too will the time in which the universe moves. The relatively recent scientific discovery of dark energy confirms as well that the power of entropic forces at work in the universe actually increases as time goes on, constantly hastening the demise of the universe and with it the demise of its time. In many respects, this scientific knowledge is consistent with the claim of the doctrine of creation that this world is passing away and that it will pass away definitively at the Last Judgment, however much science may not grasp the doctrine's hopeful addendum that in its passing away it becomes unimaginably more. The sense of an ending moves as well in the time of our lives as endings to physical and emotional liveliness of all sorts punctuate our lives and are sympathetically witnessed in the lives of others. And in the midst of the suffering that issues from these endings looms the ending of death itself, the finality and inevitability of which defines the time of our lives and stirs the searing grief of loss.

This dual resonance of eschatological time now—at once graced and yet measured by the rhythm of finite need and suffering—sets the proper Christian context for considering the tragic events that occur in the midst of the graceful beauty of events in time. We have seen that the eschatological quality of time in Christian belief defines a particular temporal aesthetic, a way that the subjectivity of the believer judges the meaning of events transpiring in time. I have argued earlier that the Christian virtue of hope is especially sensitive to the eschatological quality of time. Since Christian belief maintains that time is eschatological as both graced and in fallen need, I proposed as well that the theological virtue of faith not be traditionally imagined as a subjective certainty—a conceptualization so easily subject to fundamentalist misappropriation—but instead as an ardent hope ever yearning for God's consummation in the face of anomic time filled with tragic events. I proposed too that the virtue of love be set in the same eschatological temporality since hope's native temporality captures what Christians affirm about time now—that the tragic yet transpires within its graced ambiance, setting the course of struggle for a hoping-faith.

To speak of events as tragic and of the time that shapes such eventfulness as anomic places us in the realm of human judgment. This judgment issues from a human encounter with evil, with the death and deathliness that diminish life and liveliness. To make this point, one might imagine the world before the evolution of human life. Measured by reason, there was no tragedy in that world, even though the long, prehuman history of life was filled with pain and death. The tragic is a moral judgment made by human persons about the encounter with suffering and death in their own lives, in the lives of others, in the suffering and death that they witness in animal life, or in the ecological loss that vitiates the beauty of nature and causes suffering and death in the life-world. The literary genre of tragedy often locates the tragic in a protagonist's character flaw, thereby bringing the tragic under the power of human volition. Certainly much of what human persons encounter as the tragic, and so as evil that has befallen them, is caused by human moral failure. Whether such aberrant actions are wantonly callous or sadly ignorant, they are the source of immense suffering in the human community. Here, though, I will extend the category of the tragic to include the human encounter with any event that brings suffering and death into life—not only events that issue from human volition but also events that issue from the natural world beyond any human influence. Events such as pandemics, physical and mental illness, the debility of old age, catastrophic storms, and devastating earthquakes are "natural" in the sense that they are events that transpire ordinarily in the behavior of the natural world. In this same sense, human volition may be deemed "natural" to the degree that willfulness, like all things human, is also a product of the evolutionary history of the natural world. Philosophical and theological discourse about evil, however, often distinguishes between moral and natural evil in order to acknowledge a difference in the kind of evil that issues from human agency and the kind of evil that does not. Since evil is a matter of human judgment, I will regard both agential and nonagential events that bring suffering and death into human lives as tragic and will understand the temporality that attends such events, not only in their occurrence but also in their temporal wake, as anomic time.

To say that all time now is eschatological time is to acknowledge a most basic Christian belief—that the hope for eternal life in a time ever graced is hope that ever faces tragic events in times disturbed by the power of suffering and death. Hope's virtuous yearning is motivated by the grace of God's own presence, which is immanent to all events in time. But that yearning is aspiration instigated and deeply troubled by events that tragically manifest the death and deathliness that course through creation. This means that in the Christian aesthetic of eschatological time there is nothing unexpected about the concurrence of the graceful beauty of events and the tragic events that fill every life and all of history. Theodicy sees anomalous contradiction in this concurrence and a problem that cries for resolution. To the contrary, in hope's eschatological temporality, believers witness to the proportions of the tragic and yet, in spite of the overwhelming power of evil, profess their hope in the even greater power of grace. This is expressed in the striking words of Paul, "Where sin increased, grace abounded all the more" (Rom 5:20). This is not to say, though, that the concurrence of the beauty of events in graceful time and the disturbing actuality of tragic events in anomic time is not problematic for the life of faith. Even though this concurrence is Christianly normative, it presents a difficult emotional challenge with which the believer ever struggles. Let us consider the field of that struggle more closely.

An Unorthodox Assumption

We have seen that the Christian doctrinal tradition maintains that there is no innocent suffering. As shockingly contrary to the actual experience of believers as this claim may be, it remains the orthodox teaching of the mainline Christian churches articulated pointedly in the doctrine of original sin. According to that doctrine, all suffering is guilty, and so deserved. The death and deathliness that stretch out tragically into every life are God's just retribution for the sin of Adam and Eve and of all their descendants in the long history of sin. According to the Christian doctrinal tradition, tragic events issue from human fault, a fault that is imagined individually and corporately. The advantage of this traditional teaching is that it places responsibility for tragic events squarely on the shoulders of humanity, and not on God or on God's good creation. Death and deathliness are willed by God into human lives as divine justice required by God's need to redress sin.

This doctrine causes consternation to the life of faith for several reasons. First, it ignores the extraordinary variation in the ways that human beings face tragedy in the course of their lives. Second, and as a function of this first reason, it denies the reality of innocent suffering that common experience affirms as it encounters this variation. Third, it claims that God's power is the agency, though not the cause, of all death and suffering. Moreover, the doctrine of original sin claims this not only in the generic sense that God's omnipotence holds sway over all of creation but also in the more pointed sense that God's retributive agency is in some way behind *this* or *that*—and, indeed, every—tragic event, and so behind the anomic time that configures it and endures in its aftermath. We might call this traditional teaching the legal explanation of human suffering, since it regards death and deathliness as God's rightful, juridical response to human moral failure. Humanity in sin has broken the divine law, and justice demands that humanity must suffer God's punishment. We would do well to see the providential explanation as a pious expression of dissatisfaction with the legal explanation. Its counterposition transforms God's retribution into an act of grace and the harsh clarity of punishment into the mystery of divine design. Both the legal and providential explanations, however, share two problematic traits. Both deny the scandal of innocent suffering—the legal explanation by asserting that all suffering is guilty, and the providential explanation by claiming that suffering masks divine purpose. And both affirm that God does death—the legal explanation by teaching that death is God's just retribution for sin, and the providential explanation by offering the consolation that God's mysterious providence is really at work in the death faced by the grieving victim.

My consideration of tragic time in an eschatological aesthetic will introduce an unorthodox theological premise, though one that might be truthfully faithful to the experience of believers.[12] Let us assume that God's power has no agency in death and deathliness at all. Let us claim with the doctrine of original sin that all of humanity stands in a deep state of fallenness, itself the consequence of personal and social sin. But with our premise let us leave behind the doctrine's teaching that God has willed death as retribution for sin. Let us affirm the comfort the providential explanation finds in God's immanence to human suffering. But with our premise let us reject the view that God wills this or that death as an eventful unfolding of divine design. Let us abide by the belief of the author of the Wisdom of Solomon: "God did not make death, and he does not delight in the death of the living. For he created all things so that they might exist; the generative forces of the world are wholesome, and there is no destructive poison in them" (Wis 1:13–14). The tradition, of course, does not claim that God finds pleasure in death and deathliness. But the legal and providential explanations both claim that God finds purpose in death and deathliness. The Wisdom of Solomon is not a scriptural outlier in this teaching. Its message is no different from the testimony of the entire biblical plot—that God is the God of life. And since God is such, all of God's graceful agency is directed toward the promotion of life and against the destructive power of death that courses tragically through human lives and through the entire history of sin. We see this claim extolled in a promise articulated poetically in the book of Isaiah: "On this mountain the LORD of hosts will make for all peoples a feast of rich food, a feast of well-aged wines, of rich food filled with marrow, of well-aged wines strained clear. And he will destroy on this mountain the shroud that is cast over all peoples, the sheet that is spread over all nations; he will swallow up death forever. Then the Lord GOD will wipe away the tears from all faces, and the disgrace of his people he will take away from all the earth" (Isa 25:6–8).

The prophet's stirring eschatological vision of a world redeemed frames the promise whose realization will bring that world about. That promise—that God will destroy death forever—runs throughout the entire biblical canon and, in Christian belief, culminates in the Easter event of Jesus's resurrection from the dead, itself the graceful cause of the New Creation that a Christian reader would see in Isaiah's prophetic vision.

If God is the God of life and of the living (Matt 22:32), and if the entire biblical message is encapsulated in the promise that God will destroy death forever, then the very coherence of the promise would militate against any theological claim that God's agency causes death. To claim that God does death retributively or providentially would place God's biblical promise at work against God's own actions, as though there were a double will in God struggling within the divine volition for resolution. The purport of the biblical promise that God will destroy death forever is that God does not do death in any way at all. The enactment of the promise implies that God confronts death's power as strange and alien, utterly foreign to the divine will, as though death were an enemy against which God conducts a running battle in the history of sin and death. In this conceptualization, it is important to recognize that so much of the death and deathliness against which God's graceful energies are aligned issue from the human will in what the Christian tradition calls sin. But death and deathliness also issue from natural forces over which the human will has no power at all and which cause tremendous suffering in human lives. This so-called natural evil in the death-dealing power that courses through what Christians believe to be God's creation is not the work of human volition, and in my proposal it does not originate in God's will as just retribution for sin. Nor in my proposal is the death that comes from natural powers woven into the created order as God's plan for the world that God chose to be. Such an explanation, near and dear to the heart of the theodicist, is simply another version of the providential explanation. Here, rather, I have started from the premise that God's agency is not at work in death at all, whether in the general conditions of finitude or in the particular ways that death and deathliness make their way into individual human lives.

I need to be clear about the theological implications of this unorthodox premise that yet, I would argue, is utterly consistent with the claims of Christian faith and hope. My proposal does not sacrifice a traditional commitment to divine omnipotence. It does not claim, as would a process theology, that God's power—in this case, over death—is in any way limited or restricted. God's omnipotence, I assume, is absolute. The absence of God's agency in death does not mean that God is powerless before death. Indeed, God demonstrates God's power over death in the resurrection of Jesus from the dead, an enactment in time of the biblical promise that God will destroy death forever—not just for Jesus but for all believers. Nor does my proposal depart from the traditional Christian claim that evil is a privation. Even though the implication of the biblical promise is that God confronts the power of death as alien to God's will and indeed as utterly alien to God's own life-giving being, the death that God opposes is not a "something." It is the sheer absence of the life that God has imparted to creation in and through the eternal Word (John 1:4). The opposition between God and death in this theological imaginary should not suggest even a hint of dualism. In this theological imaginary, a tragic measure of death and deathliness issues from the human will in the terrible history of sin and death. Yet, my theological imaginary claims, there is a power of death and deathliness that courses through creation and that besets human lives that issues neither from the human will nor from the divine will, since God does not do death in any way at all. There is a life-ravaging power of death and deathliness that has no origin in volition of any sort, including and especially the omnipotent will of God. Whence, one might ask, does this privative power arise, if not from humanity and not from God? The doctrine of original sin, the providential explanation, and theodicies all try their hand at explaining the human encounter with evil in relation to God. My proposal has ventured an imaginary that, unlike all of those, removes God's agency from death. My imaginary will also differ from those in pleading ignorance on the origin of natural evil. Theologically, we would do far better to concede that we cannot explain the origin of nonvolitional evil than to claim such knowledge by placing that kind of evil, as the tradition does, under God's agency.

This admission of ignorance may be disappointing to those who seek some kind of resolution to the emotional problem that evil poses to the life of faith. But, as I have already argued, there is no such resolution. Ignorance is always situated at some point in a theological proposal, and where it is placed has significant ramifications for the imaginary offered. The doctrine of original sin pleads ignorance before the remarkable variance in suffering in the retributive history of sin, as well as before the plaintive insistence that innocent suffering truly exists. The providential explanation pleads ignorance as to how a most tragic death could actually be a matter of God's providential design. Theodicies plead ignorance before the emotional objection that a world like ours, so full of horrendous evil, could hardly be the best of all possible worlds, insisting only that logically it must be. I choose instead to situate ignorance in my theological imaginary at the point of explaining the origin of natural evil, while yet insisting against the classical Christian tradition that it is not divine punishment for sin and against some strains of modern theology that place death and deathliness within God's design for creation, which is simply another variety of the providential explanation.[13] Pleading ignorance on this matter, rather than on others, allows me to affirm that the God of life and of the living does not do death at all, and it allows me to affirm as well the truth of innocent suffering.

This theological imaginary, I propose, is far more edifying to faith and far more inspiring to hope than the traditional imaginary, which understands death as corporate punishment for sin or as the mysterious workings of divine providence. Here, the uncountable ways that death wends its way tragically into human lives are not mysterious at all, since the holy Mystery who is God has no agency in death. Death and deathliness remain the tragic events they are, cloaked no longer in God's just or good purposes. Instead, God stands on the side of those who, often innocently, suffer the tragic events that enter their lives. Christian faith that engages eschatological time confronts its tragic resonance by hoping ardently in the truth of God's promise to destroy death and believing that God's gracefulness in time does not fulfill that promise by thwarting God's own retributive or providential will. That hoping-faith affirms that one day God's victory over death will be consummate and that one day, in the words of the prophet Isaiah, the tears of every face will be wiped away. Christian hope's anticipation of that day brings us back to the issue of time, and particularly to the temporality of tragic events.

How Long, O Lord?

My theological imaginary makes God's biblical promise to destroy death forever the ballast of its understanding of God's relation to the tragic events that fill human life and history. That promise prompts the nontraditional assumption that God has no agency in death and so the removal of God's agency from tragic events in time. It is important to note that even though human sin is the cause of so much suffering, the death and deathliness that issue from aberrant moral choice and that are suffered by the victims of moral evil are yet divine retribution according to the traditional doctrine of original sin, since in the legal explanation only God's power could explain death's presence in the realm of creation. This places all tragic events in some way under God's agency in the traditional imaginary, and it is this understanding of God's relation to the tragic that my proposal considers to be at odds with the biblical promise narrated throughout the entire scriptural canon. If tragic events are neither divine punishment nor divine providence, then how should our theological aesthetics account for them? Most pointedly, how do these tragic events stand with regard to my claim that events in time mediate God's grace to creation? Even though my theological imaginary is animated by an unorthodox assumption, it is important to stress that it is extraordinarily traditional in many other ways. My account of tragic events must begin by following the contours of the traditional Christian account of evil as privation.

Creation unfolds eventfully in occurrences that take place in time's reality. The motion of temporal events is the dynamism of being that, I have suggested, reflects the perichoretic relations that eternally transpire in the inner life of the Trinitarian God. This eventfulness, like all things created, is good. The time that measures these events mediates the very presence of God to creation. For this reason, time itself is beautiful, and the gracefulness of the motion in which some events unfold in time makes them strikingly beautiful in human judgment. Although all events as events are good and beautiful, many events bring death and deathliness into human lives. Some are the events of human actions—acts of physical and psychological violence, acts of cruelty, acts of moral indifference, acts of bigotry, acts of vengeance, acts of infidelity and betrayal, the examples far too many to catalogue at length. As these tragic events are enacted by the human will out of malice or ignorance, they multiply in the history of sin and death and give rise to deeper tragedy still, as though their fallenness spills out beyond the tragic time of their own eventfulness into an anomic time far longer in duration. The classical theological tradition would explain such events—aberrant acts of the human will—as privations, as enacted events emptied of their proper faithfulness to the unbounded goodness of God's will. Although these events exist terribly in history, there to be witnessed by all, the evil that they enact has no standing in being, since that evil is an absence of the enactment of virtue's goodness. Events in nature too enter into human lives tragically, causing suffering and death that victims of disease, mental or physical disability, infirmity, earthquakes, and storms regard as evil. In analogy to the event of an aberrant act of the will, we also may regard these death-dealing natural events as privative, the analogical dissimilarity defined by the complete absence of volitional responsibility for such privation. In the traditional imaginary, the suffering that issues from natural events is divine retribution. As willed divine justice, such suffering is finally judged to be a good, as are all events that bring about God's purposes. Proceeding instead from the assumption that God has no agency in death at all, we may regard death-dealing natural events as privative of the good, while yet affirming a consequence of that unorthodox assumption—that there is no theological accounting for the origin or currency of such death in creation. We have nothing to say theologically about how (causally) or why (meaningfully) this sort of deathliness besets human lives.

To say that tragic events are privative of the good, however, is not to say that such events are ungraced or vacant of created goodness. If all time is eschatological time, then all events occur in an aesthetic shaped by the temporality of Christian hope. All events in time are graced by the divine presence and so charged with the power of eternal life that animates hope's longing. And the gift of graceful time is ever given in response to human need, to time's sense of an ending rooted in its own finitude and in its deep need before the tragic events that demand hope's courage. Tragic events are privative in their diminishment of life, not in and of themselves as creation's providential movement in time. In a Christian imaginary, events are judged to be tragic to the degree that the terrible suffering they cause diminishes human dignity, mars the ordered symmetry of the created beauty of eventfulness, and scandalously affronts the presence of the God of life to all occurrences in time. Although not evil in themselves, tragic events possess a privative power that troubles, and often deeply troubles, the believer's hoping-faith in the midst of anomic time. As I noted in chapter 2, Paul Tillich has taught the Christian tradition that this troubling, encountered experientially as the believer's doubt, is not an emotion extraneous to faith that assaults its steadfast certainty from without, but instead is an indispensable dimension of the act of faith itself. Doubt, for Tillich, must be productively negotiated by a faith—or, we might say, a hope—that ever confronts the tragic. Faith and hope should never seek to defeat doubt, lest their goal become the unrealistic avoidance of the tragic events that fill time, which faith properly engages and by which faith is authentically troubled. Unfortunately, by explaining God's relation to evil the way they do, the doctrine of original sin, the providential explanation, and theodicies do just that. Failing to recognize the legitimate troubling of faith and hope before the tragic, they offer explanations that say far too much, all of them assuming that God's relation to tragic events is a problem to be resolved by placing evil under God's agency and thus making evil providentially purposive. It would be far better to reflect on hope's struggle in the face of tragic events in light of a spirituality that attends to the eschatological time in which that struggle occurs.

In order to appreciate how important time becomes in the theological imaginary I have proposed, let us turn to the category of mystery. Theologically understood, mystery is a quality of the divine life itself. The mystery who is God is not a problem to be solved, a trail of clues to be strung together, or an ambiguity to be clarified. The divine mystery is the infinite depth of God's eternal being, ineffable goodness perfectly actualized, unbounded love without beginning or end. The divine mystery is God's otherness, God's difference from creation. Yet this difference is not at all estrangement. Quite to the contrary, God's mysterious difference nestles into the world of finite creatures thoroughly and completely without in any way losing its infinite otherness. More, when regarded for what it truly is, this divine closeness to creatures actually heightens an appreciation for the divine transcendence. Karl Rahner makes this point strikingly by speculating that the most intimate, heavenly encounter with God in the Beatific Vision will not bring the saints a clearer comprehension of God but only intensify their appreciation for the profundity of the divine mystery.[14]

God's agency in death is shrouded in mystery in the traditional imaginary, though mystery reductively imagined as the inscrutability of the divine will and not as the immanent-transcendence of God's very being. My imaginary claims that there is nothing at all mysterious about God's agency in death since God does not do death in any way. In my imaginary, there is nothing mysteriously inscrutable about God's will, since God has revealed God's providential will in the biblical promise to destroy death forever and has manifested the consummate realization of that promise paradigmatically in Jesus's resurrection from the dead. My imaginary understands mystery as God's immanent-transcendence to creation, particularly to time, and even more particularly to tragic events in eschatological time. For the purport of the biblical promise is not that God will destroy death forever only in some fulfilled future in which tragic events pass away in God's final redemptive victory. Rather, the eternal integrity of God's very person and God's abiding immanence to time have implications for how God keeps the promise. God's keeping the promise implies that God is engaged gracefully now, in and through every moment of time, in and through all eventfulness, in the redemptive work of raising the death that transpires in tragic events to new life. God's promise itself is eventful, ever being kept as God's own providential eventfulness gracefully engages tragic events in anomic time.

In this imaginary—and actually, one might say in any Christian imaginary—the time in which the struggle of faith and hope takes place stirs the spiritual challenge of believing and hoping in the face of tragic events and in the midst of anomic time. If God has promised to destroy death forever and has revealed the enactment of that promise in Jesus's resurrection from the dead, then why all the time, and tragic time at that, until its consummate fulfillment? Why does the keeping of the promise take the time of our lives, and more, in the grander duration of the Christian imaginary, the time of history itself until the Last Judgment? Why all this suffering for so long? Posed in a theological context, this question in effect asks why God has created time, and when asked with respect to tragic events in time, this question begs for an answer along the lines of a theodicy. Asking why God created time is a question about God, not a question about time, and one that rather arrogantly attempts to fathom the mystery who God is. Asking why God does not keep the biblical promise sooner or even immediately so as to shorten or eliminate tragic time seeks a reasonable justification of God's providence in the face of evil, and one that, we have seen in my analysis of theodicy, attempts the erasure of time in the instant of logical closure. Theologically, these are the wrong questions to bring to the believer's encounter with tragic events in time. A spirituality sensitive to the way the eschatological character of time defines the proper consideration of tragic events will not pose the question "why" tragedy, or "why not" the fulfillment of redemption now. Such a spirituality instead must address the question "how" the believer lives faithfully and hopefully in and through tragic time, patient of the duration that God has created time to be.

Hope is the bearing of faith especially attuned to the troubling resonance of anomic time. If it remains true to its virtuous nature, hope ever struggles through tragic time, whether in the course of our lives or in the course of history. The act of hope is an event defined by that struggle, as hope ever resists its loss to a despair seemingly justified before the relentless onslaught of tragedy, while yet ever yearning for God's redemptive victory over the powers of sin and death. Hope is motivated by grace and encouraged, drawn forward, by the graceful beauty of events in time that make their tragic distortion a scandalous affront to God's immanence to creation and to human dignity. The beauty of time proleptically beckons hope toward the promise of eschatological fulfillment. But hope remains unfulfilled. Stirred by a future that is unimaginably "more," hope yet wavers in its long anticipation. It grows and diminishes in the present, its emotional journey through time tempered in this moment by the ascendancy of the tragic and inspired in the next moment by the abounding power of grace. The dynamics of a hoping-faith are no more and no less than this precarious, ongoing state of being hopeful of, of being faithful to, time's eschatological destiny in resurrected life in spite of death's apparent victory in all the corners of creation and in so many events in time.

We would do well to imagine God's keeping of the biblical promise to destroy death forever in time, the very fulfillment for which believers hope, as God's divine accompaniment to creation's eventfulness. This saving presence that I have portrayed as mediated through the sacramentality of time is the divine mystery, God's life-giving and life-restoring immanence to events judged to be beautiful and sources of joy, as well as to events that are devastatingly tragic and sources of grief-filled anguish. The mystery of God's presence to tragic events does not bring peace to hope's struggle in anomic time. In many respects, God's presence intensifies that struggle, since the discernment of the mystery of uncreated grace in the midst of tragic time stirs hope's desire for eschatological fulfillment, for a sharing in the resurrected life of the Savior, and so for a participation in the eternal life of God. Hope does not properly hope for an imminent resolution of this struggle, or for a Gnostic-like escape from the tragic. Its gaze set on God's future, hope hopes for faithfulness in times that shake the believer's steadfast discernment of God's presence to the tragic. Eschatological hope hopes for strength in the ongoing struggle for justice that relentlessly unfolds in tragic time. Hope hopes that God's accompaniment in its journey through time will gracefully inspire acts of love that resist events motivated by hate. Hope is an orientation to God that is properly patient of the temporal aesthetic of creation that God has ordained in bringing forth all that is not-God. Its virtue is a spiritual endurance through anomic time; its stance is that of a Christian perseverance animated by its patience with the divine mystery in time and expectant that God's providence will prevail to bring about the redeemed time of the New Creation.

For the believer, all time is a period of waiting in which hope hungers for the restoration of time's created beauty. But this waiting should be an intentional Christian practice responsive to the eschatological quality of time in which the believer engages in the struggle of hope. So much of the waiting we do in our lives is unproductive, the impatient enduring of a dead time that we wish would pass as quickly as possible. The events that transpire in this time are found to be routine, or boring, or deeply problematic in a way that leads one to conflate the problem and its time and to wish for the disappearance of both. This wanton disregard for the gift of time can infiltrate the believer's judgment as well. It appears in the fundamentalist's desire for certainty and so for the erasure of the tragic time that stirs doubt. It appears in the providential explanation's desire to have the troubled time of grief and trauma disappear in the consolation that a tragic event not only is accompanied by grace but is grace itself. It appears too in theodicy's desire for a reasonable defense of God's goodness that seeks the transfiguration of tragic time into empirical evidence of that very goodness. Most of all, in the traditional imaginary, impatience with time appears as the judgment that the time of this world is of little consequence compared to the eternity that awaits, and so needs to be endured with a forbearance that ever looks past time toward the joys of heaven. All of these views fail to appreciate the eschatological character of time, its place in creation as the divinely willed métier of eventfulness, as the means—good and beautiful—of God's redemptive accompaniment to creation, and as the duration in which God's promise-keeping is being fulfilled in every moment. For the Christian believer, no time is dead time. Time is a spiritually tensive field in which hope, discerning in time the closeness of the divine mystery, struggles to yearn faithfully for God's redemption in the face of the many tragic events that threaten to eclipse hope's expectation of God's future.

How, though, is Christian waiting practiced in eschatological time? How does such waiting become an event defined at once by uncountable short moments and yet by the long duration of eschatological time, a waiting in which all these moments might be ordered into the beautiful symmetry of an ardent hope? The first response to this question must simply acknowledge the features of the theological imaginary proposed here. God's divine accompaniment to the waiting of believers in time is not only a source of grace but also a source of consolation as their hope faces the anomic time of privative events. This accompaniment is not a double bind in which God's life-giving presence is aligned against God's own agency in death, but rather a presence in saving solidarity with those who suffer the tragic effects of sin and death. This divine solidarity flourishes in all places and in all times, though it has occurred most visibly and paradigmatically in the way of the cross. There in the events of Good Friday, understood not as a sacrificial atonement, the death of the Son willed by the Father, but rather as the divine nature's accompaniment of humanity on the *via dolorosa* that life often is, God takes God's stand against death and on the side of innocent suffering. God's most public solidarity on that holy day bespeaks the mystery of divine accompaniment to events in time, especially to tragic events.[15] No matter how lonely Christian waiting through tragic time may be, the believer trusts that waiting is never a solitary practice, but one that in every moment is enacted in the company of God and in the eschatological company of the entire communion of the saints.

Christian waiting is also practiced in words. The rhetoric of divine accompaniment is offered in the revealed words of the biblical promise that God will destroy death forever. Even though the promise remains unfulfilled in tragic time, believers trust that its words are true, that the promise is ever being kept, and that it will be consummately kept, since the God of infinite love, unchangeable will, and eternal power is the maker of the promise. Believers give voice to their waiting in ways too numerous and diverse to catalogue. Hope expresses its devotion to God's redeemed future in inspired testimonies of expectation for the realized promise, testimonies often made in the face of brutal injustice, the persistence of wanton cruelty, and overwhelming grief. Hope speaks too in words of encouragement to others on the journey through time that is so often tragic. When spoken well, these words fully acknowledge the evil undergone by the one who suffers, refusing to make the tragedy into grace itself and, only when the time is right, directing the suffering believer's gaze to the graceful dimensions of eschatological time that may renew even the most broken heart and shattered hope. The language of hope, though, is most powerfully expressed in the biblical genre of the lament, the plaintive cry of the believer in the spiritual pain of waiting. Consider how the ancient psalmist searingly articulates the sensibilities of this rhetoric of troubled yearning: "How long, O LORD? Will you forget me forever? How long will you hide your face from me? How long must I bear pain in my soul, and have sorrow in my heart all day long? How long shall my enemy be exalted over me? Consider and answer me, O LORD my God! Give light to my eyes, or I will sleep the sleep of death, and my enemy will say, 'I have prevailed'; my foes will rejoice because I am shaken" (Ps 13:1–4). At first hearing, the words of the lament have a hopeless ring, as though the believer, assaulted by the unrelenting persistence of tragic time, has abandoned the patience that eschatological time demands. More, the lament seems to be an accusation of divine faithlessness, an indictment of God's apparent surrender in the battle with sin and death in time. The lament is indeed an expression of doubt, but the very doubt that we have seen is a productive dimension of an engaged faith and, we might say, an engaged hope. The lament calls God to task, but does so because God's accompanying presence is so palpable amid the intensity of tragic time. It is God's mysterious immanence that stirs the plaintive cry. The impatience of the plea "how long?" gives voice to the most ardent longing for graceful fulfillment. Yet the sigh in which the lament is prayed expresses the believer's resignation to the patient waiting for which eschatological time calls. Lament is not the rhetoric of empty complaint but of a strong, and realistically troubled, hope.[16]

Finally, Christian waiting is practiced in acts of virtuous engagement that participate in the divine resistance to suffering and death. The theological imaginary proposed here follows in the line of the Catholic theology of grace of the *nouvelle théologie* of the mid-twentieth century. I began my study by noting that Henri de Lubac's rejection of the neoscholastic concept of *natura pura* in effect denied the existence of a graceless time. De Lubac's creative exercise of *ressourcement* portrayed creation as saturated in grace from its emergence in time, thus recovering from scripture and tradition a long-lost theological theme that has since become axiomatic in modern Catholic theology. My imaginary has pushed de Lubac's critique of neoscholastic extrinsicism a step further by portraying time itself as the medium of God's grace to the universe. In a critique of de Lubac's theology that he refined throughout his career, Karl Rahner raised a point of caution for any theological imaginary that accentuates the utter gracefulness of time. Lest a strong theology of grace run the risk of imagining God's power as irresistible, he argued, it must always yet stress the capacity of the human will to respond freely to that grace, a position consonant with the Council of Trent's teaching on justification. This was Rahner's notion of the supernatural existential, which became an important motif in his own strong theology of grace.[17] With Rahner, my imaginary must recognize that a theology of grace "everywhere and always" in a Catholic style rightly insists on the integrity of moral responsibility before God's grace.

An engaged waiting in eschatological time takes many forms. Waiting can blossom in the inward actions of prayer, meditation, and contemplation, which are themselves ways of gathering the believer's hope but which flourish all the more as they motivate hope to extend its energies in communal directions.[18] Waiting can be a time to build subjective dispositions that shape hope's resolve. The tradition speaks of four cardinal virtues—prudence, fortitude, temperance, and justice—that are marks of a Christian character and that we might appreciate as virtues cultivated by the practice of hope's active waiting in the vagaries of tragic time. It is the virtue, though, of doing justice that is hope's preeminent responsibility in eschatological time. Acts of justice, which, like all virtues, are freely willed and empowered by grace, are hope's confidence in God's future. Acts of justice, which resist moral evil and work to repair its tragic effects, are anticipations of God's coming kingdom here and now in the midst of time. Acts of social justice address the insidious ways that humanly enacted evil becomes engrained in communal, economic, and political structures over long periods of tragic time, and so even more powerfully rooted in the very human dispositions that originally gave rise to them. For believers, acts of social justice are testimonies to hope's patience in the long historical arc of human fallenness, for social evil resists justice as much as acts of justice do their best to resist corporate evil. Christian waiting is not a religious quietism but an imitation of God's graceful accompaniment of suffering in tragic time. Waiting is the practice of solidarity with those who suffer the pangs of moral and physical evil, a waiting that hopefully yearns for the final peace and justice of the communion of the saints in its fully realized, eschatological glory. Christian waiting, actively and engagingly practiced, is a living into that community here and now, in expectation of what it will be when God has resurrected tragic time.

CHAPTER FIVE

THE AESTHETICS OF TRADITION AND THE STYLES OF THEOLOGY

My theological aesthetics of time thus far has unfolded as a theology of grace parsed through an eschatological aesthetic of hope. To the degree that sin and grace are mutually related Christian doctrines, my attention to the beauty of graceful time required careful consideration of the consequences of sin in tragic time and the challenging spiritual predicament of believers waiting proleptically for the fulfillment of God's biblical promise to destroy death forever. The result was a theological anthropology shaped by the believer's hoping-faith responsibly engaged in acts of love in this time of waiting, acts of love that participate in the love of uncreated grace that is the divine life itself. My entire study will consider time in its great traverse from now to forever, but to this point my focus has been on "time now" in a creation graced and yet fallen. Before we pass to a consideration of time in the eschatological forever, let us abide a bit longer in the eschatological now in order to explore the time of ecclesial tradition.

In this chapter, we turn again to aesthetics proper as a theory of beauty in order to envisage the beauty of tradition. To find something to be beautiful is, of course, a judgment, and so an act of human subjectivity. But aesthetical judgment is a claim about the way things are in the world—in this case, about the beauty of the church's tradition, which unfolds in history. Here I will consider claims that believers make about ecclesial tradition in its objectivity. Although some believers find dimensions of ecclesial tradition to be truthfully deficient or tragically deformed, all believers as believers judge tradition to be beautiful for what it is and for what it might be. We will see that in our own ecclesial moment there are two distinct Catholic sensibilities about the beauty of tradition, each with its own regard for what is pleasing and edifying in tradition's beauty.

It is not at all surprising that judgments about the beauty of tradition would come to be expressed theologically, since theology is the church's voice at its most articulate. An appreciation for the beauty of tradition has resonated in Christian faith and hope throughout theological history. But only in recent years has theology given attention to the genre of aesthetics as an explicit manner of reflecting on the beauty of tradition in all its variety. Above all, Hans Urs von Balthasar's impressive achievement in *Herrlichkeit* has led theologians to appreciate the value of aesthetics for theological interpretation. Balthasar's magnum opus draws on the category of beauty in order to contemplate God's divine life as beauty itself and the incarnation as the consummate revelation of finite beauty. The subplot of *Herrlichkeit* unfolds in an extended meditation on modernity's loss of a faithful sensibility for the beauty of the incarnate form, a reflection on the insidiousness of sin viewed through the lens of aesthetics.[1] The richness of Balthasar's multivolume work appears in a plethora of discrete studies that together advance an accomplished argument for the divine glory as the plenitude of beauty, of which, he insists, modern theologians are as obliged to take account as the ancients.

Balthasar's work has since prompted interest in putting the category of beauty to theological service, even if not necessarily in the manner of his particular project. Richard Viladesau, for example, has proposed a transcendental argument that finds God's infinite beauty posited in the conditions for the possibility of beauty's finite apprehension.[2] Alejandro García-Rivera has developed a Latinx theological aesthetics that sees the beauty of a faith-filled community in its capacity to appreciate difference, including cultural difference, within the unity of God's redemptive order.[3] Mirjam-Christina Redeker has offered a theological aesthetics that understands itself as a perception theory of faith, keen to explain both the beautiful and truthful nuances of the human relation to God that the act of faith grasps.[4]

In this chapter, we will join the company of these aesthetical-theological interpreters by continuing to reflect on the theological significance of time, particularly by bringing an aesthetical perspective to bear on the theological concept of tradition itself. A number of monographs on tradition have appeared in recent years, and none has examined the notion of tradition by appeal to the category of aesthetics.[5] The advantage of such a perspective is that it will elucidate different Catholic sensibilities about the nature of doctrinal truth, clarify an aesthetical dimension to contemporary disagreement in the church about what is authentically Catholic, and provide understanding too about competing notions of the proper task of theology in our present ecclesial moment. Finally, my hope is that the aesthetical analysis offered here can help to achieve a rapprochement between Catholic theologians committed to different aesthetical sensibilities on the beauty of tradition, and who may rather narrowly regard their notion of traditional beauty as exclusively true and the style of theology that serves their understanding of tradition as exclusively valid. Certainly, in a theologically polarized time like ours, there is need for such rapprochement.

Tradition and Aesthetics

Catholic belief has long held that the act of faith encounters God's revelation in scripture and tradition, even if this particular way of conjunctively formulating the belief only appeared in the aftermath of the Reformation. According to the Council of Trent (1545–63), Jesus Christ is the one source of the truth of the gospel message that was faithfully promulgated to the church by his apostles. Yet this saving "truth and rule [of conduct] are contained in written books and in unwritten traditions which were received by the apostles from the mouth of Christ himself, or else have come down to us, handed on as it were from the apostles themselves at the inspiration of the holy Spirit."[6] The pressing concern for the council fathers at Trent was to define the Catholic teaching on divine revelation in the face of Luther's claim that God's revelation was communicated in scripture alone and that ecclesiastical tradition was humanly invented corruption, nothing more than the popery Luther identified with all that was wrong with the Church of Rome. In defining a dimension of revelation that exceeded the biblical page, the council fathers found expression for the medieval Catholic belief that the truth of God's revelation appeared in the teachings of ecumenical councils whose definitions were inspired by the Holy Spirit, in papal teachings, and in the writings of recognized, orthodox theologians who, it was assumed, pronounced on dogmatic loci with unwavering agreement that reflected the unity of divine truth. This tradition of *Scriptura sacra* was complemented further in the teaching of Trent by all the time-honored beliefs and practices that did not take written form but that, invested with the authority of apostolic teaching, communicated the truth of the gospel.

In the aftermath of Trent, Catholic theologians advanced the distinctiveness of the Tridentine teaching against the Protestant scripture principle by accentuating both the truth and authority of Catholic tradition as a mode of revelation. As time passed, this resulted in the development of a theology of the magisterium that was informed by a marked increase in the publication of papal encyclicals since the late eighteenth century and interpretively guided by the definition of the dogma of papal infallibility at Vatican I (1870). Thus, tradition achieved a certain integrity in Catholic belief that prevented its reduction to scripture or even to the history of the interpretation of scripture, even to the point that tradition could sometimes be understood as partly conveying God's revelation that also was partly conveyed in the Bible. This "partly . . . partly" (*partim . . . partim*) conceptualization of the relationship between scripture and tradition was considered by the fathers at Trent and rejected for its disjunctive implication that there were two sources for the truth of revelation which remained incomplete in each.

Yet, as late as the initial draft of Vatican II's *Dogmatic Constitution on Divine Revelation* (*Dei verbum*), this "partly . . . partly" formulation was still seriously considered by its authors as a viable way of insisting on the integrity of tradition as a distinct dimension of God's revelation. Continued dissatisfaction with this schema, however, led the council fathers to approve a much-revised final version of *Dei verbum* (1965) that insisted that "sacred tradition and scripture . . . are bound together in a close and reciprocal relationship," that they "both flow from the same divine wellspring, merge together to some extent, and are on course towards the same end." The "partly-partly" conceptualization was excised from the final text of *Dei verbum* since "tradition and scripture together form a single sacred deposit of the word of God, entrusted to the church." This teaching of Vatican II on the unity of revelation in the truthful coherence of scripture and tradition does not mean that tradition can be reduced to the reception of scripture's truth in the history of faith and its transmission. Moreover, the council affirms that "the church's certainty about all that is revealed is not drawn from holy scripture alone," but also from sacred tradition. Thus, repeating the teaching of the Council of Trent, *Dei verbum* teaches that "both scripture and tradition are to be accepted and honoured with like devotion and reverence."[7]

It is this integrity of tradition in Catholic belief that I wish to explore through the interpretive lens of aesthetics. And since this lens can exhibit a broad, visual range, I first need to focus the aesthetical perspective that will be put to hermeneutical use here.

Any number of ancient and medieval philosophers and theologians addressed aesthetical issues and questions, but the appearance of the discipline of aesthetics as a dimension of philosophical inquiry is usually dated from Alexander Baumgarten's 1735 dissertation *Meditationes philosophicae de nonnullis ad poema pertinentibus*, which addressed the poem as a work of art. This work introduced the philosophical use of the word "aesthetics," which Baumgarten (1714–62) defined as "a science of how things are to be known by means of the senses,"[8] a formulation he would expand some years later in his 1750 work *Aesthetica* to include the phrase "the art of thinking beautifully."[9]

The epistemological orientation of Baumgarten's early definition has ever remained a concern for philosophers interested in aesthetics, though the discipline has since developed to include an extensive range of issues. Writing a generation before Baumgarten, Anthony Ashley Cooper, the third Earl of Shaftesbury (1671–1713), and Francis Hutcheson (1694–1746) strove to describe the nature of beauty itself, as well as its proper regard by human sensibility. Growing attention in the eighteenth century to the workings of creativity and genius led to the inclusion of these themes in the scope of aesthetic issues, the most systematic treatment of which appeared in Kant's *Critique of Judgment* (1790), specifically in the first part of the work, which advances a "critique of aesthetical judgment."[10] The concerns of the philosophical subdiscipline widened further under the influence of Hegel's (1770–1831) judgment that beauty appears most truthfully not in natural phenomena but in works of art that manifest the movement of Spirit in history. Hegel's influence has led to the consideration of aesthetics as a discipline devoted to the criticism of art and artistic judgment.[11] With the advent of the avant-garde in various forms of modern art, the scope of aesthetics widened further as artists intentionally eschewed responsibility for representing the beautiful and the aesthetical task turned to explaining exactly what it was that made art art.

Here, as throughout my study, I will focus on aesthetics as a theory of the beautiful. In this chapter I will not be concerned to explain how a judgment about beauty is formed, as I was in my appeal to premodern aesthetical theory in chapter 3. Rather, I will describe two different Catholic perceptions of beauty that flourish in the contemporary church. Aesthetical thought has long recognized in the notion of taste that aesthetical judgment is pluralistic and, as a consequence, that there are differing perceptions of the beautiful and the qualities that configure it. Along similar lines, I will argue that there are different Catholic perceptions of the beauty of tradition and that these differing perceptions are grounded in different Catholic sensibilities or tastes about the religiously beautiful itself. In our day, these two aesthetical sensibilities often find themselves at odds, their contrasting discernments of the beautiful extending to judgments about what is traditionally true and so to what is traditionally orthodox. I will argue that the capaciousness of Catholic tradition allows for the appreciation of these two Catholic tastes, especially in their mutual regard. Let us proceed by exploring each of these aesthetical sensibilities.

A Classical Aesthetics of Tradition

A classical Christian aesthetics measures any instance of the beautiful against faith's affirmation that God is consummate beauty itself. Christian aesthetical judgment, however, is always exercised in the midst of the created conditions of existence where experiences of beauty offer imaginative entry to transcendent beauty. Thus, in faith, created beauty is judged to be so because it participates in the divine beauty. Even more pointedly, qualities that faith ascribes to the divine nature will be qualities judged to be beautiful in God's creation. Divine qualities like mercy and love can be found in the realm of human virtue, where they may be judged beautiful not only because they are emotionally poignant and relationally redemptive but also because human mercy and love share finitely in the beauty of these qualities as divine attributes. The divine attribute of goodness behaves like the moral attributes of mercy and love, not only in the sense that it admits of analogical construal but also to the degree that faith finds goodness beautiful, a judgment affirmed most strikingly by both Pseudo-Dionysius (fl. ca. 500) and Thomas Aquinas (1225–74), who agree that goodness and beauty are the same.[12]

Not all divine qualities, however, readily admit of this analogical translation equally, and, as a consequence, some resonate more aesthetically in the Christian imagination, and others, less. God's power and presence are examples of attributes that resist analogical construal and so Christian appreciation as the beautiful. Medieval Christian theology held that all created being possesses the transcendental qualities of oneness, truth, goodness, and beauty since these are qualities of the Creator. All being as being is beautiful, as are the conditions under which being appears, such as its power or presence. Yet power and presence are not moral qualities like mercy, love, and goodness. The power and presence of finite being stand less easily in analogical relationship to the utterly divine qualities of omnipotence and omnipresence, even to the point that Christian discourse would be disinclined to speak specifically of creaturely power and presence as beautiful.

At first glance, it would seem that much the same could be said of the divine attribute of immutability. Like omnipotence and omnipresence, divine immutability does not easily admit of analogical translation to creaturely existence, which is enmeshed in time and change. Nevertheless, it is this divine attribute more than any other that epitomizes God's beauty in the Christian imagination.[13] God's immutability offers no homology to the created conditions of temporality and marks the divine transcendence with the absolute perfection that changelessness and timelessness logically require. True analogy may fail between the beauty of eternal perfection and the vagaries of created time, and yet classical

Christian definitions of beauty readily imagine the qualities of beauty against the backdrop of divine immutability. Aquinas, for example, lists three qualities of beauty: "right proportion or harmony," "brightness," since "we call things bright in color beautiful," and "integrity or perfection" (*integritas, sive perfectio*).[14] The perfection or completeness he ascribes to finite beauty, though, cannot approach the perfection of the immutable God and conveys much more an aesthetical sense of the "wholeness" of what is judged beautiful. Too distant a comparison to be judged analogy in any strict sense, the aesthetical quality of *perfectio* dimly hints at the divine quality most attractive to Christian aesthetical judgment. However much some divine attributes susceptible to analogical construal encourage the believer to find some limited coherence between finite and infinite beauty, the attribute of immutability captures the Christian imagination with a divine beauty marked by its utter difference from all that is worldly.[15]

Having offered such judgments about the attribute of immutability, I need to make a qualification that has some bearing on my present topic. As we have seen, Catholic belief maintains that tradition, along with scripture, is a mode of divine revelation, the means by which God has chosen to communicate the sublime and saving truth of the Christ event to the world. In a classical aesthetics of tradition, the doctrines and practices that make up tradition possess a definitiveness that defies time, since they are imagined to be—in the words of the fifth-century monk Vincent of Lérins—what has been believed "everywhere, always, by all." It is Vincent's "always" that carries the banner of immutability onto the field of tradition. Tradition, of course, is in time and, as the very process of "handing down" the faith, is characterized by change. Yet a classical aesthetics of tradition finds the beauty of tradition in its abiding truth as divine revelation. The teachings and practices of tradition identified as the apostolic heritage are seen in this sensibility as fixed. The words of the Nicene Creed, for example, are as permanent as the truths about the nature of God and the saving drama that they express. The practice of the eucharistic real presence is timelessly repeated in the communicant's reception of the sacrament. Papal infallibility ensures the certainty of those dimensions of tradition which are not subject to change and so, in the judgment of the church's teaching authority, worthy of the entire church's appreciation as the timeless truth of revelation. Since revelation, and thus tradition as revelation, communicates God's providential plan to save the world, and since that plan issues from God's eternal love and unchanging will, tradition, of all that dwells in the creaturely realm, can be represented in faith as a finite reflection of the divine immutability. Its beauty, like God's, lies in its difference from the ordinary conditions of temporality, which, in this Catholic sensibility, are saturated with relativity and doubt.

Immutability as a quality of God's being by definition transcends anything in creation including tradition, which as a dimension of divine revelation must conform to the human capacities for its subjective recognition and reception and so must be enmeshed in time and culture. Tradition cannot be immutable in any strict sense. For a classical aesthetic sensibility, though, its beauty lies in its ability to capture a sense of God's unchanging truth, the very content of divine revelation. In this respect, tradition's unchanging truth possesses a beauty that is more distinctive than the unchanging truth of scripture. All Christians believe that the inspired words of the Bible convey God's timeless truth. The revelatory power of scripture *and* tradition, however, is a peculiarly Catholic belief. Moreover, the immutability of a classical aesthetics of scripture appears not only in its unchanging content but also in the fixed character of the words on the page, ever the same and ever conveying the once-and-for-all events of the Savior's life that bring the world to redemption. Tradition, though, offers itself in a great variety of aesthetical forms that capture the Catholic sense of tradition's permanence, itself a reflection of God's unchanging beauty. Tradition appears in such literary forms as the teachings of ecumenical councils, papal encyclicals, and the writings of authoritative theologians. Tradition appears in such unwritten forms as the celebration of Mass, Marian devotions, and the pastoral leadership of the local bishop. This variety, which includes so many other manifestations of tradition, extends the permanence of traditional truth into every dimension of Catholic life, unifying the experience of the traditionally beautiful. In this classical aesthetics, the transcendental quality of beauty radiates in tradition in a way that illuminates the other transcendental qualities of tradition—its unity, truth, and goodness.

Beauty functions mimetically in this classical aesthetics of tradition. Early in its history, Christian theology embraced the Platonic categories that served as the intellectual lingua franca of the Mediterranean world and that satisfied the Christian desire to think and speak well of God's otherness. Like the Platonic forms or ideas, the divine nature transcends time and change and dwells in a state of metaphysical perfection. For Plato (ca. 429–347 BCE), the things of this world are merely shadowy copies of the supersensible ideas. They stand in mimetic relationship to the eternal truths to which they correspond. Yet the absence of a doctrine of creation in ancient Greek philosophy makes this mimesis disappointing. Mimesis registers its imitation in the ambit of physicality. It implicates the senses, which distract the intellect from the true objects of knowledge. Plato expresses this misgiving about mimesis most notably in book 10 of the *Republic*, where Socrates advocates the censoring of art in the ideal state on the grounds that, as a physical imitation of a physical imitation, it lures the mind away from the contemplation of the immutably true and beautiful.[16]

Christian mimesis transforms these Platonic categories in every respect by ascribing immutability and its consummate beauty to the Creator God and by positing a rich correspondence between the physical universe and its Creator. This transformation was facilitated all the more in the late antique world as Plotinus's (205–70) later interpretation of Platonism was appropriated theologically by Augustine (354–430) and through his influence came to be embraced as normative in the medieval theological tradition. This variety of Platonism eschewed Plato's disjunctive regard for the relationship between the visible and invisible worlds and saw finite being as a sharing in the power and qualities of consummate being itself, a metaphysical resonance most acceptable to the Christian affirmation of the goodness of being and God's providential presence to creation.[17] Mimesis in this Christian ontology is enabled by the participation of created being in the uncreated being of God. The exercise of sensibility in this kind of mimesis can be an occasion of sin, since the reflection of eternal being in finite being could be idolatrously distorted by human volition.[18] But even while susceptible to sinful corruption, Christian mimesis properly falls within the scope of creation's sacramentality, in which finite being is metaphysically receptive to and conveys the graceful presence of God.

A classical aesthetics of tradition presupposes this understanding of Christian mimesis, regarding finite beauty as a mirroring of God's beauty facilitated by its created participation in the fullness of being. A classical perspective on Christian mimesis assumes that this finite mirroring of the divine beauty occurs statically since tradition reflects the divine immutability. This stationary beauty of tradition appears in interesting ways—in commonly affirmed iterations of the creed, in the iconic lives of the saints, and in the repetition of the sacramental life of the church. In each of these examples, and all the others that might have served, the Catholic imagination delights in the immovability of tradition's mimesis, ever the same in its mirroring of the divine immutability. This static mimesis is truly beautiful as a representation of what is authentically catholic and of what enduringly abides as the apostolic faith of the tradition.

As we have seen, mimesis implicates the senses, and in Christian mimesis the senses, responding well to grace and resisting the pitfalls of sin, are the experiential modes of apprehending sacred beauty. Catholic Christianity richly appreciates the role of sensibility in religious experience and in that respect is especially open to the aesthetic dimensions of the encounter with God. In a distinctly Catholic aesthetics, all the senses have a share in the experience of created beauty and its transcendent arc toward eternal beauty, at least to the degree that the senses mutually draw each other into the apprehension of the world. Aquinas, though, argued that of all the senses those most cognitive—seeing and hearing—especially apprehend the beautiful. The beautiful, he claims, "is that which calms desire, by being seen or known," and it is the senses of sight and hearing that particularly minister to reason, the faculty that conceptually grasps the beautiful. Thus, he observed, "we speak of beautiful sights and beautiful sounds but not beautiful tastes and smells."[19] Although Thomas singled out the senses of seeing and hearing as inclined to the experience of the beautiful, it is interesting to note that vision has a prominence in this aesthetic grouping. Early in the *Summa Theologiae*, Thomas defines beauty as "a matter of right proportion," and a beautiful thing as that which "pleases the eye of the beholder [*quod visum placet*]."[20]

Aquinas voices widely held Catholic assumptions in the aesthetical primacy he assigns to the sense of sight. Of all the senses, vision has pride of place in a classical Catholic aesthetics. The sense of sight unifies the other senses by construing possible objects of experience, and so of aesthetical experience, in a spatial field, there to be engaged by the other senses. Viewed as a theater of creation, this field offers a host of images upon which faith-filled vision might gaze in order to contemplate the mimesis of divine beauty. Unlike a Protestant aesthetic sensibility, which is iconoclastically wary of the visual and far more attracted to the beauty of a faith that comes from hearing the Word of God purely preached (*fides ex auditu*), a Catholic aesthetics turns to the visual apprehension of creation—in Aquinas's apt phrase, *"intellectum nostrum . . . convertendo se ad phantasmata"*[21]—in order to behold finite concrescences of divine beauty, an optics supported by the ancient Christian claim that God is light (1 John 1:5). A Catholic visual aesthetics embraces the values of an Orthodox theology of the icon, which sees the static, painted image as a window to eternity and the supernatural mysteries of the faith. Latin Catholicism, however, widens this window and with it the religious efficacy of vision by regarding three-dimensional objects—religious statuary and the crucifix—as its conventional art forms that represent the sacred for visual apprehension, an aesthetical commitment that reflects a readiness to find the divine beauty in the wider realm of ordinary physical things. The openness of Roman Catholicism to the reality of extraordinary visionary events, of appearances of the Savior, the Virgin, or the saints to believers, bespeaks the primacy of vision in a classical Catholic aesthetics, as does the more ordinary Catholic experience of gazing in veneration at the consecrated bread and wine elevated by the celebrant at the ritual climax of the Mass.[22]

A classical Catholic aesthetics values all of the senses in grasping the specific beauty of tradition, though here again the sense of sight has prominence. The Christian paradigm of visual beauty is the Beatific Vision, the consummation of eschatological meaning in the vision of God. Paul spoke of this visual experience movingly early in the tradition, expressing for the first time the aim of Christian yearning: "For now we see in a mirror, dimly, but then we will see face to face" (1 Cor 13:12). Benedict XII (1285–1342) articulated the hope of believers more fully in his fourteenth-century teaching that the souls of the blessed in heaven "see the divine essence with an intuitive vision" immediately, even before the resurrection of the body and its future reuniting with the soul at the end of time, and that in this vision God is seen "nakedly, clearly, and openly" so that in the vision the theological virtues of faith and hope disappear.[23] In remarkable poetry, Dante captures the hope of believers for this wondrous sight as he recounts the final steps of his heavenly ascent in the *Paradiso*: "Thus my mind, all rapt, was gazing, fixed, motionless and intent, ever enkindled by its gazing. In that Light one becomes such that it is impossible he should ever consent to turn himself from it for other sight; for the good, which is the object of the will, is all gathered in it, and outside of it that is defective which is perfect there."[24] In Dante's supernatural imaginary, which articulated the very Christian assumptions it both confirmed and profoundly influenced, it is the beauty of the divine immutability that brings the believer to rapture, a state that shares finitely in the immutability of God. Dante describes this heavenly participation by portraying his mind as "motionless" (*immobile*), transfixed by the vision of the impassible God. It is the sense of sight in its eschatological register that enjoys this redemptive encounter with the glory of God that radiates from the unchanging perfection of the divine nature.

This most profound of Christian hopes finds an analogue in the visual apprehension of the many forms of tradition, which offer a beautiful mimesis of the divine immutability. Catholic belief in the permanence of tradition encourages this connection, as does the status of tradition as a dimension of divine revelation itself. Like great works of visual art, the forms of tradition endure, defying effective change. Their beauty lies not only in their capacity to please when seen but also in their timeless availability to sight, to be seen and to please in the unchanging beauty of their sacred form again and again. Great works of visual art, of course, are only imaginatively and not literally timeless. They can be diminished in their beauty, much in the manner of Michelangelo's Sistine Chapel ceiling frescoes, sullied in their appearance with the passage of time. Corruption here is put right through restoration, in the recovery of the most beautiful original by erasing the deleterious effects of time. Along similar aesthetical lines, the forms of tradition possess the perfection of orthodoxy, which presents itself in all its clarity before the devout eyes of believers, its beauty appearing in the abiding and ever-familiar doctrinal formulations, rituals, beliefs, practices, and authorities that convey the saving truth of redemption. Corruption in this classical aesthetics is deviation from the beauty of orthodox perfection, itself a reflection of God's unchanging being. And here too, heterodox corruption can only be addressed through restoration, in the recovery of the beautiful original by erasing novel interpretations that occasionally claim false authority, disrupting the familiar field of tradition's fixed, observable beauty.

A Developmental Aesthetics of Tradition

Before considering the features of a developmental aesthetics of tradition, I should note that the identification of this sensibility does not assume that the developmental and classical aesthetics are mutually exclusive, as though commitment to one necessarily precludes a commitment to the other. Each aesthetics can accommodate the values of the other. Nevertheless, a classical Catholic aesthetics is basic to Catholic sensibilities. Any other Catholic sensibility is a variation on its theme and issues from a sense of compatibility with it. Compatible tastes, though, often proceed from an experience of preference, and the same typically applies to these kinds of Catholic taste. Moreover, any kind of taste can be held so strongly that it judges its grasp of the beautiful alone to be adequate to its object, to the rejection of other aesthetical judgments that claim validity. We shall see that these various allegiances and alignments of Catholic taste present themselves in the encounter between a classical and a developmental aesthetics of tradition.

A developmental Christian aesthetics of tradition has only appeared in the modern period as a post-Enlightenment sensibility. It is a recent arrival in the history of Catholic taste and for that very reason is regarded suspiciously by the classical sensibility. A product of historical consciousness, a developmental aesthetics of tradition finds divine beauty in the providential unfolding of events in time, which slowly clarifies the fullness of tradition's truth. Beauty in this aesthetics is judged to dwell not only in the truthful content of tradition but also in the process that brought it to be and also too in the anticipation that this process is occurring now in the present moment.

The very notion of the development of doctrine first appeared in the early nineteenth century, initially in the work of the Protestant theologian Friedrich Schleiermacher (1768–1834) and then, through his influence, in the work of Catholic theologians at the University of Tübingen, most notably in the early writings of Johann Sebastian Drey (1777–

1853). All of these theologians, Protestant and Catholic, found in the theological principle of doctrinal development an effective response to the historical-critical interpretation of scripture and the history of doctrine that Enlightenment and post-Enlightenment thinkers presented as proof of Christianity's falsity. Historical-critical interpretation exposed all the differences in scripture that a canonical reading of its pages easily glossed over. Historical-critical interpretation of the history of doctrine likewise demonstrated that the earliest Christian church—the foundation of what Christians devoutly called the apostolic tradition—was characterized by a vast plurality of beliefs that settled on orthodox unity only over the course of centuries of Christian infighting and through the vagaries of historical events. In these respects, historical-critical interpretation, motivated by Enlightenment disdain for Christian meaning, was a direct assault on a classical aesthetics of scripture and tradition, which delights in what it judges to be the lovely permanence of Christian mimesis. The principle of doctrinal development enabled theologians to acknowledge the facts of historical data marshaled against Christianity by its modern cultured despisers while yet interpreting the facts theologically to demonstrate the ways in which the tradition gradually came to its orthodox clarity, the development itself now placed within the ambit of divine providence at the prodding of the Holy Spirit.

Johann Sebastian Drey sketched the first Catholic understanding of developing tradition in his short work on theological method, *A Brief Introduction to the Study of Theology* (1819). Here Drey averred that conceptualizing the system of doctrine "not as a dead tradition from a time gone by" but instead "as the development of a living tradition" requires thinking of it as defined by two dialectically related elements: one that is fixed ("ein *fixes*") and one that is mobile ("ein *bewegliches*").[25] The fixed element takes shape as dogma, which Drey portrayed as "the single objectively . . . valid criterion of Christian *truth*."[26] The fixity of dogma is a function of its truth being "closed" or "completed," not from any privileged state of givenness but only, Drey insisted, through a process of doctrinal development in which the finally settled state of dogma has been proven in the abiding faith of the church. This mobile element of doctrine ever dwells in the ongoing life of the church as a quality of engaged faith that "in the development . . . is still conceiving [doctrinal truth]."[27]

For Drey, an authentic understanding of tradition is one in which the fixed signposts of dogma guide the proper development of doctrine in consonance with the orthodox past. This direction, however, does not produce an utterly reflexive mimesis of authoritative dogma. Even when it lacks the recognized validity of orthodoxy, the mobile element in doctrine "can yet be Christian truth that only has not yet developed to the level that it can be recognized generally as such."[28] Indeed, Drey pointed out that truthful tradition can be misrepresented through the error of "hyper-orthodoxy," which "finally denies any mobility" to doctrine.[29] In an astonishing judgment, which expresses the Romantic assumptions that enabled this modern conception of tradition, Drey observed that persons can "distance themselves from the truth either by falling away from it or by lagging behind it [*Zurückbleiben hinter ihr*]." The latter prospect, he continued, is "inertia, a consequence of the expiring activity of the (religious) principle in its progressive development."[30] For Drey, this developmental understanding of history is the only legitimate way of rendering the mystery of God's presence to tradition, and so much so that "any historical conception and account of the [temporal] appearances of Christianity that proceed from a principle different from [a developmental one] contradicts Christianity, is unchristian and untheological."[31]

The next generation of Tübingen theologians appropriated Drey's historical understanding of tradition, most notably his influential student Johann Adam Möhler (1796–1838), who favored the imagery of organic growth for the development of tradition in his early work *Unity in the Church*.[32] It was John Henry Newman's (1801–90) *Essay on the Development of Christian Doctrine* (1845), however, that brought the notion of developing tradition into the theological mainstream. Throughout the *Essay*, Newman compared the development of doctrine to the mental clarification of an idea. In this noetic analogy, the content of the idea represents the truth of the apostolic deposit of faith, which, like any objectively true idea, is always complete in itself. Yet, like any idea of depth, the apostolic tradition, as expressed in a variety of authoritative doctrines, comes to be believed, appreciated, and understood gradually in the conditions of time and culture. "This process," Newman claimed, "whether it be longer or shorter in point of time, by which the aspects of an idea are brought into consistency and form, I call its development, being the germination and maturation of some truth or apparent truth on a large mental field."³³ Like Drey, Newman thinks that the established doctrinal tradition provides an authoritative heuristic for development. And yet, like Drey, Newman regards historical development as the means by which established orthodoxy itself came to take shape, the means by which it is meaningfully enlivened in every present moment, and the means by which a presently obscure and only latent orthodoxy achieves clarity and manifest recognition.

Even though the notion of a developing tradition fell under the suspicion of church authorities during the modernist crisis in the early years of the twentieth century, its integrity has come to be regarded as axiomatic since the Second Vatican Council. In his famous address convening the council on October 11, 1962, Pope John XXIII himself referred to the work of the council as an exercise in reinterpreting and so developing the ancient faith for the present moment, a conceptualization of the workings of tradition that gave magisterial voice to this modern understanding:

> But from the renewed, serene, and tranquil adherence to all the teaching of the Church in its entirety and preciseness . . . , the Christian, Catholic, and apostolic spirit of the whole world expects a step forward toward a doctrinal penetration and a formation of consciousness in faithful and perfect conformity to the authentic doctrine, which, however, should be studied and expounded through the methods of research and through the literary forms of modern thought. The substance of the ancient doctrine of the deposit of faith is one thing, and the way in which it is presented is another.³⁴

Although John XXIII was reflecting here on the task of the council fathers, the understanding of doctrinal development that he articulated—what we might call the reception model—has come to be accepted in the Catholic tradition as the normative way of imagining the changeability of tradition. Catholic theologians have come to understand their interpretive efforts as possible contributions to the development of doctrine that offer new ways of imagining how the ancient truth of tradition might be received meaningfully in the present moment and how novel developments might themselves take shape as future orthodoxy. Even more broadly, this reception model envisions every believer's act of faith as a hermeneutical site for meaningfully reconciling the truth of ancient doctrine and the truthfulness of contemporary experience in the ongoing life of the church.

In considering the aesthetics of this conception, it is important to note that the explicit sense that developing tradition is beautiful first requires awareness that tradition is developing, and such an explicit awareness presumes knowledge of the historicity of doctrine that can only be acquired through education. This is not to say that believers who have not been educated in the historicity of doctrine are incapable of the implicit awareness that the truth of the faith develops in their lives and in the life of the church. The ongoing experience of deeper conversion into the mysteries of the faith is a good example of implicit awareness of development that believers share as a matter of course, especially as conversion is consciously shaped by events in life that are surprisingly transformative and prompt a sense of change. This kind of experience in turn can be broadened imaginatively to the entire church throughout its history so that this implicit sense of development extends beyond the life circumstances of the believer to tradition as such. Moreover, believers who are not educated in the historicity of doctrine often have the sense that the Holy Spirit is at work in their lives and in the church in unprecedented ways. An implicit sense of development does not require education in the historicity of doctrine. Yet this understanding of tradition, however it be aesthetically judged, most commonly comes through education and even specifically theological education. Aesthetical judgments about a developmental understanding of tradition, whether appreciative or unappreciative, are typically offered by those who are theologically literate.

Those who judge the developing tradition of the church to be beautiful do so in a number of ways. If a classical aesthetics of tradition is inclined to identify the transcendental qualities of the beautiful and the good, a developmental aesthetics of tradition is inclined to identify the transcendental qualities of the beautiful and the true. Believers attracted to this modern aesthetics find special beauty in the developing conception's capacity to reconcile faithful claims for tradition's truth and the historical evidence of how doctrine actually developed. From the perspective of this Catholic taste, there is no opposition between truthful secular knowledge and the sacred knowledge that resides in the deposit of faith. The unity of truth enables the believer to embrace, rather than resist, the factual record of Christian events and yet to affirm authentic continuity amid what might otherwise be seen as time's corrosive threat to tradition.[35] This sensibility, then, finds beauty in the eventfulness of tradition that is imagined as a different kind of Christian mimesis, one that regards the development of doctrine as an ever-changing reflection of the eventfulness of the divine life, particularly in its providential outreach to the temporality of creation. This divine eventfulness mirrored in tradition can be imagined as the perichoretic dynamism of the divine life itself, as a way in which the impassible God may yet mysteriously move and be moved in love, or as the event of incarnation that unfolds in the life, death, and resurrection of Jesus Christ. Typically, though, a developmental aesthetics locates God's beauty in the many ways the Holy Spirit is believed to be eventfully present to time, and so accentuates the pneumatological immanence of God to history. The surprising ways the Spirit brings the world to sanctification are the imagined object of this kind of Christian mimesis, and mimesis reflects the eventfulness of God's graceful providence.

The beauty of eventfulness also appears in this aesthetics in the way the notion of a developing tradition enlivens the Council of Trent's teaching on the cooperative role of human agency in the encounter with divine grace. In its *Decree on Justification* (1547), Trent formally defined the long-standing Catholic belief in the responsibility of free choice in accepting the offer of divine grace, and so affirmed the indispensability of human agency in contributing to the believer's justification.[36] Drawing on this Catholic anthropology, an aesthetics of development finds beauty in the ways that believers engage the presence of the Holy Spirit in the church to enact both the recognized truth of tradition and the truth of tradition that has yet to be fully grasped. Believers are perceived as the receptive means through which the Holy Spirit works in bringing to fruition the beliefs and practices that take shape as tradition in the course of time. But more, believers are perceived as gracefully endowed with a supernatural *sensus fidei*, a sense of the faith, which enables them to discern and articulate the truth of sacred tradition that both they and the Holy Spirit bring to reality, albeit in extraordinarily unequal ways.[37]

Catholic mimesis in this aesthetical style appreciates the way the very temporality of tradition captures the truth of the economy of salvation that eventfully unfolds on this side of the Last Judgment, and perhaps, as I shall consider in my last chapter, even thereafter.

Whereas the classical aesthetics of tradition privileges the sense of sight and imagines the objects of tradition beautifully visible in a field of sacred space, the developmental aesthetics of tradition values the sense of hearing, which apprehends the sound of traditioning in the sequence of sacred time. In a reflection on Catholic aesthetics, one might assume too quickly that the aural dimensions of tradition would be bound up in some way with the art form of sacred music. In point of fact, there are different styles of liturgical music that are more or less compatible with each of the two aesthetical sensibilities of tradition. The sound of tradition that is valued in the developmental aesthetics of tradition is the resonance of believers' voices giving expression to their faith, of talk in the church about how the truth of the Holy Spirit takes shape as tradition. Often, this talk expresses the common faith of the church, as happens in creedal recitation or in the prayer of the Mass. As much as the developmental aesthetics attends to the church's common voice and finds its resonance beautiful, it encounters beauty too in the sound of faithful voices expressing new perceptions of the Spirit's presence to the present moment and also, through this act of hearing, new perceptions of beauty in the process of doctrinal development that faithful listening grasps and discerns.

These voices ordinarily express a sense of what we might call "development-in-continuity," the customary reception of the age-old faith of the church in the most recent circumstances of time and culture by which the tradition develops slowly and even imperceptibly, as past and present meanings encounter each other in the act of faith and prove to be mutually enlivening. At times, though, the voices that the community hears make claims to the faith that are strangely novel, since they are unfamiliar and even at odds with what has long been recognized and held as the orthodox tradition. For those inclined to the developmental aesthetics, such voiced claims are contributions to a genuine ecclesial dialogue about the Spirit's truthful presence. In this dialogue, listening and speaking are practices that enhance an appreciation for the beauty of tradition that has been and will always be, as well as for tradition that may be in the process of coming to be.[38] Like any authentic conversation, this ecclesial dialogue is unpredictable in its direction and characterized by all sorts of twists and turns that authentic openness to the truth requires. For those whose Catholic taste is inclined to the developmental aesthetics of tradition, this truth-seeking conversation itself is beautiful both in its devoted efforts to name the purposes of the Spirit at work in time and, when truthfully founded on the *sensus fidei*, as a possible mimesis of God's revelation in and through sacred tradition.

Catholic Aesthetics and Theological Styles

Whereas the classical aesthetics of tradition is quite old, extending from the early medieval period to our day, the developmental aesthetics of tradition is a recent arrival in Catholic history, appearing only in the nineteenth century but not flourishing until the time of Vatican II. Thus, the effective engagement of these Catholic sensibilities is a post–Vatican II phenomenon. As we have seen, these aesthetics are not mutually exclusive. Contemporary Catholics who are especially inclined to the classical aesthetics often recognize and embrace the truth and beauty of the developmental aesthetics. The foundational status of the classical aesthetics ensures that its values are affirmed and appreciated by believers inclined to the developmental aesthetics. And yet at times the ways these aesthetics are practiced in ecclesial life can become occasions for forming Catholic identities that are factional and exclusive, ironically reducing an encounter with the beauty of tradition, and through it an encounter with the beauty of God, to a fetish that claims exhaustively to represent all that is authentically Catholic.

Theologians share these same Catholic tastes and adopt interpretive styles that express their sensibilities. Those attracted to the classical aesthetics are drawn to a theological style that finds edification in the close description of the traditionally valorized reception of scripture and tradition. In this approach, tradition itself becomes a kind of canonical structure that sets the boundaries for legitimate theological reflection. Theology in this style judges the tradition to be so beautiful that any other possible theological resource is at best distracting and at worst a deviation from its sacred truth. The tradition within which theology reflects is regarded as ostensible in its clarity, its teaching as manifestly visible as the revelatory genre itself. Theology in this style is configured as a mimesis of tradition's unchanging permanence, the beauty of its constructive art being defined by its meticulous faithfulness. Those attracted to the developmental aesthetics are drawn to a theological style keen on exploring the truthful relations between scripture and tradition, on the one hand, and the changing circumstances of history and culture on the other. In this approach, the theologian often chooses some dimension of worldly wisdom judged to be truthful as a means of elucidating the meaningfulness of tradition for the present moment. This theological act of mediation is interpretively dialogical. It purports to capture the ecclesial dialogue about the Spirit's immanence to which the whole church listens, and whose truth the theologian tries to discern, in order to articulate the authentic development of doctrine. The Spirit's activity and its moving mimesis in the life of the church are what is judged beautiful in this aesthetics, and the beauty of theology in this style lies in the degree to which its constructive art captures the truthful dynamism of the Spirit's presence in developing tradition.

These theological styles, quite like the aesthetics they express, all too easily become markers of Catholic difference, and this is especially so among the theologically literate—theologians, the magisterium, and educated Catholics—whose knowledge of the historicity of tradition is a prerequisite for making explicit judgments about the comparative value of these aesthetics and their accompanying theological styles. Conflict between the styles emerges when one regards the other as deficient in principle simply because the style negatively judged is not the one prioritized. The ancient status of the classical aesthetics and its foundational character in Catholic sensibility make it especially susceptible to this sort of exclusive judgment, though both the classical and developmental aesthetics, each in its own way, can be myopic in their regard for the full extent of the traditionally beautiful.

At its best, the classical aesthetics highlights the beauty of the Christ event, which is the source of the very divine revelation that theology interprets. But this dedication to the clarity of the Christ event itself can sometimes lead to impatience with the ambiguous dimensions of a tradition that courses through time and so does change. This impatience can be and has been exercised in a variety of ways that attempt to reduce tradition's temporality, plurality, and ambiguity to a permanence, singularity, and clarity that it does not and should not have. These failures of the classical aesthetics take shape theologically in the expectations that authentic theology will be classically homogeneous and not pluralistic, that it will conform to the focused lucidity of the Catechism's propositional formulae, and that the faithful work of the theologian involves explaining and defending the teachings of the Catechism and the pronouncements of the magisterium. At its best, the developmental aesthetics of tradition appreciates the beauty of the Spirit's ongoing presence to the church and the world, as well as the beauty of the graceful discernment of that presence by the community of believers. But this attunement to the mysterious character of tradition's truthful change that unfolds in ecclesial dialogue can sometimes lead to impatience with the clearly visible parameters of the ancient tradition, in which what was once dialogue has now become devout recitation. This impatience can and has been exercised in a variety of ways that imagine the truth claims of the present moment to supersede the authority of proven tradition simply because of their contemporaneity, as though the permanence of tradition in its temporal expanse could be instantly eclipsed by the most recent novel claim for traditional truth. These failures of the developmental aesthetics take shape theologically in the expectations that human experience is the preeminent source of theology, that sinfulness is endemic in principle to the visible and hierarchical structures of the church, and that the magisterium's conservative voice cannot find a place in the kind of dialogue that this theological style judges to be beautiful.

As Elaine Scarry has observed, "Beauty, sooner or later, brings us into contact with our own capacity for making errors." "The beautiful," she continues, "almost without any effort of our own, acquaints us with the mental event of conviction, and so pleasurable a mental state is this that ever afterwards one is willing to labor, struggle, wrestle with the world to locate enduring sources of conviction—to locate what is true."[39] Often, though, the pleasure of conviction leads those who enjoy it to narrow their conceptions of the true and the beautiful for the sake of a skewed sense of their complete capture, a state of affairs that unfortunately prevails as much in the church as it does in the world. The failures of each Catholic sensibility explain much of the polarization in the church between believers and the ways these failures manifest themselves theologically explain much of the polarization in the church between theologians and between theologians and the magisterium. All these parties, which is to say the entire community of faith, would do well to reflect on how these failures, as errors of aesthetical reductionism, are detrimental to the rich unity of the church, which only appears in the wholeness of tradition's beauty, which each Catholic sensibility grasps in its own limited way.

Perhaps the analysis of Catholic taste offered here can be helpful in embracing the aesthetical pluralism that does indeed exist in the church. These deep Catholic desires for the beauty of tradition, and finally for the beauty of God, even in their difference shape the unity of the church as the one body of Christ. The failure of one sensibility to value the other and its attendant theological style diminishes the church's regard for the goodness and truth of tradition. There is an ecclesial need in our day for believers to reflect on how the Catholic sensibilities and theological styles can and should be sources of mutual appreciation rather than markers of division.

We have seen that each of the two Catholic aesthetics prioritizes a particular sense experience to which it accords special powers in apprehending sacred beauty—seeing for the classical aesthetics and hearing for the developmental aesthetics. Aquinas, we should recall, concluded that both the senses of seeing and hearing are aesthetical by nature in their shared capacity to apprehend beauty, an ability that directly eludes the other senses. As senses in the service of an aesthetics of tradition, seeing and hearing turn to different kinds of objects in order to appreciate sacred beauty that is imagined in different ways. Yearning for the consummate sight of the Beatific Vision, the eyes of faith anticipate its beautiful and unchanging perfection in the permanence of tradition, which appears in the space of tradition's sacred visibility. Enamored of the Spirit's living presence, the ears of faith strain to hear how God moves the church in time, changing it ever—sometimes slowly and sometimes suddenly—toward the fulfillment of the kingdom of God, which will eschatologically encounter the depth of the divine mystery. Finally, faithful seeing and hearing apprehend the same divine beauty in the same sacred tradition and are engaged interpretively in the same theological task. The church would be the poorer were it to lack one of these aesthetics, just as it would be poorer were it to lack either of the styles of Catholic theology that serve these sensibilities. The church is poorer now to the extent that these Catholic tastes tend to regard each other suspiciously rather than appreciate how each sensibility complements the other and how both together apprehend the beauty of tradition much more fully than either may alone.

As an aid in fostering this broader appreciation, let us consider the teaching of the Council of Chalcedon (451) as a rule of faith that extends analogously beyond the nature of the incarnation to the proper relationship between the two Catholic aesthetics. The Chalcedonian decree condemned the christological belief of the Monophysites, who claimed that only the immutable divine nature of Christ defined his person, to the exclusion of his full humanity. The Monophysites were scandalized by the thought that the Savior's unchanging divinity could dwell in real relationship to a created nature that was completely human, coursing in the finite conditions of time and change. In response, Chalcedon sanctioned the fourth-century Cappadocian theology that insisted on the hypostatic union of complete divinity and complete humanity in the incarnate person of Christ.[40] We might very well view the beauty of tradition and of its theological interpretation in a similar way. The beauty of tradition lies in the mysterious union of its permanence and its development, of its unchanging and changing dimensions, which together compose the living unity of tradition. In much the same manner, the theological styles interpretively inclined to each of these traditionally beautiful qualities are themselves only dimensions of the unity of the theological task.

Even though the teaching of Chalcedon defines the orthodox faith on the person of Christ, many Christians throughout the centuries have been tempted to imagine the Savior in the manner of the Monophysites, as fully divine but not as fully human. To some degree, this latent monophysitism stems from the status of divine immutability as an aesthetical paradigm in Christian imagination. Just as the tradition has long resisted the notion that divine immutability enters the creaturely realm divorced in the person of Christ from the definitively human, so too should contemporary believers resist an aesthetics of tradition that finds beauty only in its permanence at the expense of its development. The theological styles inclined more or less to a classical or developmental aesthetics of tradition are obliged to foster an appreciation for both senses of Catholic beauty in their theologies, for only through such a comprehensive aesthetics can they do justice to what is beautifully old and beautifully new in tradition, and, through it, to all that is old and new in our encounter with the beauty of God.

CHAPTER SIX

FOREVER AND A DAY

Resurrected Time in a Heavenly Imaginary

In this, our closing chapter, we move from considering time in the duration of now to time in the duration of forever. I will try to appreciate, even in the most limited of ways, the features of a fulfilled time consistent with my analysis thus far. My first chapter argued that the continuity of grace is well imagined in a time that extends into the resurrected life after death in which Christians believe and for which Christians hope. If grace is the divine life itself and God's immanence pervades all of creation, then that graceful presence must extend throughout the heavenly life that the blessed dead enjoy eschatologically—a state of existence that, though redeemed, remains creaturely. There is a tendency in the history of Christian imagination to conflate God's eternity and heavenly life to the point that heavenly life loses its creaturely reality, as though it were eclipsed by God's utterly unique timelessness. But this misconception violates the most basic of Christian beliefs that there ever remains a distinction between God and creatures, between God and all else that possesses being as a gift from God and so is not-God. If heavenly life is creaturely and time is a constituent dimension of creation, then imagining the creaturely life of heaven as temporal is not merely a poetic possibility but a logically consistent necessity if imagining heavenly life is to square with basic Christian belief. Moreover, were one to conceive of time's eventfulness as the medium of God's grace to creation—which is the proposal I have argued for throughout my study—then the divine self-sharing that gracefully takes place forever in resurrected life could be imagined as mediated through a heavenly time in which resurrected persons continue to live into their redemption through Christ. Theologically, one would assume that the beauty of events in heavenly time would transcend the beauty of events in the ordinary time of creation, however beautiful events in existential time may be.

There is, of course, a reason that a temporal heaven has been resisted in Christian imagination. In the experience of believers, "time now" is a fallen realm in which the power of sin and death mars the beauty of graceful time. Time now often configures tragic events that bring suffering, loss, and estrangement into the lives of believers, to say nothing of all of history, threatening the hope believers hold for God's consummation of all things. In the traditional Christian imaginary, time now is unredeemed. To the degree that anomic time is so much a dimension of time now, "time forever" seems a poor way to imagine heaven, since it seems to extend the power of sin and death into the resurrected life that Christians believe is the utter fulfillment of God's promise to destroy death forever. Little wonder that Christian claims for the hope of eternal life would be inclined to imagine that eschatological sharing in the life of God would entail the absorption of resurrected life and its heavenly ambiance into the timeless eternity that only God possesses in the traditional imaginary. But the Christian hope of sharing eschatologically in God's eternal life should not suggest that creatures lose their creatureliness in that saved state, as though redemption obliterated the difference between God and creation, including the created duration of time. Were we to frame a heavenly imaginary consistent with a classical belief in the exclusive eternity of the divine life, we would need to maintain that difference, and in doing so reflect on how time itself is resurrected and participates in eternal life without losing its own created temporality. In order to take the first step toward that heavenly imaginary, let us explore a bit further the reluctance to imagine a heavenly time by considering how Christians throughout the tradition have believed in the end of time.

Liminal Time in Traditional Catholic Belief

We will begin with a historical sketch of Christian origins. Earliest Christian faith emerged from apocalyptic sensibilities that expected the imminent end of the world, sensibilities that themselves originated in the earlier religious culture of the first Jewish Christians. The duress of the Seleucid occupation of Israel in the second century BCE gave rise to a Jewish style of apocalypticism that appeared in the literary work of the prophet Daniel. Writing in 165 BCE, Daniel described a vision of God's deliverance of the Jewish people from their enemies precipitated by the appearance of an eschatological king appointed by God, one like a son of man "coming with the clouds of heaven" (Dan 7:13). In an Exodus-like miracle, the son of man would descend into the world from the heavens above in order to vanquish Israel's persecutors. In Daniel's Jewish imagination, the world that was about to end through this great miracle was his small corner of the world—Israel, God's sacred land. And the end that Daniel imagined was the end of Israel's oppression under Seleucid captivity, as the eschatological king, God's emissary, defeated Israel's enemies and established God's kingdom on Israel's holy soil. For Daniel, this apocalyptic, saving event would not bring about the end of time. Daniel envisioned a salvation that would take place in this world, on a liberated Israel, in the existential flourishing of the Jewish people. Time would continue, renewed by God's rescue in what ancient Jews believed to be a this-worldly salvation.

The very first Christians were Jews who were shaped by apocalyptic sensibilities like Daniel's that circulated in their own religious culture. Although historians recognize the difficulty of reconstructing the actual words and deeds of Jesus of Nazareth (4 BCE–30 CE), one likely historical portrait is that Jesus was a Daniel-like apocalyptic preacher who understood himself to be a herald of the coming son of man about whom Daniel wrote. Apocalyptic strains in any religion are always a minority tradition—the belief of the few—and such strains typically are fueled by tragic cultural circumstances, bad times, as they were in Jesus's day in the long, military occupation of Israel by the imperial forces of Rome. In the context of the Roman captivity (63 BCE–70 CE), the message of the restoration of Israel preached by apocalyptic Jews like Jesus and his likeminded followers was seen by the occupiers as subversive to Roman authority. Talk of the imminent liberation of Israel through the miraculous power of God struck Roman ears as incitement to a colonized people to resist their colonizers, even if Roman authorities knew that Jesus and his message posed no real threat to their rule.[1] Imperial power is often impatient even with powerless opposition. Jesus was arrested by the Roman authorities, summarily tried, and crucified, a brutal form of capital punishment reserved under Roman law for non-Roman subalterns.

It is nearly as difficult to reconstruct earliest Christian origins as it is to reconstruct the historical Jesus, since the very first Christians, some of whom were Jesus's contemporary followers, left no literary record. But again, scholars have found that Jewish apocalypticism is a likely interpretive path. If the earliest Jewish Christians were Jesus's apocalyptic followers who ardently believed in his preaching of the coming son of man, then one would expect that the religious expectation of Daniel's vision would have shaped their experience of Jesus's resurrection from the dead. Unlike later Christians, even as early as Paul, who saw Jesus's resurrection from the dead by God as the climactic salvational event that ushered the power of eternal life into history, the earliest Jewish Christians likely imagined Jesus's resurrection and restoration to new life as a miraculous precondition for his appointment by God as the son of man of their apocalyptic imagination. Having been so appointed the savior of Israel, Jesus now, in the belief of the earliest Jewish Christians, would soon appear in the sky "coming with the clouds" to establish God's kingdom in Israel. The earliest Christians would have anticipated this eschatological event as the fulfillment of God's covenant with Israel.[2] Like Daniel, they would not have expected that Jesus's imminent return would bring about the end of time. The earliest Christians experienced the resurrection of Jesus as a saving event that was thoroughly Jewish in meaning, and ancient Jews hoped for a salvation in time, not in a heavenly afterlife.[3]

The apostle Paul was a contemporary of the earliest Jewish Christians. After his conversion to the Jesus movement he met with leaders of the early Christian communities—Peter, James, and John—and all agreed that Paul would preach the gospel to the gentiles and the first followers of Jesus would preach to the Jews (Gal 2:9). In letters he wrote to Christian communities in the 50s of the first century, some twenty-five years after the first Easter experiences, Paul taught eschatological beliefs that the earliest Jewish Christians probably did not initially hold, beliefs that would shape the later tradition. In addition to his belief that Christ's salvation was universal in scope, for Jew and gentile alike, Paul claimed that Jesus's resurrection from the dead was the graceful power that brought believers to their own resurrected life after death, as God through Christ miraculously transformed their physical bodies in the grip of sin and death into spiritual bodies that were "imperishable," resurrected bodies of "glory" and "power" (1 Cor 15:42–44). In Paul's eschatological imaginary, Christ's resurrection was the "first fruits of those who have died," and in him "all will be made alive" (15:20, 22).

Like the earliest Christians, Paul expected the imminent return of Christ. He concludes 1 Corinthians with the petition *"marana tha,"* "Come, Lord!"—an early Christian prayer in the Aramaic that Jesus and the first Jewish Christians spoke that expressed a deep yearning for the saving return of Jesus (1 Cor 16:22). But Paul likely imagined this eschatological event differently from the earliest Christians. Those who have died in Christ, he believed, will be brought to life "then at his coming" (15:23), an event that Paul seems to expect within his lifetime. In 1 Thessalonians, the earliest of his letters, written around 51 CE, Paul details this astonishing occurrence that he believes looms on the temporal horizon:

> For since we believe that Jesus died and rose again, even so, through Jesus, God will bring with him those who have died. For this we declare to you by the word of the Lord, that we who are alive, who are left until the coming of the Lord, will by no means precede those who have died. For the Lord himself, with a cry of command, with the archangel's call and with the sound of God's trumpet, will descend from heaven, and the dead in Christ will rise first. Then we who are alive, who are left, will be caught up in the clouds together with them to meet the Lord in the air; and so we will be with the Lord forever. (1 Thess 4:14–17)

Paul completes this apocalyptic imaginary in 1 Corinthians, written after the passage from 1 Thessalonians above. After Christ's coming "comes the end, when he hands over the kingdom to God the Father, after he has destroyed every ruler and every authority and power." "For he must reign," Paul continues, "until he has put all his enemies under his feet. The last enemy to be destroyed is death" (1 Cor 15:24–26). Paul does indeed seem to imagine an end-time precipitated by the coming of Christ, which heralds the resurrection of those who have died in Christ and who are joined in their heavenly ascent by living believers, who "will not . . . die, but . . .

will . . . be changed, in a moment, in the twinkling of an eye, at the last trumpet" (1 Cor 15:51–52). Safely assumed into heaven, resurrected believers are spared the apocalyptic turmoil of Christ's battle with the fallen energies of this world. And as Christ's defeat of death achieves a consummate victory, this world, now purged of evil, is made a gift to God.[4] Although Paul does not specifically address the issue of time in this somewhat sketchy imaginary, one might reasonably conclude that he believes that what we have called tragic time, time as we know it, will disappear. In that respect, Paul's eschatology includes the notion of an end-time. Paul says nothing about a heavenly time in what he elsewhere calls the New Creation (2 Cor 5:17; Gal 6:15).

Intensely apocalyptic beliefs in the early tradition did not last long, for the simple and obvious reason that Jesus did not appear. By the time the canonical gospels were written, between 70 and 100 CE, late first-century Christians already had begun to retheologize their beliefs about the return of Jesus at the end-time by imagining that this apocalyptic event would take place in a far more distant future. This initial normalizing of the ardent hopes of the earliest Christians is pointedly expressed in the closing words of the Gospel of Matthew, in which the biblical author has the resurrected Christ command his apostles to make disciples of all nations, as he assures them, "I am with you always, to the end of the age" (Matt 28:20). Jesus's promise of accompaniment "always, to the end of the age" has the ring of postapocalyptic adjustment to an ordinary time in which a nascent church struggles with its day-to-day problems. Pockets of ardent apocalypticism still punctuated late first-century Christian communities, religious expectations that undoubtedly intensified when these communities faced local persecution. The New Testament book of Revelation, written at the turn of the second century, is a clear illustration of just how frenetic the longing for the imminent consummation of the end-time could be in such dire circumstances. But as the age of persecution passed with the promulgation of the Edict of Milan in 313 CE and as Christianity was embraced as the religion of the empire by the late fourth century, eschatological impulses became thoroughly domesticated. In the late antique world and into the Middle Ages Christians increasingly became preoccupied with satisfying their sinful debt to God through virtue that would bring God's favorable judgment at the hour of one's death. In this temporal aesthetic, in which, as Peter Brown puts it, "every moment mattered"[5] as an occasion for gaining ethical merit, the apocalyptic resonance of the end-time faded in its existential relevance to Christian life.

The end-time, though, did not at all disappear from the Christian imaginary in the Middle Ages. By the time Catholic Christianity began to take shape in the Latin West with the rise of feudal society and the monastic tradition, Christians had settled on a way of conceptualizing their distinctive belief in the resurrection of the body. The Greek culture that Christianity embraced socially and intellectually in its early years offered an anthropology that allowed Christians to account for the miracle of resurrection in the face of the body's deathly decay. For the ancient Greek philosophical tradition, a human person was an unhappy union of a material body and an ethereal soul, the soul the self-identical reality of the human person and the body a corrupt and even evil impediment to the soul's fulfillment. Christians conformed these anthropological categories, so foreign to the Jewish culture from which Christianity emerged, to their belief in the goodness of all creation, understanding the identity of the human person to reside in the created unity of soul and body. At the moment of death, Christians believed, the soul was separated from the body, and the body, however disposed, underwent the dissolution that common sense verifies. The soul instantly appeared before God to be judged based on the person's lifelong conduct, and the divine verdict assigned one of two eschatological destinies—unending happiness in heaven or unending misery in hell. By the later Middle Ages, a developed doctrine of purgatory had Christians imagine that nearly all of the heaven-bound needed to spend some time in a supernatural place of suffering to be purified of their sinful debt to God before they could experience the unimaginable joy of the Beatific Vision. But in this anthropology, disembodied souls were not complete selves. Disembodied souls would dwell in heaven, hell, or purgatory while earthly time ran its course, but finally, after earthly time had reached its end, a sequence of astonishing events would reunite the soul and body of each person.

The ancient creeds professed the belief that Jesus would "come again in glory to judge the living and the dead."[6] But just how this would occur was worked out in Catholic imagination over the course of centuries. As history reached its divinely ordained temporal end, which late antique and medieval believers assumed would be in the distant future, God's archangels would sound trumpets announcing the end of time and the Last Judgment. All those who died in all of human history would be miraculously raised from the dead. Whatever corruption their bodies had suffered in death—slow decay through careful burial, swift decay through burial at sea, immediate dissolution to ash by fire—the power of grace would restore their physical selves to wholeness. Disembodied souls in heaven, hell, and purgatory would be joined again to their bodies in this world, and all would assemble in one place. Christ would appear in the sky, coming with the clouds of heaven, and descend to the place of assembly to conduct a universal judgment of the living and the dead. The particular judgment already undergone by those who had died would be reiterated, and the universal judgment of the living at the end-time would serve as their particular judgment. We have already seen that some of this imagery derives from Paul, though it more strikingly has its provenance in the Gospel of Matthew:

> When the Son of Man comes in his glory, and all the angels with him, then he will sit on the throne of his glory. All the nations will be gathered before him, and he will separate people one from another as a shepherd separates the sheep from the goats, and he will put the sheep at his right hand and the goats at the left. Then the king will say to those at his right hand, "Come, you that are blessed by my Father, inherit the kingdom prepared for you from the foundation of the world. . . ." Then he will say to those at his left hand, "You that are accursed, depart from me into the eternal fire prepared for the devil and his angels." (Matt 25:31–34, 41)

In both instances, Christ's judgment on the saved and the damned is measured by their lifelong virtuous performance, or the lack of it—their active care or disregard for the hungry, the thirsty, the homeless stranger, the unclothed, and the imprisoned (Matt 25:35–36). Catholic Christianity imagined redemption as an unequal, but nonetheless consequential, partnership between God's grace and the believer's free choice and moral energies. The particular judgment at death was based on how the believer chose ethically, how the believer acted in order to live a morally responsible life of discipleship to Christ. The universal or Last Judgment was an eschatological social event at which all could witness at once how God's justice was applied to every human life and, indeed, to all of history.

Throughout the late Middle Ages, artists rendered the Last Judgment again and again in mosaics, frescoes, and paintings, visual art that charged the religious imagination of the faithful. Whether the genre was executed by unknown artists, such as the creator of the eleventh-century wall mosaic of the Cathedral of Santa Maria Assunta in Torcello, just outside Venice, or by great masters such as Giotto di Bondone (1266–1336), Fra Angelico (1395–1455), or Michelangelo Buonarroti (1475–1564), its eschatological theme was seemingly as inexhaustible as the form of its depiction. Centered at a high point in the Last Judgment scene was the Savior, who had descended here below from his seat at the right hand of the Father. He radiates the divine light that is his glory and is attended by choirs of angels and quite often his twelve apostles, all of whom are heavenly witnesses to the final judgment. Detailing the imagery posed in Matthew 25, the artists depict the damned to Christ's left, often before the yawning jaws of hell and the vexing prods of demons who begin their infernal torture even before Christ's judgment has quite reached its conclusion. To Christ's right are the redeemed, who are often portrayed standing serene in orderly rows and slowly making their heavenly climb to the endless happiness of paradise. Time is about to end as this world passes away, and only heaven and hell remain forever more.

It is interesting to speculate on why this theme was so prevalent in Catholic medieval art, its frequent choice not simply a matter of artistic preference but as much a testimony to the artist's judgment about what his audience would find meaningful. As I have noted, the Catholic tradition accentuated the believer's moral contributions to redemption; it insisted on the indispensable role played by the believer's virtuous words and deeds in living into God's grace. Believers who contemplated Last Judgment scenes were struck by the impassive visage of their savior as he made and reiterated decisions that defined the eschatological division stretched out before him. They could contemplate the hopeless dismay on the faces of the damned and the stolid joy on the faces of all the extraordinary and ordinary saints. Believers imagined themselves in their places, as they ardently believed they would be on the last day, standing to Christ's left or right and anticipating the endless, supernatural destinies that depended on their ethical comportment now, in the ordinary time of their lives. Last Judgment scenes thus functioned as cautionary tales and as inducements to moral action in a Catholic culture fraught with anxiety about how one would fare before God's judgment, the consequences of which could not be more significant.

Catholic spirituality in this eschatological key could not help but be competitive. All believers found themselves situated in a hierarchy of discipleship defined by the quantity and quality of a person's good deeds. And in this hierarchy, all believers could see a better performance than their own in comparison with which all felt anxiety about the prospect of God's favorable judgment at death, and so at the Last Judgment. Even the great, and extraordinarily few, ascetical saints of the medieval tradition could judge themselves wanting in comparison to the ancient example of the martyrs, whose death for the Lord was incapable of imitation in the Catholic culture of their day. Medieval ascetics could judge themselves deficient in comparison to the ascetical saints, some the founders of their religious orders whom they sought to emulate—though, it was assumed, from a distance. And laypersons, the vast majority of medieval Catholics, who defined the lowest level of the hierarchy, imagined themselves deficient in comparison to all above—the martyrs, the ascetical saints, and perhaps especially ordinary ascetics, who consecrated their lives to the church, who lived in close proximity to laypersons, and who served as existential points of comparison to fuel this religious anxiety.

Contemplating the Last Judgment stirred anxiety in every present moment of Catholic merit religiosity, present moments that extended from the Middle Ages through the Tridentine tradition, all the way to the time of the Second Vatican Council (1962–65). But the very same contemplation allowed the believer to imagine the moment of consummate redemptive relief. As much as the prospect of the Last Judgment made believers anxious about their own eschatological status, its finality also enabled them to imagine the beginning of their unending happiness in heavenly life. All believers—or, just to account for the very small number of possible aberrations, nearly all believers—assume, as believers, that they are among the saved. Within merit religiosity, claiming faith while presuming one's damnation would be emotionally incoherent. For nearly all, eschatological anxiety, though troubling, was manageable. It was an emotional measure of the believer's commitment to the reality of the heavenly paradise. Moreover, in spite of some degree of suspense about the eschatological future, the believer trusted that God's judgment on the last day would be favorable and that he or she would stand resurrected at Christ's right hand and enter the communion of the saints forever.

The eschatological finality of the Last Judgment meant that it stood on the cusp between time and what the faithful in the traditional imaginary believed to be eternity. To be an event so historically unusual made the time of the Last Judgment liminal—a kind of extraordinary temporality that straddled the natural and the supernatural realms. In its liminal temporality, the Last Judgment was not unique in the Catholic imaginary. The notion of liminal time flourished in the late medieval Catholic belief in purgatory. As the third supernatural "place," purgatory was distinguished from heaven and hell because it was temporal, at least in the sense that its time, and so purgatory itself, came to an end and finally passed into nothingness. But even more, purgatory was saturated with time. Those consigned there in the particular judgment—nearly all, it was assumed—were remitted to purgation for a specified time commensurate with their sinful debt to God. Each individual's consigned time in purgatory was different, some relatively short and some relatively long, but all measured by the church in years and days. Although these earthly temporal categories chronicled a purgatorial stay, the actual time of purgatory behaved strangely. One can gather a sense of this by considering the Catholic practice of earning indulgences that flourished from the late Middle Ages to the Second Vatican Council.

An indulgence is an ecclesiastical pardon that remits some or all of the time in purgatory that a sinner has accrued to any point in his or her life. It is granted through the satisfaction of prescribed devotional practices, including almsgiving. Believers applied their devotional energies to the earning of specific indulgences associated with the celebration of Masses, the saying of certain prayers, the observance of holy days or seasons, pilgrimage to sacred sites, and the veneration of sacred objects, including relics. Indulgences could be earned for oneself or for a suffering soul in purgatory. Partial indulgences for the remission of a certain number of days or, more typically, years in purgatory could be earned by the indulgent penitent depending on the devotional time or rigor required for the satisfaction of the indulgence. In any case, though measured in earthly categories, purgatorial time was distorted by its supernatural proximity to eternity. Carlos Eire notes that by the early sixteenth century it was accepted that "one day of suffering on earth equaled a thousand years in purgatory."[7] This calculation did not mean that purgatorial suffering was little compared to earthly suffering but, quite to the contrary, great. In this imaginative metric, suffering was stretched out into a liminal, supernatural time that was daunting. Hence, partial indulgences were typically offered in spans of time that were quite large. The recitation of a short, simple prayer, for example, could earn an indulgence of five hundred years. On November 1, All Saints' Day, the veneration of the extensive relics collection of Martin Luther's prince, Frederick the Wise of Saxony (1463–1525), granted the believer an indulgence of 1,902,202 years and 207 days![8] That this papally approved indulgence was not plenary, a full remission of purgative time, bespeaks how long Catholics imagined the time of purgation would typically be before the suffering soul was sufficiently purified to encounter the Beatific Vision. On the one hand, the liminal time of purgatory assuaged the anxiety caused by the competitive spirituality of the hierarchy of discipleship. Purgatory's time extended the duration of competition beyond one's years in earthly life, allowing those who were behind to "catch up" to the virtuous paradigms of martyrs and ascetical saints whose spiritual achievement was marked by suffering. In many respects, purgatory was imagined as a supernatural monastery in which all—especially laypersons—could make redemptive progress by suffering that brought one closer to God.[9] On the other hand, purgatory's liminal time in the afterlife yet reflected the anxiety of merit religion. Its mind-boggling duration filled with suffering comparable to the torments of hell reminded believers who expected it to be their first otherworldly destination that every moment in one's life here and now mattered for its profound supernatural effects.

The liminal time of the Last Judgment was not at all as imaginatively detailed as purgatorial time. Its liminality was bound up with its being the final event to transpire in time. Nearly all of the time of history was filled with moral occasions for believers to live into their redemption and to secure God's favorable judgment. The Last Judgment, though in time, was not an event that unfolded in this ordinary time. The Last Judgment quite literally defined the boundary that separated time from eternity. Its liminality made other times behave strangely. The time of purgatory provides an interesting example. In the traditional imaginary, all things temporal would pass away after the Last Judgment took place. Of all things created, only heaven and hell would remain. Purgatory too would pass into nothingness, but first it had to be emptied out so that all the suffering souls could be joined to their bodies and participate in the Last Judgment. But at the sound of the archangel's trumpet that announced the great event, the suffering souls were still enduring the pains of the purgative sentence imposed by God at their particular judgment. Many still had to undergo thousands of years of suffering in order to complete their purification for entry into heaven. There were only two ways to solve this problem in the Catholic imaginary. One could imagine a divine amnesty that commuted the purgatorial sentences of the suffering souls to allow their participation in the Last Judgment. In Catholic sensibilities, however, this possible solution violated God's consistent justice, to say nothing of God's timeless divine foreknowledge of when the Last Judgment would occur. The only other, and viable, solution was to imagine that the purgative torment of many of the suffering souls was intensified and compressed into an astonishingly brief time so that purgative justice for all could be served and the suffering souls would not be late for the most anticipated social event of all time. This interesting distortion of purgatory's own strange time was caused by its drift into the currents of the Last Judgment's liminal time.

The Last Judgment took place in time, but in a time in which time was up. Medieval Christians who contemplated the Last Judgment scene in mosaics and paintings encountered this quality in the iconic presentation of the genre. Whatever variations medieval artists offered to make the scene their own, the representational theme was largely the same—the judging Christ centered the frame, and the damned to his left and the saved to his right balanced his eschatological judgment. This consistency in portrayal had the effect of "freezing" the end-time in whatever representation by any artist, as though that last moment of time endured forever. And in a way it did. In the Catholic imaginary, the last event in the last moment of time—the division of the saved and the damned—was about to be transformed into what were imagined to be the timeless durations of heaven and hell. The liminal time of the Last Judgment was bolstered by the finality of Christ's judgment, which conveyed something of the eternity of the divine decision in time's last moment. The social character of the Last Judgment contributed to this liminal temporality as well. As the entire human race was raised from the dead and assembled for judgment before the Savior, all times were unified into one final moment. And to the degree that the moments of all these lives were invested in the judgment of each and every one, every one of those many moments of time was distilled into this final moment in which time was on the verge of winking out.

Thomas Aquinas (1225–74) describes this most liminal moment of transition in the last pages of the *Summa Contra Gentiles*. As the Last Judgment draws to a close, he states, "human nature will be entirely established in its goal." But because God created all material existence for the sake of humanity, all material creation after the Last Judgment must be aligned with the incorruptible nature of resurrected persons, at least when it can be. For that to happen, the "state of generation and corruption will then be taken away from the whole bodily creation."[10] In Aquinas's cosmology, natural movement in the entire field of creation is induced by the movements of the heavenly bodies, which, in Aquinas's hierarchical worldview, are closer to the divine First Mover. Thus, "generation and corruption in inferior bodies are caused by the movement of the heavens."[11] Since the airy realms high above are a vestibule to the heavenly abode of resurrected persons, their motion must cease after the Last Judgment so that the heavenly bodies are conformed to the incorruptible state of resurrected life. And as heavenly motion ceases, so too does time: "Therefore, that generation and corruption may come to a stop in the inferior bodies, the movement of the heavens must also come to a stop. And on this account, the Apocalypse (10:16) says 'that time shall be no longer.'"[12] Time and motion will cease in the heavenly heights, where its loss is a sign of the transfiguration of creation. But time's loss in the earthly world here below marks the corruptible distance between resurrected bodies and non-human corporeality. "The other animals, the plants, and the mixed bodies, those entirely corruptible both wholly and in part," Aquinas asserts, "will not remain at all in that state of incorruption [achieved by the heavenly bodies]. In this way, then, must the saying of the Apostle be understood: "'The fashion of this world passeth away' (I Cor. 7:11)."[13] Yet, for the Angelic Doctor, though the bodily forms of these non-human creatures will cease to be, their ontological substance, created by God and so good, will endure eschatologically, be purified by fire, and "achieve a kind of resplendence in its own way."[14]

Aquinas's claim that there will be no time in this resplendence of the New Creation articulates the assumptions of the traditional imaginary. As the mark of corruption, time will no longer endure in the state of redemption fully realized. The very possibility of supernatural time threatens the constancy of the eschatological states of the saved and the damned, as though, were they still in time, the otherwise timeless alignment of their respective wills to God or to evil could shift and divine judgment be undone. The liminal time of the Last Judgment defines the consummate cusp between time, in which the power of sin and death tragically flourish, and eternity, in which sin, death, and time have ceased to be. The brief time of the Last Judgment stirs a sense of an absolute temporal ending as history itself ceases and Christ's judgment is passed not simply on the actions of individuals in their own times but on the transhistorical consequences of sin. In that brief, liminal time, all times are reduced to the eschatological moment of Christ's judgment, and with that judgment on time all time ceases. As the Last Judgment is completed, the "physical body" will be miraculously transformed into a "spiritual body" and time will come to an end—its deathliness left behind as the New Creation flourishes in its incorruptible state. Let us imagine all this differently.

Heavenly Time

Throughout my study, I have argued that imagining time as the sacramental medium of God's grace would do wonders for the doctrine of creation and, through the doctrine of creation, for the doctrine of grace. The Platonic influence on Christian doctrine for too long has led believers to devalue time, to imagine a rift that separates creation on this side of the eschaton from creation on the eschaton's heavenly side, and so to fail to appreciate the continuity of grace through all the dimensions of God's creation. Were we to affirm the continuity of God's graceful presence to creation, from creation's beginning through its eschatological renewal in resurrected life, and were we to see time's eventfulness as the way in which the Spirit of God is ever-present to creation, then the sacramentality of time would need to extend to all the times of creation, including the time of resurrected heavenly life. My study began with a proposal that time, as the medium of grace, needs to be considered not only in the ordinary time of "now" but also in the extraordinary time of "forever." In spite of the reluctance to do so in the traditional imaginary, there yet may be theological advantage to such speculation, both for our appreciation of the Christian hope in the resurrection of the body and for our appreciation of the beauty of time as a dimension of God's creation.

I have rehearsed all the reasons for the tradition's reluctance to imagine a heavenly time, and, for that matter, to speculate fulsomely about the nature of a heavenly time. Time, as I have noted, shares in creation's lapse through the sin of humanity, as evinced by the tragic time that courses through history. Heaven and resurrected life are typically conflated with God's eternity and so are imagined to be timeless in the manner of the divine life, as though heaven were not a creaturely state. And simply the mystery of heavenly life, centered in the joy of the Beatific Vision as it is in traditional belief, leads to a proper apophatic reluctance to speak about "what God has prepared for those who love him," "what no eye has seen, nor ear heard, nor the human heart conceived" (1 Cor 2:9). But even if one were theologically willing to follow the kataphatic path of the heavenly scenes rendered by medieval artists or Dante's moving poetic imagery in the *Paradiso*, one would still need to address the fundamental issue of what a heavenly time would be and why a heavenly time would be a consistent way of imagining the continuity of God's grace.

As has already been suggested in chapter 1, the notion of heavenly time is bound up meaningfully with the doctrine of the resurrection of the body. The traditional imaginary appealed to the most literalistic imagery to conceptualize the meaning of the Christian belief in life after death. To many modern believers, the depiction of the flesh of the dead miraculously restored on the last day to be reunited with souls beckoned from their supernatural destinies seems terribly unsophisticated and fundamentalistically naïve. That literalistic imagery, however, is actually a very good place for theological reflection to begin in considering the Christian hope for life after death, if only because such imagery is a clear assertion of the reality of bodily resurrection. The resurrection of the body should not be reduced to a metaphor for life after death, nor should it be regarded as a symbol that points to a reality other than the one it affirms. Admittedly, the resurrection of the body is an anthropological mystery that eludes all conceptualization, and even all efforts precisely to delineate its meaning. However the resurrection of the body might transpire, the belief at the very least affirms that the human person in his or her entirety, in all that makes the person who he or she is, inner life and outer life, is redeemed by God's grace and enters into the fullness of life in communion with God and all the saints. Resurrection is a transformed state of life without end in the eternal love who God is. In this respect, the tradition speaks of resurrection as eternal life. Human persons who are resurrected are and remain creatures, and so even in resurrected life are not eternal, as God alone is. But resurrected life, the tradition affirms, is graceful participation in the eternal life of God, and in that qualified way the tradition, as early as Paul's letters, speaks of the "imperishable," glorious, unending life of the redeemed as eternal (1 Cor 15:42; Rom 6:23).

As much as the doctrine of the resurrection of the body expresses the Christian hope for the redemptive transformation of the believer beyond the powers of sin and death and into a graceful state of existence that shares in the eternal life of God, it yet affirms a real continuity between the human person in history and the resurrected self. That continuity comprises all that the person is and has become in the course of her or his life—an individual's personality, character, thoughts, intentions, emotions, imagination, memory, sense of humor, hopes, commitments, and, of course, the physicality that enables the transcendence of these subjective states into words, deeds, and relationships. The doctrine of bodily resurrection reminds believers that physicality shares in resurrected continuity just as much as the distinctive qualities of the inner life.[15] This holistic understanding of the human person expresses the values of the doctrine of creation. Like all creatures, human persons are created good in their very being. But even more, they are created in the image and likeness of God (Gen 1:27) and so stand in intimate relationship to God that distinguishes their dignity from the goodness of other creatures. The ancient biblical author does not explain the anthropology of the creation story in detail. No account is given of what being created in the image and likeness of God means. A Christian reading of the ancient Jewish story, though, would need to understand the *imago Dei* as the gifted capacity of the human person for eternal communion with God and the saints in resurrected life and, in that reading, would need to presuppose the holistic, personalist anthropology that the doctrine of bodily resurrection affirms.

In this anthropology, the capacities of the self that lie in the person's inner and outer life are indeed gifted in the act of creation, which is to say that the very being of the human person is an act of grace. And it is grace that brings human persons in their deep fallenness to resurrected life. The Catholic tradition yet claims that the moral contributions of the believer—the believer's words and deeds that live into the gift of grace—are consequential for the formation of the resurrected person who the believer hopes eschatologically to be. This belief, clearly articulated in the Council of Trent's *Decree on Justification* (1547), claims that those assisted by grace "turn towards their own justification by giving free assent to and co-operating with this same grace."[16] Trent defined this classical Catholic anthropology in opposition to the teaching of the sixteenth-century Protestant Reformers who asserted that God's grace is the utter power of salvation. Grace, in their view, is only received by the believer in faith, and even that reception must be credited to the work of grace. The believer makes no choice that is redemptively efficacious, because any choice is so deeply immersed in humanity's fallen state that it can only perpetuate the history of sin and death. Thus, in the classical Protestant imaginary, resurrected life tends to be conceived dialectically, as a state of existence so discontinuous with the current state of human fallenness that its glory is unimaginable. The blessed dead are distant in Protestant sensibilities, and not simply because grace fulfilled is conceived in such sharp contrast to human fallenness.[17] The heavenly differentiation of the blessed dead that Catholics regarded as a function of the hierarchy of discipleship, itself a hierarchy of virtuous deeds, was leveled out in the Protestant doctrine of grace alone. The blessed dead were assumed to be different resurrected persons, of course, but their heavenly glory was utterly corporate, personally indistinguishable as the sole work of grace. Their worldly words and deeds, sinful through and through, were believed to be so thoroughly transformed in resurrected life that nothing remained of them to imagine. Nor, typically, was there a Protestant impetus to imagine the blessed dead now in heaven acting on the side of grace's victory. Since human works were dialectically opposed to the saving power of grace, the notion of heavenly works proved to be oxymoronic and, as well, raise the specter of the Catholic cult of the saints, which initially gave rise to the Protestant critique of Catholic merit religion. Heaven here is happily occluded from human view.

I intend no criticism at all in this account of the Protestant eschatological imaginary. Its steadfast devotion to the power of grace as the sole source of resurrected life configures a Christian imaginary of remarkable beauty. But that judgment of beauty derives from a sensibility quite suspicious of continuity between this world and the next in its intentionally thin account of resurrected life. If there is continuity in the Lutheran and Reformed eschatology of *sola gratia*, it lies in the doctrine of predestination, the classical Protestant belief that God has eternally chosen some for eternal life in heaven, and no human willfulness in time on the part of the elect could compromise God's determination of the saved. This continuity in God's predestinating will that brings the elect to eternal life is utterly timeless. The eternal decree may pass through time in the graced lives of the elect, but its continuity—from its pronouncement before the foundation of the world to the heavenly fulfillment of the chosen—is impervious to time. The Catholic eschatological imaginary is quite different. Here, time is consequential to the passage to resurrected life because virtuous deeds, events in time, contribute in some small but yet indispensable way to the resurrected life of the believer. Even though all traditional Christian imaginaries, regardless of denominational commitments, have tended to imagine an eschatological divide between time and an eternal afterlife, such a separation is most inconsistent in Catholic sensibilities, which affirm the role of moral eventfulness in shaping the resurrected persons who believers hope to be. In the Catholic imaginary, resurrected persons are invested with events in time, not only in the commonly Christian sense that our resurrected selves will be our created selves fulfilled but also in the more particularly Catholic sense that virtuous character enacted in time endures in resurrected life and marks the distinctiveness of each resurrected person.

Especially in the Catholic tradition, then, the continuity affirmed between virtuous works in earthly time and the contribution they make to the believer's heavenly resurrection begs for an eschatological imaginary in which time continues to transpire in heaven. That resurrected life in heaven is a creaturely state ever distinguished from the eternity of the one God is reason enough for all Christian traditions to resist the popular and theologically thoughtless understanding of resurrected life as transpiring timelessly. But the Catholic anthropology, which in the wider arc of Christian belief must also be an eschatological anthropology, seems to require the notion of heavenly time in order consistently to portray the moral eventfulness that grace has assisted to the point of its constitution in the eschatological character of the resurrected person. Moreover, the theological proposal offered throughout my study presents an even stronger reason to insist on a heavenly time. If time configures the motion of events, and time, as I have proposed, be imagined as the medium of God's grace to creation, then theologically representing God's grace to creatures in resurrected life would seem to require the notion of a heavenly time were the continuity of grace to be posited in all dimensions of creation—in this world and the next. Even more, the doctrine of bodily resurrection affirms a holistic conception of life after death. Its claim is that our eschatological selves in redemption will transcend the selves that we are now. Yet the blessed dead, the tradition affirms, are the selfsame persons they were in earthly life. Although extraordinarily "more" through the power of grace, resurrected persons continue to be who they became through the cultivation of virtue in earthly life. An eschatological anthropology is obliged to be faithful to the contours of a more general theological anthropology if the personal continuity affirmed in the doctrine of bodily resurrection is to hold true eschatologically.

A Catholic theological anthropology in line with the teaching of Trent insists that personal existence is shaped by the way that a believer lives virtuously into the divine offer of grace through the believer's exercise of free choice. But for resurrected selves to be who they are, to abide in the character shaped by the moral events in their lives, they must continue to engage in virtuous acts in heaven.[18] Resurrected persons must live into the unbounded grace of resurrected life in order to continue to be the selves who they are. The eventfulness that marks personal existence could only be excluded from the heavenly imaginary at the cost of sacrificing the very integrity of character that the doctrine of bodily resurrection affirms. And in order for moral eventfulness to transpire so that persons in resurrection can still be persons, to say nothing of persons continuous with the persons who they have been, a consistent heavenly imaginary must include the notion of a heavenly time.

How, though, to imagine this heavenly time? Doing so would be a variation on the theme of imagining the resurrection of the body, replete with all the limitations and possibilities of that traditional exercise of spiritual reflection. In however limited a way, the believer envisages God's redemptive victory over sin and death in a way that affirms the goodness of creation now taken up into the continuity of grace's miraculous consummation of the things that God has made, whether human persons or created time. In that exercise, the reluctance to imagine a heavenly time issues from the deleterious power of change that believers meet in their lives in what we have called tragic time, a time that configures the events of sin and death. Heavenly time would be this tragic time with which we are so familiar, now resurrected—time brought by grace into a state of participation in Christ's resurrected life and so miraculously transformed into a creaturely state of heavenly glory. We can take some small steps toward imagining such resurrected time by speculatively walking the path of a *via negativa* that thinks the thought of tragic time's loss in God's eschatological consummation.

Tragic time is time distorted by fallen events in the history of sin and death. Believers have been tempted to imagine resurrected life as timeless in order to portray the utter fulfillment of God's biblical promise to destroy death forever (Isa 25:8). As death is destroyed, the traditional imaginary assumes, so too is the time in which deleterious change unfolds. This conceptualization, however, fails to respect the tradition's belief in resurrected life as the redemptive continuity, and not the loss, of creatureliness. Tragic time's loss is not the loss of time, for time's creaturely goodness gracefully participates in Christ's resurrection, as does the goodness of all creation. Rather, a doctrinally consistent portrayal of resurrected life would have the eschatological victory of grace witness the loss of time's privation through the tragic events that distort its created beauty. Theological speculation that imagined a heavenly time would represent the ambiance of heavenly eventfulness as configured by time made eschatologically more through its graceful elevation beyond sin and death. The saints in heaven are best imagined as dwelling in resurrected time so that the unique eventfulness of each of their lives, virtue brought by grace to redemption, can be continuous with their ongoing moral eventfulness in heaven as they live into their resurrection to be the persons who they have been and, in heavenly time, will be. Heavenly time, I propose, still comprises a past, a present, and a future.

As I have already considered in my study, eschatological time is not just heavenly. All time is eschatological time—time now, as well as time forever. I have considered that time now, in its earthly proportions, is eschatological for several reasons. Like all creatures, time is created through the Son of God, and so is filled with the power of his redemptive life. All time is graced, and so always already courses in eternal life. And all time now, to the degree that it is created and graced, evokes in the believer a sense of an ending molded by its very creatureliness and by its hopeful anticipation of God's consummate victory over sin, death, and the anomic time that configures these tragic events. The sense of an ending that accompanies every moment of earthly time is measured both by time's fragility, a fragility that Augustine described so well, and also by the liminal time of the Last Judgment, at the conclusion of which time now—in the traditional imaginary, all time—disappears. Were we to imagine a heavenly time, these qualities of the eschatological now would be transformed in the resurrection that time would undergo in order to participate in the Savior's resurrection from the dead. Time in the eschatological forever would continue to be created, as all things heavenly are and as heaven itself is. Time, as not-God, remains creaturely; time is not eternity. Yet time's creation through the Son of God, as revealed in the Gospel of John (1:3), ensures its predestination to the New Creation. A resurrected time would be continuous with time in the eschatological now, though not merely in sequence. In this continuity time is fulfilled in its goodness, raised beyond anomic time so that its beauty can shine forth in every heavenly moment. These graceful moments keep the time of heavenly events that continue to manifest the redemption of the saints in the presence of God. Time in the eschatological forever would continue to be graced, its grace undiminished by sin and death, which in the eschatological forever have passed away into their privative nothingness. In the fullness of grace, resurrected time would lose the tensive quality of time in the eschatological now, where grace struggles with sin and death and where hope's yearning for the resolution of this struggle, for the consummate victory of grace, is stirred as the believer's fundamental disposition toward God's future.

While these qualities of resurrected time—its creatureliness and its graceful continuity—evince analogical similarity-in-difference to time in the eschatological now, the quality of earthly time that evokes in the believer a sense of an ending proves to be more strikingly different in one crucial way. The sense of time's ending emerges in the believer's apprehension of time's created fragility. A heavenly time would indeed convey a sense of creation's fragility, for all of creation, including heavenly time, is dependent on God's providence for its abiding existence. Time is an unusual form of creatureliness. Its moving accompaniment of created events provides an ephemeral ambiance within which eventfulness transpires. Time's moments ever continue to end as the present moment's anticipation of the future slips away into the past. For a heavenly time to be time, and not eternity, the momentary endings that configure eventfulness would need to continue in the New Creation. These momentary endings in time forever, though, would be devoid of the anomic qualities of time's flow now. Time would never stultify in boredom, nor be empty in loneliness, frozen in trauma, or devastated in grief. Time would never be measured in periods before and after betrayal, before and after love withered, before and after despair. In resurrected time, dead time has passed away. The eschatological hope in anomic time for the end of sin and death has been fulfilled. In time forever, all time is thoroughly graceful, the motion of its eventfulness swept up into the divine presence without remainder and its tempo measuring acts of love in the communion of the saints. In heavenly time, however, the sense of time's ending consummately, as it does in the traditional imaginary's anticipation of the Last Judgment, would cease in the imaginary I have proposed. Since time has been resurrected into eternal life, time, like heaven itself and the resurrected life of the blessed dead, continues on forever as a time in which God will be all in all.

If resurrected time is never-ending, as all dimensions of the New Creation are, then a time abundantly continuous in its grace raises questions about the existence of hope in heavenly time. Eschatological time, we have seen, stirs the temporality of hope. But in time now, hope is evoked especially by the believer's encounter with tragic events and the disturbing resonance of anomic time. One hopes in the face of suffering, and hope yearns for God's fulfilled future in which our lives, and indeed all of history, are healed and made whole. In time forever, time has been fulfilled. God has fully realized God's biblical promise to destroy death forever.

Hope's tensive temporality in time now has been resurrected and gracefully transformed into a time that would seem to make hope superfluous.[19] The eschatological anthropology developed in my study, however, has made much of the virtue of hope—even to the point of imagining that the act of faith can be understood as hope so that hope's temporality frames the more creaturely of the theological virtues. Indeed, I proposed too that hope's eschatological temporality was the proper experiential field in which to situate the virtue of love. The blessed dead are readily imagined as dwelling in God's love throughout heavenly time, especially since that creaturely virtue participates most intensely in the very reality of love who God is. The virtue of love in heavenly time abides forever in God, as God abides in the resurrected lives of the saints (1 John 4:16).

But hope is another matter. Its virtue in time now is so closely aligned with anomic time that we could imagine the heavenly fulfillment of hope's yearning as its disappearance. Certainly the traditional imaginary's conception of a timeless afterlife would have it that way. Paul acknowledges hope's this-worldly situation in his testimony that "now we see in a mirror, dimly, but then we will see face to face. Now I know only in part; then I will know fully. . . . And now faith, hope, and love abide" (1 Cor 13:12–13). How, though, might we imagine hope—or, better, an act of faith as hope—not only now, but in a never-ending heavenly time? To be hope, hope must yearn in the present for a future that is "more." Time, to be time in heaven, must transpire in the measure of past, present, and future, as I have already noted. Thus, the temporal dynamics that would make hope intelligible would remain in resurrected life. Heavenly hope, however, would encounter nothing of the tragic, nothing of sin and death, nothing of time distorted by the privation of creation's graceful eventfulness, and so hope's yearning would not pine for God's redemption in the midst of human fallenness. Hope in the eschatological forever could be imagined as a virtue continually practiced as the saints in heaven live into their salvation. The very notion of a heavenly future suggests that resurrected life is not a settled, static state but a time in which God's redemption increases as grace abounds all the more (Rom 5:20), though in the time of forever a "more" no longer in comparison to the deathly power of sin but to the heavenly present of God's gift of grace. Heavenly hope on the part of the blessed dead can be imagined as their unceasing yearning for this unending increase in God's self-sharing, an imparting of grace commensurate with God's eternity that continues to assist the saints all the more in their heavenly virtue. Heavenly hope too can be imagined as the never-ending desire to be worthy of this ever-excessive gift, and so an act of hope that pervades the communion of the saints as eschatological humility and gratitude.

The Beatific Vision and the Beauty of Heavenly Diversity

Time's eschatological defeat in the traditional imaginary is reflected clearly in the liturgical prayer for the dead: "Eternal rest grant unto them, O Lord, and let perpetual light shine upon them. May the souls of all the faithful departed, through the mercy of God, rest in peace." In this common Catholic sensibility, the perpetual light of the timeless divine glory embraces the blessed dead into a quiescent state of motionless repose. It would seem that the saintly beneficiaries of redemption reap the harvest of grace by doing nothing, except, of course, basking in the glory of God's heavenly illumination. In a Catholic tradition that stresses the believer's meritorious words and deeds in heavenly reward, the imaginary of a heavenly rest expresses the desire for the end of anxious struggle in the midst of tragic time. In the traditional imagery of heavenly redemption, the hierarchy of discipleship in earthly time is supernaturally fixed in eternity, one's heavenly status a reflection of one's earthly merits. Let us continue in our task of imagining all this differently.

The traditional imaginary sees the particular judgment at the hour of death as the event of divine decision that assigns the believer to one of two supernatural destinies—unending joy in heaven or unending torment in hell. The Last Judgment affirms this eschatological division, reifying the eternal boundary that forever separates the saved and the damned. In many respects, the symbolic line that separates heaven and hell justifies the pernicious borders created in the history of sin and death that give rise to untold human suffering—borders that separate races, nations, the wealthy and the poor, the powerful and the disenfranchised, the healthy and the sick, the free and the incarcerated. Let us instead think along with that ancient, minority Christian belief that the power of God's grace brings all to salvation, a belief that the great twentieth-century Catholic theologian Hans Urs von Balthasar insisted is utterly worthy of Christian hope.[20] Were we to imagine that hope truthfully realized, then the hour of one's death would no longer be the moment in which God's judgment accepted some and rejected others. Instead, God's judgment would reveal all the egregious ways in which God's grace was rejected and neglected by the person under judgment, who, faced with the truth of that self-revelation, would find grace's unyielding power, itself the love of God's own divine life, irresistible. In effect, we are imagining the particular judgment as an encounter with the Beatific Vision, and the Beatific Vision, no longer reserved in a heavenly holy of holies and available only to the saints purged of sin, instead as God's relentless embrace of the *imago Dei*, no matter the depths of its sinful distortion. In such a heavenly imaginary, God would quite literally be all in all. The New Creation would be inclusive without remainder. The harrowing of hell would transpire with God's supernatural reckoning and graceful embrace of every person's life.

A heavenly imaginary of universal salvation need not at all undermine the Council of Trent's teaching on justification. Believers are indeed obliged to live into God's grace through their own freely-willed assent. Virtue, however, is not grace, which is the unearned gift of eternal life. With Paul, we can affirm that God's judgment and God's grace are not at all the same. Human persons, in this life or the next, are undeserving of grace. Virtue matters, not only in earthly time but also, as we have proposed, in heavenly time. But virtue does not bring about the miracle of resurrection, nor does it give rise to a moral hierarchy of more and less, either in this life or the next. Grace, as Kathryn Tanner has reminded us, is noncompetitive,[21] and so too should be the Christian life that lives into God's unconditional gift, which, by its very nature, is not subject to the workings of self-interest and exchange. "Our lives as individuals," Tanner notes, "should be constituted and enhanced in their perfections as we share our lives with others in community, identifying ourselves thereby as persons in community with others and not simply persons for ourselves. We perfect one another in community as our operations to perfect our own gifts and talents enter into and supplement the operations of others in a combined venture for goods otherwise impossible."[22] This communal living into God's noncompetitive grace can serve as a way of imagining the Christian life not only in time now but also in time forever. If the doctrine of the resurrection of the body means that the saved—in my proposal, every human person—must continue to be herself or himself or theirself in heaven, then all the saints, as we have seen, must continue to act in a resurrected time in which the noncompetitive power of grace fosters the communal building of the heavenly kingdom of God.

This shared eschatological virtue in the time of forever can be troubling to imagine in time now. If the power of God's noncompetitive grace is so efficacious that all are redeemed, then one must imagine a time forever filled with relationships between those who were truly saintly in their earthly lives and those who were purveyors of the most egregious crimes against humanity, eschatological relationships between perpetrators and their victims, between those in the traditional imaginary who were deserving of heavenly reward and those who were deserving of hellish damnation. It can be challenging enough to imagine a heavenly community in which God's grace, no different from God's love, abounds so completely that even the most egregiously undeserving are overwhelmed by its irresistible power and stand in the ranks of the redeemed. But it is even more challenging to imagine a heavenly community in which the time of forever is unendingly filled with virtuous solidarity among all of its members, a solidarity that requires mutual commitment and reciprocity in the service of the good, however much earthly purveyors of even horrendous evil forever participate fully in the joy of resurrected life.

We can imagine this communal heavenly virtue as the moral work of negotiating the effects of sin. In my first chapter, I noted that the doctrine of the resurrection of the body requires a heavenly time in which resurrected persons continue to act as persons in the communion of the saints, and that in order for their personal integrity to be continuous from time now to time forever the effects of sin, though not sin itself, must continue to define their eschatological identity. The effects of sin have shaped the character of the saints, both through the sin they suffered and through the sin they enacted that others suffered. In time now, the effects of sin make persons who and what they are. To imagine resurrected life emptied of sin's effects would be to imagine a redemption in which the power of grace violated, rather than transformed, the moral histories that constitute the substance of our actual selves, as though our lives as they really came to be in the goodness of creation's time were of no account.

The strongest scriptural testimony to support this view is found in the resurrection stories that conclude the Gospels of Luke and John. In these later Gospels, the resurrected Jesus appears to his disciples and makes the wounds of his crucifixion the proof of his identity. "Why are you frightened?" Luke's Jesus asks his disciples, who are startled by his miraculous appearance. "And why do doubts arise in your hearts? Look at my hands and my feet; see that it is I myself. Touch me and see; for a ghost does not have flesh and bones as you see that I have" (Luke 24:38–39). John's Jesus confronts the doubts of his disciple Thomas, who was absent from an earlier and first appearance of the resurrected Lord to his disciples. Incredulous, Thomas himself made the wounds of Jesus's crucified body the measure of his belief in Jesus's resurrection. A week later, Jesus appeared again to his disciples and, after a greeting of peace to all, said to Thomas, "Put your finger here and see my hands. Reach out your hand and put it in my side. Do not doubt but believe" (John 20:27). In resurrected life, Jesus's open wounds endure, wounds that were the effects of terrible sin that he suffered in time now. Faith assumes that these wounds on his resurrected body cause no suffering in time forever. His wounds share in his glory. But the Gospel stories imply that in time forever and, in Jesus's unique case, eternally, the effects of the sin he suffered remain. They mark his identity, defining in a consequential way who he was, and so who he will be forever.

We can imagine that the effects of sin in the communion of the saints set an unending agenda for the practice of heavenly virtue. The effects of sin that transpired in anomic time in broken relationships, between nations and races, in acts of violence, through callous economic and social policies, in the systemic power of evil institutions in their own immediate present or transhistorically—all these lingering effects of sin that make resurrected persons who they continue to be require responsible moral redress in the New Creation. Resurrected time is filled with infinite occasions for the saints in heaven to engage in such eschatological virtue—acts of forgiveness, reconciliation, compassion, understanding, and love—that live into the grace that is the eternal love of God's own self. Resurrected time individuates these virtuous events, their graceful motion unfolding in the beauty of offers and acceptances of healing that increase the joy of redemptive solidarity all the more. Hope in heaven is a yearning for this redemptive "more," which in no way suggests that grace is incomplete or even, for that matter, that the redemption that grace brings is incomplete. Heavenly hope does presuppose that resurrected persons, as the creatures they forever are, can always be "more" in their love of God, their love of neighbor, in their redemptive joy in a time full of grace. And heavenly hope, as I have noted, is an inexhaustible desire to be worthy of an unbounded grace, ever mediated through time and of which the saints are forever undeserving. Such is the source of their gratitude's long duration.

Christian faith affirms God's omnipresence to all of creation, and so expresses the belief that God is everywhere, that all space is filled with the divine life. The tradition, however, has been reluctant to speak explicitly of God's omnitemporality. The strikingly univocal attribute of eternity, which professes God's absolute difference from time, has militated against such a conceptualization. Here I have attempted to recover time's theological significance by imagining time's eventfulness as the sacramentality of grace and as the continuity of time now through time forever in the resurrected community of all the saints as created beauty. Any Christian imaginary affirms that at the heart of this heavenly community, ever animating its redemptive solidarity, is the extraordinary eventfulness of the divine Trinity. Throughout the Christian tradition, resurrected life has been portrayed as the saints' unceasing contemplation of God. In the traditional imaginary, the Beatific Vision exhausts the heavenly experience of the saved. It has been imagined as the profound bliss of redemptive fulfillment, as the believer's encounter with the ineffable divine mystery in which all of the joys and sorrows of life find their consummate resolution in the love of God.

My approach to a heavenly imaginary has walked a kataphatic path. I have speculated not about God but about creatures. My proposed imaginary was constructed by pursuing both a *via negativa* and a *via positiva* from time now to time forever in order to develop a theological anthropology set within an eschatological aesthetic. I have had little to say about the divine aseity itself, rightly content to speak of God's disposition toward creation in and through grace. I have said even less about the Beatific Vision of God in heaven, except to note with the tradition that this sublime object of Christian hope is the complete realization of hope's deepest yearning and to propose that the Beatific Vision lies at heaven's boundary as well as at its center. This proper theological reticence has been consistent throughout Christian history. Although Paul anticipates that resurrected life will bring the believer face to face with God, he yet assumes that the joy of this encounter eludes imagination and words (1 Cor 13:12; 2:9). Aquinas's careful treatment of the Beatific Vision in the *Summa Contra Gentiles* has little to say about what the saints see as they contemplate God, except to assure his readers that every desire is fulfilled in the ultimate happiness of the vision.[23] Instead, Aquinas explores the conditions for the possibility of such creaturely intimacy with God, noting that the vision requires the saints' graceful elevation into the divine glory, that the vision is perpetual, that God is seen in and through God's own essence, and that yet, even in this consummate experience, the created intellect cannot comprehend God.[24] But of all the tradition's theologians who have embraced this theological reticence about the substance of the Beatific Vision, Dante deserves pride of place.[25]

The entire otherworldly journey of *The Divine Comedy* can be read as the pilgrim's progress through the supernatural hierarchy to the Beatific Vision in the highest heights of heaven. In the closing scene of *Purgatorio*, Dante emerges from purgatory into the earthly paradise where Adam and Eve enjoyed the short time of a creation unspoiled by sin. There he is entrusted by the ancient poet Virgil, his spirit-guide through hell and purgatory, to the care of Beatrice, Dante's youthful love long-lost to death, who now serves as guide for the heavenly ascent nearly all the way to the journey's glorious end. The poem's concluding tome, *Paradiso*, charts this ethereal course as Beatrice leads Dante through the lower reaches of heaven into the realm of the fixed stars, higher into the *primum mobile*, and finally to the tenth and highest heaven of the Empyrean, the "Celestial Rose," as Dante calls it, in which all the souls experience the vision of God, no matter where they are situated in the heavenly hierarchy by the merit of their earthly deeds. So close now to the Beatific Vision, Beatrice is about to hand over her task as guide to Saint Bernard, but before she does she prepares Dante for the wonder he is about to witness: "We have issued forth from the greatest body to the heaven which is pure light: light intellectual full of love, love of true good full of joy, joy that transcends every sweetness. Here you shall see the one and the other soldiery of Paradise [angels and humans], and the one in those aspects which you shall see at the last judgment."[26] Now, his heavenly instructor Bernard encourages Dante to reflect on the grace that filled the Empyrean with the saints, whose ranks include those who lived before and after the incarnation; children who died before they could responsibly exercise free choice; and the tradition's celebrated disciples—John the Baptist, Francis, Benedict, and Augustine.[27]

Bernard continues his tour of this redemptive gallery by calling Dante's attention to the Virgin Mother, in whose "womb was rekindled the Love under whose warmth this flower [of the incarnation] in the eternal peace has thus unfolded."[28] Bernard offers a long prayer of praise to Mary, which seems to serve as a devotional vestibule to the vision of God that will complete the spiritual journey of every life. Dante listens with silent reverence, and as the prayer ends Bernard beckons him to turn his eyes on high. "Thenceforward," Dante marvels, "my vision was greater than speech can show, which fails at such a sight, and at such excess memory fails."[29] The great poet testifies that his talent flags in the face of the divine light, whose radiance is overwhelming. "Now will my speech fall more short," he confesses, "even in respect to that which I remember, than that of an infant who still bathes his tongue at the breast."[30] In that sublime moment of spiritual vision, Dante makes out the Trinity in the "profound and shining subsistence of the lofty Light" as "three circles of three colors and one magnitude," each reflected by the other "as rainbow by rainbow." And within these three circles that yet glowed as one, Dante is able to see God's graceful providence to humanity in the human face of Christ:

> O Light Eternal, who alone abidest in Thyself, alone knowest Thyself, and, known to Thyself and knowing, lovest and smilest on Thyself!
>
> That circling which, thus begotten, appeared in Thee as reflected light, when my eyes had dwelt on it for a time, seemed to me depicted with our image [*la nostra effige*] within itself and in its own color, wherefore my sight was entirely set upon it.[31]

The poet had introduced his account of this marvelous sight, still on the cusp of the Beatific Vision, by admitting the difficulty of his task: "O how scant is speech, and how feeble to my conception! and this, to what I saw, is such that it is not enough to call it little."³² Yet Dante ventures a little more, if only to express his wonder at the mystery of the incarnation: "As is the geometer who wholly applies himself to measure the circle, and finds not, in pondering, the principle of which he is in need, such was I at that new sight. I wished to see how the image [*l'imago*] [of Christ's humanity] conformed to the circle and how it has its place therein; but my own wings were not sufficient for that."³³ And that frailty of thought and word is evinced most of all in the last lines of the *Paradiso*, as the poet chooses to portray the unbounded ecstasy of the Beatific Vision not in lavish metaphor or even in simple words but finally in the silence that the poem's closure brings: "[But then] my mind was smitten by a flash wherein its wish came to it. Here power failed the lofty phantasy; but already my desire and my will were revolved, like a wheel that is evenly moved, by the Love which moves the sun and the other stars."³⁴

We can only learn from the poet-theologian. My proposal for a heavenly imaginary has engaged in speculation grounded in traditional Christian doctrine. This speculative endeavor has issued in an eschatological anthropology framed in the temporality of hope. Theological speculation, however, has nothing to do before the anticipated, overwhelming joy of the Beatific Vision. With the tradition, our attention to the Beatific Vision must be properly reticent, our approach simply apophatic. The vision of God is an encounter with the divine mystery itself, and, as Dante noted so well, in the face of such mystery words and thoughts fail. As much as my study has taken issue with Augustine's theological treatment of time in the *Confessions*, I will bring it to a close by affirming Augustine's sharp distinction between time and eternity and his traditional assumption that eternity is solely a divine, and not a creaturely, attribute. This study has insisted that this distinction holds, and should never be blurred, throughout heavenly time. It is that very difference between eternity and time that will enable one last speculation about the beauty of time in heaven.

Throughout the history of aesthetical thought, beauty has proved to be a value difficult to define. I have found advantage in a classical explanation of beauty that attends to qualities in the object that stir the judgment of beauty, rather than to modern accounts that focus much more on the subjectivity of taste. Beauty is inescapably subjective, to the degree that it remains a human judgment, but a classical theory does its best to describe what it is in the thing of beauty that elicits the edifying judgment. Beauty, the classical explanation claims, lies in a symmetry that the perceiver finds in the object. Apprehended in sight or sound, this sense of proportion gathers a diversity of parts into an ordered whole, the blend drawing the diversity into a harmony that is pleasing, perhaps most of all because the diversity is not lost but remains in the beautiful order. Medieval theology identified beauty, along with unity, truth, and goodness, as one of the transcendentals, qualities of created being that reflect the being of creation's divine source. God is beauty itself. Were we to make this belief the measure of the insight captured in the classical notion of beauty, then we could say that the beauty of God's Trinitarian life is the paradigm for the judgment of created beauty in the classical sensibility. The exquisite harmony of the one, eternal life of God mysteriously embraces the diversity of the divine Persons, just as the diversity of the Persons—Father, Son, and Spirit—channels the unity of divine love into the graceful activities of creation, redemption, and sanctification. The divine Persons, of course, are not "parts" of God, any more than the divine unity is a "whole." The simplicity of God's being prevents any univocal alignment between the beauty of composite creatures and the beauty of God. Faith, though, can find an analogical model for the representation of beauty in creation in the beauty of the Trinitarian God.

The beauty of this harmonious unity of diversity appears in the divine life not only in the Triune being of God but also in the abiding presence of the incarnation within the Trinity. The incarnation itself is a paradigm of beauty in the unity of such different natures—one divine, one human; one eternal, one temporal—in the person of Jesus of Nazareth. But the beauty of the incarnation, so apparent on every page of the Gospels, also contributes its own measure to the beauty of the divine life. The human nature of Christ is not an outsider to the Trinitarian perichoresis. The human nature of Christ is created. In the teaching of Chalcedon, Christ's humanity is "like us in all respects except for sin,"[35] and so is not in any respect eternal. And yet there is a sense in which the human nature of Jesus is taken up into the eternal life of God while still retaining the integrity of its creaturely existence.[36] Even though Jesus's humanity is unique by virtue of its incarnational embrace by the eternal nature of God, it represents all of humanity, and through his human nature all humanity too participates in the timeless life of God. This astonishing truth of the Christian message—that God's own nature assumed human nature to itself and in doing so gracefully brought human nature to eternal life—also expresses the beauty of the union of difference in the divine life of God. This is the beauty of the incarnational paradox whose futile understanding Dante compares to a geometer seeking "to measure the circle," prompted by the "new sight" of "how the [human] image conformed to the [divine] circle and how it has its place therein."[37]

This beauty radiates into the heavenly kingdom in the vision of God. My imaginary proposed that the Beatific Vision, the unbounded love of God, is not reserved for some, the saints who have been purified even of the effects of sin, but instead is encountered by all in the hour of death in the particular judgment. It is this vision that brings judgment as the self-revelation of utter unworthiness to all, as well as the conversion of all by the irresistible power of grace. Thus converted, all the saints are ever faithful to grace's redemptive project and forever hopeful of being worthy of the divine love. In such an imaginary of universal salvation, the Last Judgment becomes a celebration in which the good news of all of history is that no one stands outside the divine love—all, in the wholeness of their persons and their lives, enter the eschatological community to live into the graceful time that permeates the heavenly realm. The time of the Last Judgment is no longer liminal, a divide between tragic time and heavenly timelessness, but instead an affirmation of the continuity of graceful time from this world to the next. Although the effects of sin remain in heavenly time, the deforming power of sin and death has been destroyed forever. In the victory of grace, only virtue remains, virtue whose acts of forgiveness, reconciliation, understanding, and love endlessly increase the joy of redemption. The virtuous acts ever done in the heavenly community are individuated as events in heavenly time, their redeeming motion and the time in which they are set thoroughly graceful and uncompromisingly beautiful. These heavenly events continue to shape the resurrected character of heavenly diversity as all resurrected persons continue to be themselves forever, their personal integrity, and so their eschatological diversity, ever "more" as heavenly time continues. The beauty of the heavenly community is shaped by this resurrected diversity of sin vanquished and the effects of sin ever being healed, a diversity forever harmonized by the vision of God that animates the saints in their active heavenly love. The beauty of heavenly time is that it preserves this diversity of selves and action in the unity of the communion of the saints.[38] Heavenly time is God's way of keeping the joy of redemptive eventfulness from happening all at once.

The Beatific Vision offers its own unfathomable beauty to those who encounter the mysterious diversity-in-unity of the Trinitarian life of God, not just initially in judgment at the boundary of heaven but in every moment of resurrected time. But all of heavenly beauty, we can imagine, is accentuated as well in the contrastive harmony of God's eternity and the diversity of resurrected persons and their graceful virtue in the aesthetic of heavenly time. Creaturely diversity in time is God's providential plan, begun, scripture records, in the six days of creation in time now and consummated endlessly in time forever. Human diversity, unified in the *imago Dei*, which all persons share, is sinfully distorted in tragic time as the mark of alienating difference. It is grace that assists virtue in the restoration of diversity to its providential goodness in time now through works of inclusion, justice, and love that are true to the noncompetitive character of grace. This diversity intensifies and grows in resurrected time as the heavenly character of the saints increases, as all the saints become even more themselves in resurrected life. And this creaturely diversity—beautiful, good, and true—unfolds in a heavenly time that ensures its eventfulness forever and that transpires not simply before but within the Beatific Vision, whose eternity is the very grace that time mediates to creation.[39] The beauty of this heavenly symmetry of diversity, in the redemptive unity of the eternal God and the resurrected temporality of all that is creaturely, is the very same beauty that dwells in the gracefulness of time now. Even though the eyes of faith struggle so often to see and appreciate that beauty, it abides in every moment, there to be beheld as the tempo of God's graceful presence to creation—the beauty of eternity in time, now and forever.

NOTES

Chapter One Eschatology, Time, and the Continuity of Grace

1. Jürgen Moltmann, *The Coming of God: Christian Eschatology*, trans. M. Kohl (Minneapolis: Fortress, 1996).

2. John E. Thiel, *Icons of Hope: The "Last Things" in Catholic Imagination* (Notre Dame, IN: University of Notre Dame Press, 2013). In his review of *Icons of Hope*, Leo J. O'Donovan, S.J., observed that its argument "highlights the need for a contemporary theology of time" ("Closed for Repair?," *Commonweal* 141 [October 24, 2014]: 36). My goal in this work is to take some steps toward meeting that need for a contemporary theology of time. In no respect, though, is the present study a sequel to *Icons of Hope* that presupposes the reader's knowledge of that earlier work.

3. On the history of theological encyclopedia, see Edward Farley, *Theologia: The Fragmentation and Unity of Theological Education* (Philadelphia: Fortress, 1983). For the notion of functional specialties in theology, see Bernard J. F. Lonergan, S.J., *Method in Theology* (New York: Herder and Herder, 1972), 125–45.

4. Johannes Weiss, *Jesus' Proclamation of the Kingdom of God*, ed. L. Keck (Philadelphia: Fortress, 1971); Albert Schweitzer, *The Quest of the Historical Jesus*, ed. J. Bowden (Minneapolis: Fortress, 2001).

5. Hans Urs von Balthasar, *The Glory of the Lord: A Theological Aesthetics*, vol. 5, *The Realm of Metaphysics in the Modern Age*, trans. O. Davies et al. (San Francisco: Ignatius, 1991), 48–204.

6. Karl Rahner, "The Hermeneutics of Eschatological Assertions," in *Theological Investigations*, vol. 4, trans. K. Smyth (Baltimore: Helicon, 1966), 323–46.

7. Joseph Ratzinger, *Eschatology: Death and Eternal Life*, trans. M. Waldstein (Washington, DC: Catholic University of America Press, 1988).

8. Moltmann, *Coming of God*.

9. Miroslav Volf, *Exclusion and Embrace: A Theological Exploration of Identity, Otherness, and Reconciliation* (Nashville: Abingdon, 1996).

10. Elizabeth A. Johnson, *Friends of God and Prophets: A Feminist Theological Reading of the Communion of the Saints* (New York: Continuum, 1998).

11. Cyril O'Regan, *Theology and the Spaces of Apocalyptic* (Milwaukee: Marquette University Press, 2009), 34–60.

12. Henri de Lubac, S.J., *The Mystery of the Supernatural*, trans. R. Sheed (New York: Crossroad Herder, 1998), 37.

13. Ibid., 34–35.

14. Ibid., 42.

15. Ibid., 36, 37.

16. See Henri de Lubac, *Surnaturel: Études historiques* (Paris: Aubier, 1946), 431–71.

17. "L'esprit, en effet, ne désire pas Dieu comme l'animal désire sa proie. Il le désire comme un don. Il ne cherche point à posséder un objet infini: il veut la communication libre et gratuite d'un Etre personnel" (ibid., 483). Joseph Flipper has argued, more broadly, that de Lubac's early theology was saturated with eschatological concerns that issued from the apocalyptic currents of the Second World War and postwar politics. Joseph S. Flipper, *Between Apocalypse and Eschaton: History and Eternity in Henri de Lubac* (Minneapolis: Fortress, 2015). For a lucid account of the issues at stake in the neo-Thomist–de Lubac debate, see Nicholas J. Healy, "Henri de Lubac on Nature and Grace: A Note on Some Recent Contributions to the Debate," *Communio: International Catholic Review* 35 (2008): 535–64. See also Hans Boersma, *Nouvelle Théologie and Sacramental Ontology: A Return to Mystery* (New York: Oxford University Press, 2009), 90–97.

18. De Lubac, *Mystery of the Supernatural*, 68.

19. C. Harold Dodd, "The Eschatological Element in the New Testament and Its Permanent Significance," *The Interpreter* 20 (1923–24): 20.

20. C. H. Dodd, *The Apostolic Preaching and Its Developments* (New York: Harper & Row, 1964), 83.

21. Ibid.

22. Ibid., 84.

23. Ibid., 85.

24. Ibid.

25. Ibid., 86.

26. Ibid.

27. C. H. Dodd, *The Parables of the Kingdom* (New York: Charles Scribner's Sons, 1961), 159.

28. Ibid., 163–64.

29. Ibid., 168.

30. C. H. Dodd, *The Interpretation of the Fourth Gospel* (Cambridge: Cambridge University Press, 1965), 447n1.

31. Oscar Cullmann has most developed the notion of an "inaugurated eschatology" as a corrective to Dodd's position, even though he did not use the term "inaugurated" himself. See Oscar Cullmann, *Christ and Time: The Primitive Chris-*

tian Conception of Time and History, trans. F. V. Filson (Philadelphia: Westminster, 1964), 84–88. Cf. Cullmann, *Salvation in History*, trans. S. G. Sowers (New York: Harper & Row, 1967), 173–85.

32. Ironically, neo-scholasticism's efforts to rebuff the Enlightenment critique of Christianity actually embraced the broad features of the Enlightenment worldview by imagining a reality in which the supernatural and natural orders are divided.

33. A fine Protestant example of this theology of grace from the perspective of systematic theology is found in the work of Kathryn Tanner: "In the first place, my [Tanner's] account of the nature with which we are created does not allow one to imagine humans properly existing without the actual gift of grace in the way a Thomistic account of our created nature in terms of a simple desire for grace might. To be created as a human being means to be created with grace and not simply with a desire for what grace supplies. Human life therefore seems utterly wrecked apart from the actual gift of grace. In the second place, grace, understood as a strong form of participation in God, is necessary for the excellent exercise of our ordinary functions as human beings, and not merely for the achievement of distinctly supernatural ends such as eternal life. God, it seems, must give it to us; God is required to give us grace by God's intent to create us as the sort of creatures we are" (Kathryn Tanner, *Christ the Key* [Cambridge: Cambridge University Press, 2010], 108–9).

34. Thomas Aquinas, *Summa Contra Gentiles*, book 4, *Salvation*, trans. C. J. O'Neil (Notre Dame, IN: University of Notre Dame Press, 1975), 325 (4.86.1).

35. Ibid., 338–41 (4.92.1).

36. Medieval theologians developed a host of categories to portray heaven as a metaphysical halfway house between eternity and time, as a sempiternity of time without beginning or end that "may be regarded as divided by any moment into two eternities: the past eternity (*aeternitas a parte ante*) and the future eternity (*aeternitas a parte post*)" (Carlos Eire, *A Very Brief History of Eternity* [Princeton: Princeton University Press, 2009], 139). Such distinctions evince a resistance to imagining the continuity of "time now" and "time forever."

37. All quotations from the Bible in English are from the New Revised Standard Version.

38. Karl Rahner, "The Life of the Dead," in *Theological Investigations*, 4:353–54.

39. Karl Barth, *Church Dogmatics* III/3, ed. G. W. Bromiley and T. F. Torrance, trans. G. W. Bromiley and R. J. Ehrlich (Edinburgh: T&T Clark, 1960), 424–25.

40. Augustine, *City of God*, trans. H. Bettenson (New York: Penguin, 1984), 1081–91 (22.29–30); Thomas Aquinas, *Summa Contra Gentiles*, book 4, *Salvation*, 297–349 (4.79–97); Jonathan Edwards, "Heaven Is a World of Love," in *The Works of Jonathan Edwards*, vol. 8, *Ethical Writings*, ed. P. Ramsey (New Haven: Yale University Press, 1989), 366–97.

41. Specifically, Gisbert Greshake, "Das Verhältnis 'Unsterblichkeit der Seele' und 'Auferstehung des Leibes' in problemgeschichtlicher Sicht," in *Naherwartung, Auferstehung, Unsterblichkeit: Untersuchungen zur christlichen Eschatologie*, by Gisbert Greshake and Gerhard Lohfink (Freiburg: Herder, 1976), 92–97.

42. Ratzinger, *Eschatology*, 184–85 (italics added).

43. International Theological Commission, *Some Current Questions in Eschatology*, 2.2, available at the Vatican website, http://www.vatican.va/roman_curia/congregations/cfaith/cti_documents/rc_cti_1990_problemi-attuali-escatologia_en.html.

44. This is, of course, simply the current state of our knowledge of the physical universe. For a discussion of the relationship between time and matter, see Sean Carroll, *From Eternity to Here: The Quest for the Ultimate Theory of Time* (New York: Plume, 2010), 67–81.

45. Gregory of Nyssa, *Gregory of Nyssa: The Life of Moses*, trans. A. J. Malherbe (New York: Paulist Press, 1978), 113.

46. This point on the persistence of the effects of sin in heaven is developed in Thiel, *Icons of Hope*, 52–54, 171–88.

47. Hans Urs von Balthasar, *Dare We Hope "That All Men Be Saved"?*, trans. D. Kipp and L. Krauth (San Francisco: Ignatius, 1988).

48. Jürgen Moltmann has described the mutual implication of past, present, and future in experience as the "interlaced times of history." Jürgen Moltmann, *God in Creation*, trans. M. Kohl (San Francisco: HarperCollins, 1991), 124–39.

Chapter Two The Virtues in Time: An Eschatological Anthropology

1. Immanuel Kant, *Critique of Pure Reason*, trans. N. K. Smith (New York: St. Martin's Press, 1929), 66 (B 35).

2. Ibid.

3. Ibid., 67 (B 36).

4. Ibid., 86 (B 66).

5. Immanuel Kant, *Kritik der reinen Vernunft*, ed. J. Timmermann (Hamburg: Felix Meiner Verlag, 1998), 93. The German word *Ästhetik* can be translated into English as "aesthetic" or "aesthetics." I will use the English word "aesthetic" to refer to a field of possible experience and the word "aesthetics" to refer to a philosophical or theological theory of beauty. The German word could convey either of these meanings.

6. Charles Péguy, *The Portal of the Mystery of Hope*, trans. D. Schindler Jr. (Grand Rapids, MI: Eerdmans, 1996).

7. Augustine describes the inseparable bonds of faith, hope, and love in his *Enchiridion* on the theological virtues: "Love is not without hope, hope is not with-

out love, and neither hope nor love are [sic] without faith" (Augustine, *Enchiridion on Faith, Hope, and Love*, in *Augustine: Confessions and Enchiridion*, trans. A. Outler [Philadelphia: Westminster, 1955], 341 [8]). For a traditionally minded account of the interrelationship of the theological virtues that follows Aquinas's treatment, see Dominic Doyle, "'A Future, Difficult, Yet Possible Good': Defining Christian Hope," in *Hope: Promise, Possibility, and Fulfillment*, ed. R. Lennan and N. Pineda-Madrid (Mahwah, NJ: Paulist Press, 2013), 23–30.

8. Avery Dulles, S.J., *The Assurance of Things Hoped For: A Theology of Christian Faith* (New York: Oxford University Press, 1994), 170–72.

9. Ibid., 172.

10. Ibid., 174–75.

11. Ibid., 175–76.

12. Ibid., 176–77.

13. Ibid., 179.

14. Ibid.

15. Ibid., 181.

16. Søren Kierkegaard, *Repetition*, in *"Repetition" and "Philosophical Crumbs,"* trans. M. G. Piety (New York: Oxford University Press, 2009), 3.

17. Ibid.

18. Ibid., 4.

19. "The dialectic of repetition is easy, because that which has been repeated has been, otherwise it could not be repeated. . . . When one says that life is repetition, one also says that that which has existed now comes to be again" (ibid., 19). In *Repetition*, Kierkegaard does not explicitly unpack the category of his title with direct reference to the experience of faith. He does, though, make this connection explicit in a later work: "For in faith repetition begins" (*The Concept of Dread*, trans. W. Lowrie [Princeton: Princeton University Press, 1957], 16–17).

20. Thomas Aquinas, *Summa Theologiae* II-II.1.1 (hereafter abbreviated *ST*). Translations of the *ST* are taken from the Blackfriars edition (New York: McGraw Hill, 1964–1981).

21. Ibid., II-II.2.1.

22. Ibid., II-II.6.1.

23. Ibid., II-II.2.1.

24. Ibid., II-II.2.4.

25. Ibid., II-II.4.1.

26. Ibid., II-II.4.8.

27. Gerhard Ebeling, *The Nature of Faith*, trans. R. G. Smith (Philadelphia: Fortress, 1968), 167.

28. Ibid., 177.

29. Ibid.

30. Kierkegaard, *Repetition*, 75.

31. The Christian tradition offers many instances of this testimony to faith's certainty. The following words of the sixteenth-century Reformer John Calvin (1509–64) are an influential example: "Now, therefore, we hold faith to be a knowledge of God's will toward us, perceived from his Word. But the foundation of this is a preconceived conviction of God's truth. As for its certainty, so long as your mind is at war with itself, the Word will be of doubtful and weak authority, or rather of none. And it is not even enough to believe that God is trustworthy . . . , unless you hold to be beyond doubt that whatever proceeds from him is sacred and inviolable truth" (*Institutes of the Christian Religion*, trans. F. L. Battles [Philadelphia: Westminster, 1977], 1:549 [3.2.6]). "Now we shall possess a right definition of faith if we call it a firm and certain knowledge of God's benevolence toward us, founded upon the truth of the freely given promise in Christ, both revealed to our minds and sealed upon our hearts by the Holy Spirit" (ibid., 551 [3.2.7]).

32. Athanasius, *The Life of Antony*, in *Athanasius: "The Life of Antony" and "The Letter to Marcellinus,"* trans. R. C. Gregg (New York: Paulist Press, 1980), 33–41.

33. Teresa of Ávila, *Interior Castle*, trans. E. A. Peers (New York: Doubleday, 1989), 131.

34. St. John of the Cross, *The Dark Night*, in *The Collected Works of St. John of the Cross*, trans. K. Kavanaugh (Washington, DC: Institute of Carmelite Studies, 1973), 335–36.

35. Paul Tillich, *Dynamics of Faith* (New York: Harper and Row, 1957), 100.

36. Ibid. Cf. Paul Tillich, *The Courage to Be* (New Haven: Yale University Press, 1952), 171–78; Tillich, *Systematic Theology: Three Volumes in One* (Chicago: University of Chicago Press, 1967), 3:238–40.

37. Tillich, *Dynamics of Faith*, 101.

38. Ibid., 102.

39. Ibid., 100.

40. Aquinas does speak of hope's certainty in this life, but regards such certitude as derivative and not the issue of hope's own nature. Rather, he understands hope's certainty as "a derivation from faith's certitude found in the cognitive power" (*ST* II-II.18.4). In this regard, Aquinas speaks of hope's certitude as a function of the divine truthfulness, which is the object of faith.

41. See Nancy Pineda-Madrid, "Hope and Salvation in the Shadow of Tragedy," in Lennan and Pineda-Madrid, *Hope*, 85–92.

42. Paolo Prosperi has spoken of the "hoping" dimensions of the act of faith. See Paolo Prosperi, F.S.C.B., "Believing and Seeing," *Theological Studies* 78 (December 2017): 927–28.

43. My discussion of the temporalities of faith, hope, and love and my conclusion that all time is eschatological time have avoided a discussion of the nature of time parsed theologically, in the manner, say, of Augustine's well-known reflections in book 11 of the *Confessions* or Jürgen Moltmann's account of what he calls the

"interlaced times of history" in his Gifford Lectures of 1984–85 (*God in Creation*, trans. M. Kohl [San Francisco: HarperCollins, 1991], 124–39). Rather, the various phenomenologies of time offered here have more locally described ways in which time has been, and should be, imagined to suffuse the theological virtues. I will consider Augustine's influential meditation on time in the *Confessions* in the next chapter.

44. Katherine Sonderegger, *Systematic Theology*, vol. 1, *The Doctrine of God* (Minneapolis: Fortress, 2015), 23.

Chapter Three   Toward a Theology of Events in Time

1. Pope John Paul II, *Man and Woman He Created Them: A Theology of the Body*, trans. M. Waldstein (Boston: Pauline Books and Media, 2006).
2. Ian A. McFarland, *The Divine Image: Envisioning the Invisible God* (Minneapolis: Fortress, 2005).
3. Dwight N. Hopkins, *Being Human: Race, Culture, and Religion* (Minneapolis: Fortress, 2005).
4. Peter Brown, *Augustine of Hippo: A Biography* (Berkeley: University of California Press, 1967), 158–84.
5. Augustine, "To Simplician—On Various Questions," book 1, in *Augustine: Earlier Writings*, trans. J. Burleigh (Philadelphia: Westminster, 1953), 376–406.
6. Augustine, *Confessions*, trans. R. S. Pine-Coffin (New York: Penguin Books, 1961), 197 (9.10).
7. Ibid., 197–98 (9.10).
8. Ibid., 254 (11.2).
9. Ibid., 256 (11.3).
10. Ibid., 257 (11.5).
11. Ibid., 261 (11.10).
12. Ibid., 262 (11.12).
13. Ibid., 263 (11.13).
14. Ibid., 259 (11.7).
15. Ibid., 264 (11.14).
16. Ibid.
17. Ibid., 266 (11.15).
18. Ibid., 266 (11.16).
19. Ibid., 269 (11.20).
20. Ibid., 274 (11.26).
21. Ibid., 276 (11.27).
22. Ibid., 277 (11.28).
23. Ibid., 280 (11.31).

24. Sean Carroll, *From Eternity to Here: The Quest for the Ultimate Theory of Time* (New York: Plume, 2010), 10.

25. Ibid., 11.

26. Ibid., 14.

27. Ibid., 15.

28. Ibid., 21.

29. Ibid.

30. Ibid., 24.

31. Quoted in ibid., 10.

32. William R. Stoeger, S.J., "Scientific Accounts of Ultimate Catastrophes in Our Life-Bearing Universe," in *The End of the World and the Ends of God: Science and Theology on Eschatology*, ed. J. Polkinghorne and M. Welker (Harrisburg, PA: Trinity Press International, 2000), 19–28.

33. Claiming that the particularity of time frames the beauty of certain events raises the issue of the contributions of space to that same particularity. Natural reality always courses in both space and time since natural reality ever transpires in these dimensions. No doubt, then, that the particularity of space in space-time frames as well eventful beauty. In some respects, the condition of space more powerfully individuates such beauty. Coming "home," arriving at the sacred destination of the pilgrimage, visiting yet again one's favorite city, are events localized in spaces whose beauty seems to transcend time, or, to be more precise, whose beauty seems to extend through all times. My focus here, though, will continue to be on an aesthetics of time.

34. Aristotle, *Poetics*, trans. K. Telford (Chicago: Henry Regnery Company, 1961), 15 (1450). In addition to an ordered arrangement of parts, Aristotle also notes that "magnitude" or, better, a certain magnitude is required in the object of beauty that allows the contemplation of the ordered unity of its parts.

35. Aristotle, *Metaphysics*, trans. R. Hope (Ann Arbor: University of Michigan Press, 1966), 276 (1078b).

36. Thomas Aquinas, *ST* I.5.4.

37. Glenn Parsons, *Aesthetics and Nature* (New York: Continuum, 2008), 7.

38. Vasily Seseman maintains that "the difference between artistic and natural beauty is inessential and not qualitative." For "we assign [the beauty of art and nature] an aesthetic valuation on account of the expressiveness of their sensory appearance and, in attempting to re-create them in one or another way, we aim to bring out and fix on precisely that feature of their nature that is grounded on a certain harmonious cohesion of sensuous elements and complexes (*Aesthetics*, trans. M. Drunga [Amsterdam: Rodopi, 2007], 90).

39. Aristotle observes that "the synthesis of the most beautiful tragedy ought to be, not simple, but complex and imitative of things fearsome and piteous" (*Poetics*, 22 [1452]).

40. *ST* I-II.27.1.
41. Martin Luther, *Heidelberg Disputation*, in *Luther's Works*, vol. 31, ed. H. Grimm (Philadelphia: Fortress, 1957), 52–54.
42. John Calvin, *Institutes of the Christian Religion*, trans. F. L. Battles (Philadelphia: Westminster, 1960), 1:47–51 (1.4).
43. Ibid., 68–69 (1.5.14).
44. Ibid., 41 (1.2.2).
45. See John S. Dunne, C.S.C., "St. Thomas' Theology of Participation," *Theological Studies* 18 (1957): 504.
46. Katherine Sonderegger, *Systematic Theology*, volume 1, *The Doctrine of God* (Minneapolis: Fortress, 2015), xx. For an account of the argument in this volume, see John E. Thiel, "Sonderegger's Systematics: The Divine Attributes as the Divine Being," *International Journal of Systematic Theology* 19 (2017): 188–99.
47. Sonderegger, *Systematic Theology*, 1:39–40.
48. Ibid., 83.
49. Ibid., 84.
50. Ibid., 79.
51. Ibid., 108.
52. Ibid.
53. The classical account of analogy is offered by Thomas Aquinas in *ST* I.13.
54. Sonderegger, *Systematic Theology*, 1:200, 108.
55. Ibid., 201.
56. Ibid., 202.
57. Augustine, *Confessions*, 144 (7.9).
58. Stephen Hawking, *A Brief History of Time: From the Big Bang to Black Holes* (New York: Bantam Books, 1988), 16.
59. Ibid., 83–84. Cf. T. Padmanabhan, *After the First Three Minutes: The Story of Our Universe* (Cambridge: Cambridge University Press, 1998), 126–70.
60. This is not to say, however, that physicists have no aesthetical judgment to offer about natural phenomena from the perspective of their disciplinary inquiry. See A. Zee, *Fearful Symmetry: The Search for Beauty in Modern Physics* (Princeton: Princeton University Press, 2015). Zee's aesthetical paradigm is resonant with the classical model adopted here.
61. Dante Alighieri, *The Divine Comedy*, trans. C. S. Singleton, 6 vols. in 3, Bollingen 80 (Princeton: Princeton University Press, 1975), *Paradiso*, part 1, p. 381 (canto 33, line 145).
62. See Alejandro García-Rivera, *The Community of the Beautiful: A Theological Aesthetics* (Collegeville, MN: Liturgical Press, 1999). García-Rivera addresses the mutual relationship among the transcendentals of the true, the good, and the beautiful.
63. Chalcedonian Creed, in *Decrees of the Ecumenical Councils*, ed. N. P. Tanner, S.J. (Washington, DC: Georgetown University Press, 1990), 1:86.

64. Gregory of Nazianzus, *Epistle 101: To Cledonius against Apollinaris*, in *Christology of the Later Fathers*, ed. E. Hardy (Philadelphia: Westminster, 1954), 215–24.

65. The insight that the character of Jesus, his personal identity, is most manifest in his resurrection is Hans Frei's (*The Identity of Jesus Christ: The Hermeneutical Bases of Dogmatic Theology* [Philadelphia: Fortress, 1975], 136, 142, 151).

66. The most extensive study of the beauty of the incarnation is Hans Urs von Balthasar's *Herrlichkeit* (*The Glory of the Lord: A Theological Aesthetics*, ed. J. Fessio, S.J., and J. Riches, 7 vols. [San Francisco: Ignatius Press, 1982–91]). Balthasar's attention to an aesthetics of the saintly life in volume 5 of that work offers another striking example from the Catholic tradition of the contrastively beautiful event.

67. Nicene Creed, in Tanner, *Decrees of the Ecumenical Councils*, 1:24.

68. Catherine Mowry LaCugna, *God for Us: The Trinity and Christian Life* (San Francisco: HarperSanFrancisco, 1991), 271.

69. Gregory of Nyssa, *An Answer to Ablabius: That We Should Not Think of Saying There Are Three Gods*, in *Christology of the Later Fathers*, ed. E. Hardy (Philadelphia: Westminster, 1954), 261–62.

70. Plato, *Timaeus*, in *Plato: The Collected Dialogues*, ed. E. Hamilton and H. Cairns (Princeton: Princeton University Press, 1971), 1167 (37d).

71. I have not offered anything resembling a developed Trinitarian theology in my proposed analogical relationship between the motion of events in time and the "motion" of Trinitarian relations and missions. Nevertheless, I trust this analogy avoids the problem of latent subordinationism in modern Trinitarian theologies identified so well by Linn Tonstad. I have used the traditional doctrinal and theological categories to describe Trinitarian relations and missions and by their use only intend to call attention to the tradition's affirmation of "motion" in the divine life. In spite of the latent subordinationism inherent in these categories, I assume, with Tonstad, the uncompromised mutuality of the Trinitarian persons and that "the aim of the trinity's action in the world is to give all human beings," and, indeed, all of creation, "a sharing in the life of God" (Linn Marie Tonstad, *God and Difference: The Trinity, Sexuality, and the Transformation of Finitude* [New York: Routledge, 2016], 238).

Chapter Four Tragic Time in an Eschatological Aesthetic

1. Hans Urs von Balthasar, *The Glory of the Lord: A Theological Aesthetics*, vol. 1, *Seeing the Form*, trans. E. Leiva-Merikakas (San Francisco: Ignatius Press, 1982), 241–57.

2. G. W. Leibniz, *Theodicy: Essays on the Goodness of God, the Freedom of Man and the Origin of Evil*, trans. E. M. Huggard (London: Routledge & Kegan Paul, 1952), 267–68 (par. 225).

3. John Hick, *Evil and the God of Love* (San Francisco: Harper & Row, 1978), 257.

4. John E. Thiel, *God, Evil, and Innocent Suffering: A Theological Reflection* (New York: Crossroad Publishing, 2002).

5. For a sustained, systematic argument against the providential explanation, see David H. Kelsey, *Human Anguish and God's Power* (Cambridge: Cambridge University Press, 2021).

6. Leibniz, *Theodicy*, 385.

7. Hick, *Evil and the God of Love*, 256.

8. See, for example, Terrence W. Tilley, *The Evils of Theodicy* (Washington, DC: Georgetown University Press, 1990).

9. Leibniz, *Theodicy*, 385.

10. Hick, *Evil and the God of Love*, 255.

11. A possible exception to theodicy's erasure of time is process theology, understood as a theodicy. One could argue that the very purpose of a process theology, which situates God in time, is to offer a theologically intelligible response to the problem of evil. Here the tension between God and evil is resolved by plunging God into time, thus sacrificing the divine eternity and with it the timeless attributes of unchangeable perfection—omnipotence and omniscience. God faces evil in much the same way that human persons do. We have not addressed this "best-of-all-possible-gods" theodicy because its claims deviate quite far from classical Christian belief, unlike the "best-of-all-possible-worlds" theodicies.

12. I have developed the argument for this position in detail in *God, Evil, and Innocent Suffering*, 76–99. See also John E. Thiel, "Creation, Contingency, and Sacramentality," *The Catholic Theological Society of America: Proceedings of the Sixty-Seventh Annual Convention*, ed. K. Lasnoski, 67 (2012): 46–58 (http://ejournals.bc.edu/ojs/index.php/ctsa/article/view/2178).

13. Karl Rahner is a fine representative of this position, so commonplace in modern theology. See *Foundations of Christian Faith: An Introduction to the Idea of Christianity*, trans. W. Dych (New York: Seabury, 1978), 115; "Ideas for a Theology of Death," in *Theological Investigations*, vol. 13, trans. C. Ernst (New York: Seabury Press, 1975), 180.

14. Karl Rahner, "The Concept of Mystery in Catholic Theology," in *Theological Investigations*, vol. 4, trans. K. Smyth (Baltimore: Helicon, 1966), 41–42.

15. For a compelling account of the way of the cross from the perspective of African-American history and experience, see M. Shawn Copeland, *Knowing Christ Crucified: The Witness of African American Religious Experience* (Maryknoll, NY: Orbis Books, 2018).

16. For a discussion of lament with regard to the hope for ecclesial reform, see Bradford Hinze, *Practices of Dialogue in the Roman Catholic Church: Aims and Obstacles, Lessons and Laments* (New York: Continuum, 2006). For a theological

reflection on the relationship between lament and time, see Rebekka A. Klein, "A Phenomenology of Lament and the Presence of God in Time," in *Evoking Lament: A Theological Discussion*, ed. E. Harasta and B. Brock (New York: T&T Clark, 2009), 14–24. Most strikingly, the ancient Jewish form of the lament has been taken up and transformed in African-American worship and music. See James H. Cone, *The Spirituals and the Blues: An Interpretation*, 2nd ed. (Maryknoll, NY: Orbis Books, 1992); Dolores S. Williams, *Sisters in the Wilderness: The Challenge of Womanist God-Talk* (Maryknoll, NY: Orbis Books, 2013).

17. Karl Rahner, "Eine Antwort," *Orientierung* 14 (1950): 141–45; Rahner, *Foundations of Christian Faith*, 127–28. For a discussion of the development of Rahner's notion of the supernatural existential, see David Coffey, "The Whole Rahner on the Supernatural Existential," *Theological Studies* 65 (2004): 95–118.

18. Gustavo Gutiérrez makes this point especially well in the context of his liberation spirituality. See Gustavo Gutiérrez, *We Drink from Our Own Wells: The Spiritual Journey of a People* (Maryknoll, NY: Orbis Books, 2003).

Chapter Five The Aesthetics of Tradition and the Styles of Theology

1. Hans Urs von Balthasar, *The Glory of the Lord: A Theological Aesthetics*, ed. J. Fessio, S.J., and J. Riches, 7 vols. (San Francisco: Ignatius Press, 1982–91).

2. Richard Viladesau, *Theological Aesthetics: God in Imagination, Beauty, and Art* (New York: Oxford University Press, 1999).

3. Alejandro García-Rivera, *The Community of the Beautiful: A Theological Aesthetics* (Collegeville, MN: Liturgical Press, 1999).

4. Mirjam-Christina Redeker, *Wahrnehmung und Glaube: Zum Verhältnis von Theologie und Ästhetik in gegenwärtiger Zeit* (Berlin: de Gruyter, 2011).

5. Kathryn Tanner, *Theories of Culture: A New Agenda for Theology* (Minneapolis: Fortress, 1997); David Brown, *Tradition and Imagination: Revelation and Change* (Oxford: Oxford University Press, 1999); Brown, *Discipleship and Imagination: Christian Tradition and Truth* (Oxford: Oxford University Press, 2000); John E. Thiel, *Senses of Tradition: Continuity and Development in Catholic Faith* (New York: Oxford University Press, 2000); Terrence W. Tilley, *Inventing Catholic Tradition* (Maryknoll, NY: Orbis Books, 2000). Brown's volumes might seem an exception to my judgment that none of these works examines tradition through the lens of aesthetics, since he attends to art as a dimension of the content of tradition. Yet in Brown's work, aesthetics is not invoked as a perspective for appreciating the beauty of tradition itself.

6. Council of Trent, *First Decree of Session 4* (April 8, 1546), in *Decrees of the Ecumenical Councils*, ed. N. P. Tanner, S.J. (Washington, DC: Georgetown Univer-

sity Press, 1990), 2:663. For a more detailed discussion of the Catholic belief in the authority of tradition as a mode of revelation, see Thiel, *Senses of Tradition*, 13–25.

7. *Dei verbum* 9, in Tanner, *Decrees of the Ecumenical Councils*, 2:974–75. For a sketch of these developments at the council, see John E. Thiel, "*Dei Verbum*: Scripture, Tradition, and Historical Criticism," *Horizons* 47 (Fall 2020): 207–31.

8. Alexander G. Baumgarten, *Meditationes philosophicae de nonnullis ad poema pertinentibus* (1735), quoted in Paul Guyer, "The Origins of Modern Aesthetics: 1711–35," in *The Blackwell Guide to Aesthetics*, ed. P. Kivy (Oxford: Blackwell, 2004), 15.

9. Alexander G. Baumgarten, *Ästhetik*, trans. D. Mirbach (Hamburg: Felix Meiner Verlag, 2007), 1:11.

10. Immanuel Kant, *Critique of Judgment*, trans. J. H. Bernard (New York: Hafner, 1951), 37–202.

11. Mary Mothersill, *Beauty Restored* (Oxford: Clarendon, 1986), 388.

12. Viladesau, *Theological Aesthetics*, 115.

13. One of the most famous testimonies to this classically aesthetical judgment is found in Augustine's account of the mystical experience of God's timelessness that he and his mother Monica shared in Ostia shortly before her death, as recorded in book 9 of the *Confessions*. See chapter 3 above.

14. Thomas Aquinas, *ST* I.39.8.

15. See the discussion of the beauty of God's unchanging perfection in David Bentley Hart, *The Beauty of the Infinite: The Aesthetics of Christian Truth* (Grand Rapids: Eerdmans, 2003), 178–249.

16. Plato, *Republic*, in *Plato: The Collected Dialogues*, ed. E. Hamilton and H. Cairns (Princeton: Princeton University Press, 1971), 819–33 (10.595a–608a).

17. See Stephen Halliwell, *The Aesthetics of Mimesis: Ancient Texts and Modern Problems* (Princeton: Princeton University Press, 2002), 313–43.

18. In her study of Augustine's aesthetical thought, Carol Harrison highlights Augustine's abiding concern that the materiality of finite beauty easily becomes a source of sinful temptation. See *Beauty and Revelation in the Thought of Augustine* (Oxford: Clarendon, 1992), 271.

19. Aquinas, *ST* I-II.27.

20. Aquinas, *ST* I.5.4. The priority accorded to vision as the aesthetical sense also stems from the medieval belief that color is the cause of beauty. See Umberto Eco, *History of Beauty*, trans. A. McEwen (New York: Rizzoli, 2010), 99–129. See also his detailed study of Aquinas's aesthetics: Umberto Eco, *The Aesthetics of Thomas Aquinas*, trans. H. Redin (Cambridge, MA: Harvard University Press, 1988).

21. Aquinas, *ST* I.84.7. Even though Aquinas speaks more generally in this article of sense images, it is interesting to note that visual experience prevails in the examples he offers of how the senses inform acts of understanding.

22. Carolyn Walker Bynum notes an extreme form of this pious practice in late medieval German devotion. In the practice of what scholars have come to call *Shaufrömmigkeit*, some believers were satisfied to "receive" the Eucharist simply by encountering the host visually. See *Wonderful Blood: Theology and Practice in Late Medieval Northern Germany and Beyond* (Philadelphia: University of Pennsylvania Press, 2007), 10.

23. Pope Benedict XII, *Enchiridion symbolorum definitionum et declarationum de rebus fidei et morum*, ed. H. Denzinger and A. Schönmetzer, S.J., 34th ed. (Freiberg im Breisgau: Verlag Herder, 1967), 297 (1000–1001).

24. Dante Alighieri, *The Divine Comedy*, trans. C. S. Singleton, 6 vols. in 3, Bollingen 80 (Princeton: Princeton University Press, 1975), *Paradiso*, part 1, p. 377 (canto 33, lines 96–104).

25. Johann Sebastian Drey, *Kurze Einleitung in das Studium der Theologie mit Rücksicht auf den wissenschaftlichen Standpunct und das katholishe System*, ed. M. Seckler (Tübingen: Francke Verlag, 2007), 133 (par. 256).

26. Ibid., 134 (par. 258).

27. Ibid., 133 (par. 256).

28. Ibid., 134 (par. 258).

29. Ibid., 135 (par. 260).

30. Ibid., 127 (par. 240).

31. Ibid., 97 (par. 175).

32. See Bradford E. Hinze, "The Holy Spirit and the Catholic Tradition: The Legacy of Johann Adam Möhler," in *The Legacy of the Tübingen School*, ed. D. J. Dietrich and M. J. Himes (New York: Crossroad, 1997), 79–87.

33. John Henry Newman, *An Essay on the Development of Christian Doctrine* (Notre Dame, IN: University of Notre Dame Press, 1989 [repr. of 2nd ed., published 1878]), 38.

34. Pope John XXIII, *Opening Address to the Council*, in *The Documents of Vatican II*, ed. W. Abbott, S.J. (New York: America Press, 1966), 715. John XXIII's formulation has since been supported by a teaching of the Congregation for the Doctrine of the Faith, *Mysterium ecclesiae* (June 24, 1973), which claims that the content of revelation may legitimately be conveyed in the changing forms of time and culture. See "In Defense of Catholic Doctrine" (*Mysterium ecclesiae*, June 24, 1973), *Origins* 3 (July 19, 1973): 110–11.

35. On traditional continuity through the vagaries of time, see John E. Thiel, "The Analogy of Tradition," *Theological Studies* 66 (2005): 358–80.

36. Council of Trent, *Decree on Justification*, in Tanner, *Decrees of the Ecumenical Councils*, 2:671–78.

37. Second Vatican Council, *Lumen gentium* 12, in Tanner, *Decrees of the Ecumenical Councils*, 2:858.

38. On dialogue in the church, see Bradford E. Hinze, *Practices of Dialogue in the Roman Catholic Church: Aims and Obstacles, Lessons and Laments* (New York: Continuum, 2006).

39. Elaine Scarry, *On Beauty and Being Just* (Princeton: Princeton University Press, 1999), 31.

40. Council of Chalcedon, *Definition of the Faith*, in Tanner, *Decrees of the Ecumenical Councils*, 1:86–87.

Chapter Six   Forever and a Day: Resurrected Time in a Heavenly Imaginary

1. Paula Fredriksen, *Jesus of Nazareth, King of the Jews: A Jewish Life and the Emergence of Christianity* (New York: Vintage Books, 1999), 266–67.

2. Paula Fredriksen, *When Christians Were Jews: The First Generation* (New Haven: Yale University Press, 2018), 74–107. Based on his judgment that Matt 19:28 is an authentic saying, E. P. Sanders argues that "Jesus looked for the restoration of Israel," a belief that one could reasonably extend to the early Jesus movement (*Jesus and Judaism* [Philadelphia: Fortress, 1985], 103).

3. For a fine overview of the various scholarly positions on the role of Jewish apocalypticism in Christian origins and a defense of the apocalyptic matrix for the preaching of Jesus and the belief of the early church, see John J. Collins, *The Apocalyptic Imagination: An Introduction to Jewish Apocalyptic Literature* (Grand Rapids, MI: Eerdmans, 2016), 261–84.

4. The most thorough study of Paul's eschatology is Christian Settler, *Das Endgericht bei Paulus* (Tübingen: Mohr Siebeck, 2017). For a broader treatment of judgment-eschatology, see Christian Settler, *Das Letze Gericht: Studien zur Endsgerichtserwartung von den Schriftpropheten zur Jesus* (Tübingen: Mohr Siebeck, 2019).

5. Peter Brown, "The Decline of the Empire of God: Amnesty, Penance, and the Afterlife from Late Antiquity to the Middle Ages," in *Last Things: Death and the Apocalypse in the Middle Ages*, ed. C. W. Bynum and P. Freedman (Philadelphia: University of Pennsylvania Press, 2000), 54.

6. Nicene Creed, in *Decrees of the Ecumenical Councils*, ed. N. P. Tanner, S.J. (Washington, DC: Georgetown University Press, 1990), 1:24.

7. Carlos Eire, *A Very Brief History of Eternity* (Princeton: Princeton University Press, 2009), 110–11.

8. Ibid., 111.

9. See John E. Thiel, *Icons of Hope: The "Last Things" in Catholic Imagination* (Notre Dame, IN: University of Notre Dame Press, 2013), 59–93.

10. Thomas Aquinas, *Summa contra gentiles*, book 4, *Salvation*, trans. C. J. O'Neil (Notre Dame, IN: University of Notre Dame Press, 1975), 346 (4.97.1).

11. Ibid., 347.

12. Ibid.

13. Ibid., 348 (4.97.5).

14. Ibid., 349 (4.97.7).

15. The most accomplished study of the doctrine from Christian origins through the medieval period is Carolyn Walker Bynum, *The Resurrection of the Body in Western Christianity, 200–1336* (New York: Columbia University Press, 1995).

16. Council of Trent, *Decree on Justification*, in Tanner, *Decrees of the Ecumenical Councils*, 2:672.

17. Carlos M. N. Eire, *Reformations: The Early Modern World, 1450–1650* (New Haven: Yale University Press, 2016), 753–54.

18. Although a Catholic anthropology strongly supports a heavenly imaginary filled with saintly virtuous deeds, and stands at odds with a classically Protestant apophasis about the afterlife, there are Protestant exceptions that prove the rule. Most notable is the American Congregationalist theologian Jonathan Edwards (1703–58), whose treatises and sermons occasionally offer detailed descriptions of the beauty of heaven and the unceasing virtue of the saints in heavenly life. See Jonathan Edwards, "Heaven Is a World of Love," in *The Works of Jonathan Edwards*, vol. 8, *Ethical Writings*, ed. P. Ramsey (New Haven: Yale University Press, 1989), 366–97; "Serving God in Heaven," in *The Works of Jonathan Edwards*, vol. 17, *Sermons and Discourses, 1730–1733*, ed. M. Valeri (New Haven: Yale University Press, 1999), 253–62. Edwards's account of virtue in heaven offers a Protestant paradigm for a heavenly time in which the saints perform the doctrine of sanctification, manifesting God's grace in acts of love that are themselves the work of grace.

19. This is the traditional teaching of Benedict XII that hope, and faith too, disappear in the believer's apprehension of the Beatific Vision. See *Enchiridion symbolorum definitionum et declarationum de rebus fidei et morum*, ed. H. Denzinger and A. Schönmetzer, S.J., 34th ed. (Freiberg im Breisgau: Verlag Herder, 1967), 297 (1000–1001). See also Bynum, *Resurrection of the Body*, 283–85.

20. Hans Urs von Balthasar, *Dare We Hope "That All Men Be Saved"?*, trans. D. Kipp and L. Krauth (San Francisco: Ignatius Press, 1988).

21. Kathryn Tanner, *Jesus, Humanity, and the Trinity: A Brief Systematic Theology* (Minneapolis: Fortress, 2001), 90.

22. Ibid., 93.

23. Thomas Aquinas, *Summa Contra Gentiles*, book 3, *Providence*, part 1, trans. V. Bourke (Notre Dame, IN: University of Notre Dame Press, 1975), 206–9 (63).

24. Ibid., 175–206 (51–62).

25. For a discussion of *The Divine Comedy* as theology, see the essays in *Dante's "Commedia": Theology as Poetry*, ed. V. Montemaggi and M. Treheme (Notre Dame, IN: University of Notre Dame Press, 2010).

26. Dante Alighieri, *The Divine Comedy*, trans. C. S. Singleton, 6 vols. in 3, Bollingen 80 (Princeton: Princeton University Press, 1975), *Paradiso*, part 1, p. 337 (canto 30, lines 38–45).

27. Ibid., 359–61 (canto 32, lines 1–48).

28. Ibid., 371 (canto 33, lines 7–9).

29. Ibid., 375 (canto 33, lines 55–57).

30. Ibid., 377 (canto 33, lines 106–8).

31. Ibid., 379 (canto 33, lines 114–19, 124–34).

32. Ibid., 379 (canto 33, lines 122–25).

33. Ibid., 379 (canto 33, lines 135–40).

34. Ibid., 381 (canto 33, lines 140–45).

35. Council of Chalcedon, *Definition of the Faith*, in Tanner, *Decrees of the Ecumenical Councils*, 1:86.

36. Karl Barth implied this untraditional position in his doctrine of election. His claim that God chose humanity in Jesus Christ implies that the humanity of Christ is eternal and so dwells timelessly in the nature of God (*Church Dogmatics* II/2, trans. G. W. Bromiley et al. (London: T&T Clark International, 2004), 94–194 (par. 33). Cf. Paul Dafyyd Jones, *The Humanity of Christ: Christology in Karl Barth's "Church Dogmatics"* (London: T&T Clark, 2008), 60–102.

37. Hans Boersma argues that the traditional understanding of the Beatific Vision has not made Christology sufficiently central and that the proper "telos of all human desire is the vision of the incarnate Christ—the Form of beauty in Christ's glorified human flesh" (Hans Boersma, *Seeing God: The Beatific Vision in Christian Tradition* [Grand Rapids, MI: Eerdmans, 2018], 53). This is an interesting position, though it may reflect an impatience with the Trinitarian mystery and indirectly elevate anthropology to a status inappropriate to the Beatific Vision. Better, I think, to stand with Dante in marveling at how "the image [of Christ's humanity] conformed to the [divine] circle and how it has its place therein." A notion of divine beauty defined by classical aesthetical sensibilities seems to call for a Trinitarian situation of Christology.

38. I have appreciated the beauty of heavenly diversity by focusing on resurrected persons. But Ian McFarland reminds us that such diversity includes a host of other heavenly creatures (*From Nothing: A Theology of Creation* [Louisville: Westminster John Knox, 2014], 162–64).

39. Following Aquinas's eschatology closely, Matthew Levering puts this nicely: "The consummation of the Church's faith occurs in the radical intimacy of the beatific vision, in which we are not onlookers but real participants in the Trinitarian life" (*Jesus and the Demise of Death: Resurrection, Afterlife, and the Fate of the Christian* [Waco, TX: Baylor University Press, 2012], 124). Of course, were one to follow Aquinas all the way, there would be no talk of *all* persons being real participants in the Trinitarian life.

INDEX

aesthetic, of time, 26–28, 182n.5
aesthetics, 182n.5
   Catholic aesthetical sensibility, 128
   classical aesthetical theory, 63–64,
      79, 81, 117, 122, 191n.20
   classical aesthetics of scripture, 125
   modern aesthetical theory, 81, 122
   Protestant aesthetical sensibility, 128
   of time, 50, 77, 81, 117
   See also beauty
analogy, 123, 165
   Catholic doctrine of, 67, 71, 75
   for God's presence to time, 60, 63,
      75, 79–80
anthropology, 25, 28
   eschatological, 47, 49–50, 117, 166,
      174
Antony of Egypt, 37
anxiety, eschatological, 152, 154, 167
Aquinas, Thomas, 14, 15, 123, 183n.7,
      195n.39
   on the act of faith, 33–34
   on aesthetics, 63–65, 124, 127–28,
      191n.21
   on the Beatific Vision, 172
   on the end-time, 156–57
   on hope and certainty, 184n.40
Aristotle, on aesthetics, 63–65,
      186n.34, 186n.39
Athanasius, 37

Augustine, 15, 77, 92, 126, 164, 173,
      174, 182n.7, 184n.43, 191n.18
   meditation on time and eternity in
      the *Confessions*, 51–60, 71–72
   mystical experience at Ostia, 53–54,
      59, 191n.13
   narrative of grace in the *Confessions*,
      52–53, 60
   reflection on the origin of time,
      54–55

Balthasar, Hans Urs von, 4, 23, 77,
      82–83, 118, 168, 188n.66
Barth, Karl, 15, 30
   on the eternal humanity of Christ,
      195n.36
Baumgartner, A. G., 26, 121
Beatific Vision, 7, 8, 14, 22, 23, 108,
      128–29, 149, 154, 158, 171, 177,
      195n.37, 195n.39
   at the particular judgment, 168,
      171–72, 176
   theological apophasis with regard to,
      171–74
   See also Dante Alighieri
beauty
   of the Christ event, 138
   classical conception of, 63–64, 74,
      124, 174–75, 195n.37
   of a contrastive event, 64, 74–75

beauty (*cont.*)
   of events in time, 63–66, 74, 75, 81, 144, 174
   of God, 60, 75, 77, 118, 122–23, 126, 135, 175, 195n.37
   and goodness, 123
   of grace, 83
   modern conception of, 174
   of a series of events, 64, 76–77
   and truth, 138
   See also aesthetics; creation; incarnation; time; tradition
Benedict XII, 128
Big Bang, 62, 73
Boersma, Hans, 195n.37
Bonhoeffer, Dietrich, 30
Brown, David, 190n.5
Brown, Peter, 149
Buddhism, 84, 86
Bultmann, Rudolf, 30

Calvin, John, 67, 184n.31
Carroll, Sean, 60–62
Chalcedon, Council of, 75–76, 141, 175
communion of the saints, 23, 112, 115, 153, 165, 169–71, 176
Congregation for the Doctrine of the Faith, 192n.34
Constantinople I, Council of, 78
Cooper, Anthony Ashley, 121
Copeland, M. Shawn, 189n.15
creation, 25, 58, 62, 72–73, 78, 82–83, 91, 94, 98, 110, 114, 117, 126, 157, 165
   beauty of, 74, 122–23
   goodness of, 20, 66, 80, 83, 86–87, 101, 106, 126, 169
Cullman, Oscar, 180n.31

Dante Alighieri, 15, 74, 128–29, 158, 195n.37
   on the heavenly ascent to the Beatific Vision, 171–74
de Lubac, Henri, 6–9, 12–13, 20, 77, 114
Dodd, C. H., 9–13, 20, 180n.31
Drey, Johann Sebastian, 130–33
Dulles, Avery, 30–31

Ebeling, Gerhard, 35
Edwards, Jonathan, 15, 19n.18
Enlightenment, 131, 181n.32
eschatology, 1, 2, 9
   earliest Christian, 144–46
   Jewish, 145
   Pauline, 146–48
   realized, 10–12, 41, 115
   "thick," 4
   "thin," 4–5
   See also anthropology
eternity, 36, 58, 59
   sempiternity, 181n.36
eventfulness
   as the medium of grace, 88, 97
   as motion, 65–66
   as the resonance of eternity, 79
   tragic events, 82, 99–101, 105–6, 109, 111–12, 144
   —privative character of, 106–7, 163
   See also time
evil, 85, 92–96, 107–8, 113, 148, 189n.11
   moral, 100, 106, 114
   natural, 99–100
   —theological ignorance regarding the origin of, 104–5
   as privation, 83, 164

problem of, 87–89, 96
social, 115
extrinsicism, 8, 9, 77, 114

faith
  atemporal temporality of, 34–36, 39–40, 42–43
  certainty of, 34–37, 40, 43, 99
  conceived as hope, 30, 40, 42, 43–45, 49, 99, 105, 107, 110, 117, 166
  and doubt, 34, 37–39, 108
  as repetition, 32–33, 41
  traditional conceptions of, 30–32
  See also virtues
Florovsky, Georges, 12
Fra Angelico, 151
Frei, Hans, 188n.65

García-Rivera, Alejandro, 118
Giotto di Bondone, 151
Gnosticism, 84–86, 111
God
  divine accompaniment to eventfulness, 110–12
  eternity of, 14, 16, 21, 47, 76–77, 79, 144, 158, 162, 174–75, 177. *See also* Augustine
  freedom of, 6, 8
  God's agency in death, 101, 106, 108
  God's lack of agency in death, 102–6, 108–9, 112
  immutability of, 123–29
  missions in the Trinitarian life of, 78–79
  "motion" in the Trinitarian life of, 78–80, 188n.71
  as mystery, 108–9
  omnipotence of, 88–92, 103–4, 123, 189n.11
  omnipresence of, 97, 123, 171
  omniscience of, 90, 189n.11
  processions in the Trinitarian life of, 78–79
  as Trinity, 1, 78, 106, 171, 173, 175, 177
  See also beauty: of God
grace
  continuity of, 6–8, 13, 24, 143, 157–58, 162–63
  gracefulness of motion, 65
  noncompetitive, 168–69, 177
  as providential presence, 60, 77, 135, 157
  as source of created beauty, 74
  theology of grace as a resource for a theology of time, 59–60
  uncreated, 46, 60, 75, 80, 111
  See also eventfulness; time
Gregory of Nyssa, 22, 63, 79
Greschake, Gisbert, 17–18
Gutiérrez, Gustavo, 190n.18

Hattison, Carol, 191n.18
Hawking, Stephen, 73–74
heaven, 14–15, 151, 153, 155
  in Catholic sensibilities, 160–61
  heavenly diversity, 176–77
  heavenly future, 166–67, 181n.36
  misconceived as eternal, 16–17, 143, 158, 167
  in Protestant sensibilities, 160–61
  redemptive joy of, 15, 167, 171
Hegel, Georg, 122
hell, 150–51, 153, 155, 167–68
Hick, John, 91–95
hierarchy of discipleship, 152–54, 167
Hinduism, 84, 86
Holy Spirit, 134–39, 158

hope
  and doubt, 108
  heavenly, 166–67, 170–71
  and justice, 114–15
  patience in time, 111, 113
  temporality of, 40–45, 96–100, 107, 110–11
  —eschatological temporality of, 40–45, 47, 99, 164–66
  See also virtues
Hutcheson, Francis, 121

incarnation, 78, 118, 135
  contrastive beauty of, 75–76, 175–76
indulgences, 153–54
infallibility, 120, 124
International Theological Commission, 17–19
Irenaeus of Lyon, 91
Islam, 86

Jeremias, Joachim, 12
Jesus Christ, 55–56, 75–76, 78, 97, 119, 124–25, 135, 141, 144–51, 155–56, 164, 173–75, 195n.36
John of the Cross, 37
Johnson, Elizabeth, 4
John XXIII, 133
Judaism, 85–86. *See also* eschatology: Jewish

Kant, Immanuel, 121
  Kantian a priori aesthetic, 26–27, 50
  Kantian conception of the thing-in-itself, 51
  Kantian epistemology, 14
Kierkegaard, Søren, 32–33, 36, 41, 183n.19

lament, 113–14, 190n.16
Last Judgment, 4, 17, 23, 42, 80, 98, 109, 136, 151–53, 155, 157, 164–65, 167, 176
  liminal time of, 153, 155–57
  in medieval art, 151–52, 155–56
  particular judgment, 150, 155, 167–68
Leibniz, Gottfried, 90, 92–95
Levering, Matthew, 195n.39
Lonergan, Bernard, 3, 30
love, 99, 123
  as creaturely virtue, 46
  as the divine essence, 29, 46, 47, 49
  heavenly, 166, 177
  no temporality uniquely its own, 45
  in the temporality of hope, 45
  See also virtues
Luther, Martin, 67, 119, 154

magisterium, 138–39
Maximus the Confessor, 30, 78
McFarland, Ian, 195n.38
Michelangelo Buonarroti, 129, 151
Möhler, Johann Adam, 132
Moltmann, Jürgen, 1, 4, 184n.43
Monica of Thagaste, 51, 53–54, 191n.13
Monophysitism, 141

Neoplatonism, 67, 72
neo-scholasticism. *See* theology: neo-scholastic
New Creation, 42, 45, 76, 80, 97, 103, 111, 148, 157, 164–65, 168, 170
Newman, John Henry, 132–33
Nicaea I, Council of, 78

O'Donovan, Leo, 179n.1
O'Regan, Cyril, 4

Parsons, Glenn, 63
participation, medieval doctrine of, 67–68, 70, 72, 126
Paul, 14, 16, 19, 28–29, 30, 45–46, 52–53, 76, 82, 87, 100, 128, 146–48, 150, 158, 167, 172
Péguy, Charles, 28
perichoresis, 78–79, 135, 175
physics, 25, 27, 50, 59, 83, 98
Plato, 16, 126
Platonism, 17, 20, 59, 72, 125–26, 157
Plotinus, 126
predestination, 35, 42, 97, 161
Prosperi, Paolo, 184n.42
providential explanation (of suffering), 88–89, 92, 96, 101–2, 104–5, 108
   denial of innocent suffering, 89, 92, 101
   See also theodicy
Pseudo-Dionysius, 123
pure nature, 6–8, 77, 114
purgatory, 149, 150, 153
   liminal time of, 154

Rahner, Karl, 4, 14, 30, 77, 108, 114
Ratzinger, Joseph, 4, 18
Redeker, Mirjam-Christina, 118
resurrection
   of the body, 14–15, 18–19, 22–23, 80, 110, 146–49, 157–62, 169
   Greschake's notion of resurrection in death, 17–19
   of Jesus, 2, 10, 11, 13, 21, 50, 103–4, 109, 111, 146–47, 163, 170
   —as an event in time, 76
Rousselot, Pierre, 30

Sanders, E. P., 193n.2
Scarry, Elaine, 139

Scheeben, Matthias Joseph, 30
Schillebeeckx, Edward, 30
Schleiermacher, Friedrich, 30, 130
Schweitzer, Albert, 3, 9, 12
Seseman, Vasily, 186n.38
Simplicianus, 52
sin
   effects of sin in heaven, 22–23, 189–90
   original, 87–88, 102, 104, 106, 108
   —denial of innocent suffering, 88, 101
Sonderegger, Katherine, 47, 68–71
   on analogy, 71
   on divine immanence, 69–70
space, 61, 186n.33
supernatural existential, 114

Tanner, Kathryn, 168, 181n.33
Teresa of Ávila, 37
theodicy, 88–96, 100, 108, 110, 189n.11
   as evil, 94
   Hick's theodicy, 90–95
   issue of time in theodicy explanation, 94–96
   Leibniz's theodicy, 90, 92–95
   See also providential explanation (of suffering)
theology
   liberation, 30, 77
   neoscholastic, 6, 7, 30, 77, 114, 18n.32
   nouvelle théologie, 6, 13, 77, 114
   Orthodox, 128
   process, 1, 189n.11
   in the style of a classical aesthetics of tradition, 137–42
   in the style of a developmental aesthetics of tradition, 138–42

theology (*cont.*)
  theological encyclopedia, 2
  theological subdisciplines, 2
  transcendental, 30, 50
Tillich, Paul, conception of faith, 37–39, 42, 107–8
time
  beauty of, 21, 24, 51, 72, 96, 106–7, 110, 117, 158
  as a coordinate system, 61
  end-time, 148–49, 151, 156–57
  eschatological, 5, 23, 42–43, 46, 96–100, 110–13, 164–66
  and eventfulness, 51, 60–66, 72
  heavenly, 15, 17–19, 22, 24, 144, 157–77
  —past, present, and future of, 164
  as a human sensibility, 25–26, 58, 61–62
  individuating power of, 64–65, 72, 79, 80, 162
  as a measure of duration between events, 61
  as a medium of grace, 5, 74, 77, 81–83, 96, 106, 143, 157–58, 162, 171
  pacific time, 41–42
  practice of Christian waiting in, 111–15
  resurrected time, 163, 165, 170
  time and space, 61
  time "forever," 5, 12–24, 117, 143, 157–77
  time "now," 5–12, 21, 42, 46, 97–98, 117, 143–44, 158, 164, 177
  tragic (anomic, fallen) time, 21, 37, 41, 46, 80, 82, 99, 100, 106, 109, 111, 113, 115, 117, 158, 163–66, 170, 176

See also aesthetics; eschatology; eventfulness; grace
Tonstad, Linn, 188n.71
tradition
  beauty of, 117, 118, 119
  Catholic belief in scripture and tradition as divine revelation, 119–21, 124, 125
  classical conception of the beauty of, 122–30, 136, 137
  —privileging the sense of sight, 127–30, 136
  modern, developmental conception of the beauty of, 130–37
  —privileging the sense of hearing, 136–37
tragedy
  as literary genre, 99
  See also eventfulness: tragic events
transcendentals, 97, 123, 125, 175
Trent, Council of, 8, 114, 119–20, 135, 160, 162, 168

universal salvation, 167–69, 176

Vatican Council I, 120
Vatican Council II, 13, 120–21, 137, 152
Viladesau, Richard, 118
Vincent of Lérins, 124
virtues, 28–43, 184n.43
  cardinal, 114
  faith and hope as more creaturely, 29, 39, 41, 46, 47, 166
  heavenly, resurrected, 162–64, 167–70, 176, 177
  temporal aesthetic of, 28
  See also faith; hope; love
visions, 128
Volf, Miroslav, 4

Walker, Carolyn Walker, 192n.22
Weiss, Johannes, 3

Wesley, John, 30
Wheeler, John Archibald, 62

JOHN E. THIEL

is the Aloysius P. Kelley, S.J. Professor of

Catholic Studies Emeritus, Fairfield University.

www.ingramcontent.com/pod-product-compliance
Lightning Source LLC
Chambersburg PA
CBHW030623230426
43661CB00053B/2119